International Developments in Investigative Interviewing

International Developments in Investigative Interviewing

Edited by

Tom Williamson, Becky Milne and Stephen P. Savage

WILLAN
PUBLISHING

Published by

Willan Publishing
Culmcott House
Mill Street, Uffculme
Cullompton, Devon
EX15 3AT, UK
Tel: +44(0)1884 840337
Fax: +44(0)1884 840251
e-mail: info@willanpublishing.co.uk
website: www.willanpublishing.co.uk

Published simultaneously in the USA and Canada by

Willan Publishing
c/o ISBS, 920 NE 58th Ave, Suite 300
Portland, Oregon 97213-3786, USA
Tel: +001(0)503 287 3093
Fax: +001(0)503 280 8832
e-mail: info@isbs.com
website: www.isbs.com

First published 2009

ISBN   978-1-84392-276-6 hardback

British Library Cataloguing-in-Publication Data

A catalogue record for this book is available from the British Library.

FSC
Mixed Sources
Product group from well-managed
forests and other controlled sources
Cert no. SGS-COC-2482
www.fsc.org
© 1996 Forest Stewardship Council

Project managed by Deer Park Productions, Tavistock, Devon
Typeset by GCS, Leighton Buzzard, Bedfordshire
Printed and bound by T.J. International Ltd, Padstow, Cornwall

Contents

List of abbreviations

ACPO	Association of Chief Police Officers
APA	American Psychological Association
BPS	British Psychological Society
BSCT	Behavioural Science Consultation Teams
CBCA	criteria-based content analysis
CCRC	Criminal Cases Review Commission
CEAS	Committee for the evaluation of criminal cases that have been concluded
CFIS	Centre for Investigative Skills
CI	cognitive interview
CIA	Central Intelligence Agency
CM	conversation management
CPT	European Committee for the Prevention of Torture and Inhuman or Degrading Treatment or Punishment
CPTU	Central Planning and Training Unit
CRIME	Code of Practice for Custody, Rights, Investigation, Management and Evidence
CSI	Crime Scene Investigation
DCI	Detective Chief Inspector
DNA	Deoxyribonucleic acid
DOD	Department of Defense
DWP	Department for Work and Pensions
ECHR	European Convention on Human Rights
ECI	enhanced cognitive interview
EEG	Elecroencephalograms

EI	educing information
EIP	educing information professional
ERISP	Electronic Recording of Interviews with Suspected Persons
FTP	Federal, Provincial and Territorial
GEMAC	greeting, explanation, mutual activity, closure
GKT	Guilty Knowledge Polygraph Test
GSS	General Security Services
HUMINT	Human Intelligence
ISB	Intelligence Science Board
KREATIV	**K**ommunikasjon, **R**ettssikkerhet, **E**tikk og empati, **A**ktiv bevisstgjøring, **T**illit gjennom åpenhet, **I**nformasjon, **V**itenskaplig forankring (Communication, Rule of law (due process), Ethics and empathy, Active awareness, Trust through openness, Information (not confirmation), Valid scientific foundation)
MJ	mechanical jurisprudence
MOS	military occupational speciality
NNPL	Nordic Network for Psychology and Law
NPIA	National Policing Improvement Agency
OPI	Office of Police Integrity
PACE	Police and Criminal Evidence Act
PE	prolonged exposure
PEACE	Planning and preparation; Engage and explain; Account; Closure; Evaluation (Model of Interviewing)
PENS	Psychological Ethics and National Security
PICI	police interview competency inventory
PIP	Professionalising Investigation Programme
RM	reality monitoring
PinS	Professionalism in Security
SCI	spaced cognitive interviews
SOC	sense of coherence
SPOT	Screening Passengers by Observation Technique
SUE	strategic-use-of-evidence
TIM	tactical interview model
TJ	therapeutic jurisprudence
USG	United States Government

Figures and tables

Figures

Tables

Notes on contributors

Randy Borum is a behavioural science consultant on counter-intelligence and national security issues. As a professor at the University of South Florida, he has taught courses on terrorism, custodial interrogation, intelligence analysis, and criminal psychology, and he is the author or co-author of more than 100 publications. Dr Borum is a board-certified forensic psychologist who previously served as a sworn police officer and worked as a senior consultant to the US Secret Service for more than a decade. He serves on the Forensic Psychology Advisory Board for the FBI's Behavioral Science Unit and on the United Nations Roster of Experts in Terrorism.

Peter Bull (BA, MA, PhD, CPsychol, FBPsS) is a senior lecturer in the Department of Psychology, University of York, UK. He has over 80 academic publications, principally in the form of articles in internationally recognised academic journals; he has also written five books, as well as numerous book chapters. His published output has been primarily concerned with the analysis of interpersonal communication. His most recent books are *The Microanalysis of Political Communication: Claptrap and Ambiguity* (2003) and *Communication Under the Microscope: The Theory and Practice of Microanalysis* (2002). He is to be listed in the 2009 edition of Marquis' *Who's Who in the World*, and in the 2008 edition of the *Dictionary of International Biography*.

Ray Bull is Professor of forensic psychology at the University of Leicester. His major research topic is investigative interviewing. In July 2008 Ray received from the European Association of Psychology and Law an 'Award for Life-time Contribution to Psychology and Law'. In June 2008 he received from the British Psychological Society the 'Award for Distinguished Contributions to Academic Knowledge in Forensic Psychology'. In 2005, he received a Commendation from the London Metropolitan Police for 'Innovation and professionalism whilst assisting a complex rape investigation'. He has authored and co-authored a large number of papers in quality research journals and has co-authored and co-edited many books, including *Investigative Interviewing: Psychology and Practice* (1999 – a second edition is now being written) and *Witness Identification in Criminal Cases* (2008). In recognition of the quality and extent of his research publications, he was in 1995 awarded a doctorate (DSc).

Sylvie Clément earned a postgraduate degree in sociology at the University of Evry-Val-d'Essonne in France. She has worked since 2000 for the French Gendarmerie Nationale. As a member of the Centre de Prospective, she has conducted several internal studies on social aspects. One of her major studies was on interrogations and interview techniques in the French Gendarmerie Nationale. She is preparing a PhD thesis on the same subject.

Ivar A. Fahsing is Detective Superintendent and Assistant Professor at the Norwegian Police University College. He has published in the field of investigative interviewing, eyewitness testimony, detective skills, knowledge management and organised crime. He is used as an expert-witness in courts and has for several years conducted training of law-enforcement personnel in Scandinavia. He has 15 years of experience as a homicide detective in the Oslo Police department and at the National Criminal Investigation Service of Norway.

Ronald Fisher is Professor of psychology at Florida International University (Miami), where he is the director of the legal psychology programme. He is on the editorial boards of *Journal of Experimental Psychology: Applied, and Legal and Criminological Psychology*. Dr Fisher is the co-developer of the Cognitive Interview (CI) procedure for enhancing witness memory, and has conducted training seminars on the CI with many police and other investigative agencies (e.g. FBI, British Police, NASA, Israeli Air Force, NTSB, and NASA). Dr Fisher served on the Planning Committee and the Technical Working Group for the US Department of Justice to develop national guidelines on collecting eyewitness evidence. His research interests also examine the cognitive principles underlying detecting deception, and the relation between consistency of witness recollection and accuracy of testimony.

Michael G. Gelles is currently a senior manager with Deloitte Consulting, LLP Federal practice in Washington, D.C., consulting in the areas of human capital management and systems and operations. Dr. Gelles is a thought leader in critical mission areas. He also leads projects in the areas of strategic planning, workforce planning and deployment and leadership development that directly support mission related programs in several federal law enforcement agencies. Previously, he was the chief psychologist for the Naval Criminal Investigative Service (NCIS) for more than 16 years. He was the lead psychologist for the behavioral consultation team for the Criminal Investigations Task Force, and was a leader of numerous other task forces in the areas of workplace violence, insider threat and ethics in consultation to national security. Prior to joining the NCIS in 1990, Dr. Gelles served as a clinical psychologist for the U.S. Navy. Dr. Gelles is also a frequent lecturer and has published numerous professional papers on topics related to organizational management in operational settings, forensic psychology, law enforcement, terrorism and counterintelligence.

Ulf Holmberg (BSc, MSc, PhD) is a veteran police officer of 30 years' service in Sweden. He has worked in a number of different departments, including 15 years as a detective inspector, and investigator of violent and sexual crimes. Nowadays, he is a senior lecturer and programme director in psychology at the Centre of Psychology, Kristianstad University College, Sweden, where he is also the course leader of distance-learning courses in forensic psychology. Besides his activities at Kristianstad University College, he has trained police officers, prosecutors and judges in investigative interviewing. Ulf has a research interest focusing on the interaction of investigative interviewing, its relation to therapeutic jurisprudence and the interview outcome.

Steven M. Kleinman (BA psychology, MS forensic science, MS strategic intelligence) is a career intelligence officer with over 25 years of operational and leadership experience in human intelligence, special operations, and special survival training. He has served as an interrogator during three major military campaigns and as the director of the US Air Force Combat Interrogation Course. He has been guest lecturer on intelligence and interrogation policy at an array of US and international venues, including the Conference on Intelligence and Terrorism in London, the City University of New York School of Law, the American Psychological Association, the Singapore Home Team Academy, and the Naval Postgraduate School. He has also testified on interrogation policy before the US Senate Select Committee on Intelligence and the Armed Services Committee.

Sharon Leal (BSc (Hons), PhD) is a research fellow at the International Centre for Research in Forensic Psychology, University of Portsmouth (UK). Her doctoral research focused on the central and peripheral physiology of attention and cognitive demand. Her current research focuses on the behavioural and physiological effects of cognitive load during deception. This research is very relevant to detecting how people engaging in 'high-stake' deception respond verbally, non-verbally and physiologically. Her work involves cooperation with national and international governments and police.

Samantha Mann (BSc (Hons), PGDip, PhD) is a research fellow at the Department of Psychology, University of Portsmouth. She has been researching in the area of deceptive behaviour and deception detection for over a decade, commencing with her innovative PhD thesis which looked into the behaviour of highly motivated liars (suspects in their police interviews) and police officers' ability to detect those lies. She is currently employed on a project to develop interview techniques designed to enhance deception detection.

Becky Milne (BSC (Hons), PhD, CPsychol, CSci, AFBPsS) is a principal lecturer at Institute of Criminal Justice Studies, University of Portsmouth. She is the course leader of the FdA Investigation and Evidence, a distance-learning degree programme specifically for investigators. She is a chartered forensic psychologist, an associate fellow of the British Psychological Society, and an associate editor of the *International Journal of Police Science and Management*. Becky is a member of the Association of Chief Police Officers Investigative Interviewing Strategic Steering Group, and has worked closely with the police and other criminal justice organisations through training in the Enhanced Cognitive Interview, witness interview advising, and the interviewing of vulnerable groups (i.e. Tiers 3 and 5) and providing case advice.

Rod Morgan is professor of criminal justice at the University of Bristol and visiting professor at the Police Science Institute, Cardiff

University and the London School of Economics. Until 2007, he was chairman of the Youth Justice Board for England and Wales and prior to that (2001–4) HM Chief Inspector of Probation for England and Wales. He is an ad hoc expert adviser to the Council of Europe and Amnesty International on custodial conditions and the prevention of torture, and he is co-author of the Council of Europe's official guide, *Combating Torture in Europe* (Strasbourg: Council of Europe, 2001), to the European Convention for the Prevention of Torture.

Stephen Moston (BSc (Hons), MSc, PhD) is a senior lecturer in forensic psychology, James Cook University (Australia). Stephen is the coordinator of the postgraduate professional training programmes in forensic psychology at that university. Stephen was a former member of the Association of Chief Police Officers Investigative Interviewing Strategic Steering Group. He has conducted several major studies on police interviewing styles and suspect behaviour in England and Australia, for bodies such as the UK Home Office, and the Royal Commission on Criminal Justice. His current research interests include evaluating police interviewing styles and tactics, public perceptions of police interviewing, and denial strategies by suspects.

Nicole Nierop (MSc and LLM) has degrees in clinical psychology and criminal law. She is a senior behavioural adviser at the behavioural analysis unit of the Dutch National Police Agency, where she has worked since 1994, providing case advice in sexual assault cases and doing research. Her areas of expertise are psychological and judicial aspects of interrogation and the assessment of allegations of sexual abuse. These areas are also the subject of the dissertation she is writing. Nicole has been a member of the National Expert Committee for Sexual Abuse Allegations since it was established in 1999.

Asbjørn Rachlew is a detective superintendent at Oslo Police district, Norway. He is currently on leave of absence to complete his PhD at the Faculty of Law, University of Oslo. Rachlew completed his MSc in investigative psychology at the University of Liverpool in 1999. He lectures at the Norwegian University College in investigative interviewing. He has published and testified as an expert witness on the subject. Rachlew has worked as a detective for the UN in Lebanon and the Norwegian Ministry of Justice in various projects.

Stephen P. Savage is Professor of Criminology and Director of the Institute of Criminal Justice Studies, University of Portsmouth, which he founded in 1992. He has published widely on policing and the politics of criminal justice policy, including his most recent books, *Police Reform: Forces for Change* (Oxford University Press 2007) and *Policing and the Legacy of Lawrence* (with Nathan Hall and John Grieve, Willan Publishing 2009). He has recently researched and published on miscarriages and justice, and his current research is on the independent investigation of complaints against the police.

Andrea Shawyer is a senior lecturer in psychology at the Institute of Criminal Justice Studies, University of Portsmouth. She studied forensic psychology at the University of Surrey, and her current research interest, and the topic of her PhD thesis, is investigative interviewing with specific focus on fraud investigation and detecting deception.

Michel St-Yves has been a forensic psychologist with the *Service de l'analyse de comportement* [behavioural analysis service] of the Sûreté du Québec since 2002. He works as a critical-incident specialist and is actively involved in criminal investigations, both in the preparation of psychological profiles and the preparation of interrogations. Since 1997, he has taught the psychology of interrogation at the *École nationale de police du Québec* [Quebec Police Academy]; more recently, he has taught crisis negotiations at that institute. As well, since 2002 he has been a lecturer at the Université de Montréal's School of Criminology. He worked at the Correctional Service of Canada from 1988 to 2002, first, in risk assessment of adult offenders, and later in research on sexual offenders. His publications and papers focus on sexual assault, crisis negotiation, and police interrogation. He is the author of *Psychologie des entrevues d' enquête: de la recherche à la recherche de la pratique* [The psychology of investigative interviews: from research to practice], published in 2004 by Éditions Yvon Blais.

Marc van de Plas is a Belgian police officer, with degrees in criminology and industrial psychology. He implemented psychological support in the Special Forces and created the Belgian Behavioural Sciences Unit, which developed expertise in profiling, hostage negotiation and interview techniques, in particular in child interviewing and polygraphy. He wrote a book about basic interview techniques. At this moment, he is the head of the central department to combat crimes against physical integrity (murder, sexual assault, violence and missing persons).

Paul van den Eshof (MSc and LLM) has degrees in social psychology and criminal law. He is the head of the behavioural analysis unit of the Dutch National Police Agency, where he has worked since 1989, providing case advice, doing research, teaching and policymaking. His areas of expertise are sexual assault, psychological aspects of interrogation, the assessment of allegations of sexual abuse and missing persons. Paul has been the coordinator of the National Expert Committee for Sexual Abuse Allegations since the start in 1999.

Aldert Vrij is a professor of applied social psychology in the Department of Psychology at the University of Portsmouth (UK), and he is the contact person for E-PRODD. He has published more than 300 articles and book chapters to date, mainly on the subjects of non-verbal and verbal cues to deception (i.e., how do liars behave and what do they say?), and lie detection. He has developed a cognitive approach to lie detection, and his book *Detecting Lies and Deceit: Pitfalls and Opportunities*, published by Wiley in 2008, provides a comprehensive overview of deception and lie detection research. He advises the police about conducting interviews with suspects, and gives invited talks and workshops on lie detection to practitioners and scholars across the world. He has held research grants from the British Academy, the Dutch Organisation for Scientific Research (NWO), the Dutch government, the Economic and Social Research Council (ESRC), the Leverhulme Trust, the Nuffield Foundation, the UK government and the US government. He is at present editor of *Legal and Criminological Psychology*, a forensic journal published by the British Psychological Society.

Tom Williamson was a visiting professor at the Institute of Criminal Justice Studies, University of Portsmouth until his death in March 2007. A chartered forensic psychologist, he had a doctorate from the University of Kent for his research into investigative interviewing. He was one of the founders of the PEACE method of interviewing. A former police officer, he retired from the post of Deputy Chief Constable of the Nottinghamshire Police in 2001 and was previously a commander at New Scotland Yard.

Foreword

John G.D. Grieve

Tom Williamson

Building from the analysis of mishandled interrogations and miscarriages of justice contained in his 1990 Kent University PhD, Williamson was at the forefront of a radical shift in police interview techniques and training, determined that the one-time emphasis on 'getting a cough' at any cost should be replaced by a neutral search for reliable and durable evidence. A committed Christian, the drive towards what Williamson called 'ethical policing' dominated his working life, from his time as a young officer in the early 1970s in A10, the Metropolitan Police anti-corruption branch set up by the commissioner Sir Robert Mark.

After retiring from the service in 2001, Williamson's second, already-burgeoning academic career bloomed further, as a senior research fellow at Portsmouth University's Institute of Criminal Justice Studies – Britain's biggest criminology department and a body that, ten years earlier, Williamson had been instrumental in establishing. At the time of his death from mesothelioma, the cancer linked with exposure to asbestos, *he was still working on several academic pieces and books, and friends report that he retained his sweeping intellectual curiousity to the end.*

Aside from his role as a thinker, writer and reformer, Williamson was also an operational detective *par excellence*.

(David Rose, *Guardian* obituary, 14 March 2007)

(my italics)

This book is one of those projects referred to by David Rose, and it is a labour of love to write this foreword – I knew Tom for over 30 years. I worked closely with him several times, first meeting as detective sergeants in the 1970s when he was in A10, the new police complaints branch in the Met (Metropolitan Police of London), when he investigated me! He left a very different service from the one we joined. Modestly, he never agreed that he had influenced it greatly.

Tom's most notable long-term strategic contribution to policing followed three years at university reading psychology (1979–82) at York, when, virtually single-handed, he designed, crafted, and then began the delivery of the strategic and tactical thinking that underpinned the police response to suspect interviews. This was due legally in response to the dramatic, paradigm-shifting demands on investigators of the Police and Criminal Evidence Act but also due ethically, as identified by Tom some years earlier. Initially and unbelievably, this was done as a detective inspector (in spite of some ill-informed senior obstruction) and was based on his research in his Third Year undergraduate degree. In turn, this was then informed by his doctorate studies as a senior officer, and, finally, as a well-respected academic, he unwaveringly drove investigative interviewing. In the Met, then nationally and ultimately internationally, he pursued his moral vision of what was practical and showed what was possible, when talking to suspects.

He was an excellent staff officer, thoughtful about the turbulent time ahead and the nature of current problems. Junior officers, like his students later, benefited from his patient and detailed challenges and tuition. His role in mentoring officers writing dissertations, not just in psychology but across a range of disciplines, has had wide beneficial consequences for the intellectual strata of policing.

He was in the best sense, almost guileless, in his absolute, unwavering conviction that there was only the right way to carry out some policing tasks. He had a simple faith in what he was doing that survived the complex, messy, ambiguous, sometimes corrupt, dirty world of policing in the fetid gutters of London. Human rights became one of his passions. He wrote about it, and he and I jointly taught some investigative courses where it figured at the forefront of his teaching. He was a regular attendee at church throughout his life.

He was still writing and editing material prolifically about his vision of a police science, knowledge based, that shared information with communities, and I was still discussing concepts with him when he was ill a fortnight before his death. Widely read in law, history and policing, he was a great walker and conversationalist. Latterly, he was a meticulous writer on research and a skilled editor of others' works including my own.

This emphasis on Tom in no way diminishes the role played by his collaborators and contributors here; but I know they all saw this volume as his posthumous tribute, a continuing contribution by one of the great police reformers of our times.

John G.D. Grieve, CBE, QPM
University of Portsmouth

Introduction

This book emanated from papers presented and discussions during the Second International Investigative Interviewing Conference, held at the University of Portsmouth on 5–7 July 2006, which attracted nearly 300 delegates from many countries. The late Dr Tom Williamson, our esteemed colleague, who first initiated the ideas for this book and who gathered the group of contributors together, aimed that this second book in the series would develop from the first publication: *Investigative Interviewing: rights, research, regulation,* which emanated from the first Investigative Interviewing Conference in Quebec, Canada, in 2004. That book was concerned with investigative interviewing practices, including the abuse of detainees at Guantánamo Bay by the US military. It provided a critical analysis of the most common interviewing training methodology in North America, the 'Reid model', began to identify the common features of best practice in investigative interviewing, and concluded with a discussion of factors that contribute to effective regulation.

This new book aims to address a different set of issues. There is growing interest in investigative interviewing in many countries around the world. One reason for this is that, as in England and Wales, miscarriages of justice cases have brought public disgrace on the criminal justice system of these countries, leading to political initiatives and legal changes that have encouraged the development of modern investigative interviewing methods and training programmes. Although each country has developed its own training programme, there is evidence of transfer of knowledge between countries, with training programmes having some common features.

Examination of the miscarriage of justice cases that have stimulated the reform programmes reveal common features, including over-reliance on confession evidence and 'tunnel vision' by investigators and prosecutors. It was seen from the papers presented at the Second International Investigative Interviewing conference that it can be argued that there seems to be a paradigm shift under way across the globe from the traditional interrogation model with its emphasis on persuading suspects to confess to the new investigative interviewing paradigm where the emphasis is on a search for the truth and the collection of accurate and reliable information.

There are three paradigmatic differences that can be observed between the two models. The first is that the over-reliance on confession evidence led to poor investigations, as this was often a short cut to a conviction, and improvements in investigative interviewing have forced investigators to conduct more thorough investigations, including making greater use of forensics, and evidence from witnesses and victims. This supports the research finding that one of the most important factors in whether people will confess or not is their perception of the weight of the evidence (e.g. Moston *et al.* 1990).

The second difference is that the emphasis on gathering accurate and reliable information from suspects, victims and witnesses is part of a new information-led approach to investigation where new models of managing investigations rely on information coming in from various specialisms, including crime scene examinations, forensics, covert surveillance and the interrogation of a specialist database of crimes. Investigative interviewing therefore fits well with the development of these new information- or knowledge-based models of investigation.

The third difference is that the intended outcome under the interrogation model was a conviction, and a confession was a powerful means of achieving a conviction. Recent research (Holmberg 2004), however, has shown that more humane methods of interviewing suspects and witnesses yield more information, and this information is of higher quality. Therefore, interviewing people in a humane way has utilitarian benefits for investigators. It also opens up the possibility of a different outcome from that of conviction. In the emerging model, the preferred outcome becomes managing the risk of the suspect going on to commit further offences. Humane interviewing is a vital component of an approach to offender management that looks to therapeutic and restorative outcomes. The old model, for example, did not look beyond the conviction, for example, of a sex offender, and to subsequent attempts at rehabilitation. The new model takes a different perspective and engages with suspects in ways that will enable some, if not all, to make the journey towards being safely reintegrated into the community. For those who represent a continuing risk, it provides a basis for continuing to work with them to manage the risk. This represents a significant theoretical development for the concept of investigative interviewing in the direction of risk management and therapeutic justice.

This book therefore examines international developments in investigative interviewing and will be in two parts. Part 1 will examine the cases leading to the paradigm shift in a number of countries. Part 2 will consider issues that are of current interest to practitioners and academics, including the continuing calls for the use of torture; whether it is possible to detect deception; and the contribution of investigative interviewing methods to concepts of therapeutic and restorative justice.

Part 1: Investigative interviewing and interrogation around the world

Part 1 of the book opens with a chapter written by Dr Stephen Moston, James Cook University, Queensland, who examines the area of investigative interviewing in Australia. Moston makes a critical historical review of cases and research examining interviewing in this jurisdiction. He also examines the use of video recording within the interview room, which was pioneered in Australia. The book then travels to Europe, and three chapters examine investigative interviewing and interrogation in the UK; the Nordic region; and France, Belgium and The Netherlands.

In Chapter 2 Shawyer, Milne and Bull provide a historical overview of the development of investigative interviewing in the UK and examine the reasons for the change in ethos in the UK from interrogation to investigative interviewing, which resulted in the move to a more professional approach to investigation as a whole. The chapter ends with an examination of the recent developments in the UK, including the new arrangements for the management of investigative interviewing by the police.

In Chapter 3, superintendents Ivar Fahsing and Asbjørn Rachlew of the Norwegian Police University, who are also psychologists, describe the miscarriage of justice cases that led to the movement towards investigative interviewing in Norway. They also document cases and developments in the other Nordic countries, Denmark, Sweden,

Finland, and Iceland. Finally, they describe a technique developed in Norway called KREATIV, which is an information-gathering approach to the interviewing of suspects of crime.

The final chapter in this European trio, Chapter 4, was written and edited by Marc van de Plas, Head of the Behavioural Science Unit of the Belgium National Police, assisted by Sylvie Clément, of the French gendarmerie, and Paul van den Eshof and Nicole Nierop of The Netherlands Police Agency. The chapter provides an overview of developments in these countries, Belgium and France having suffered from miscarriage of justice cases that as a result brought politicians and judges together to make fundamental changes. Some of these changes were discussed at a conference held in Paris in January 2006, sponsored by the EU AGIS programme and organised by the French gendarmerie. Similarly, the sub-section of this chapter concerning the Netherlands examines controversial interrogation strategies and miscarriage of justice cases that have led to great changes in The Netherlands.

The book then moves across the Atlantic Ocean to North America, and two chapters document the positions of interrogation and interviewing in Canada and the USA. The first written by Michel St-Yves, a psychologist with the Behavioural Science Unit of the Sûreté du Québec, describes several miscarriage of justice cases in Canada that led to a search for more effective methods of investigative interviewing. He describes the developments in Canada which continue to be strongly influenced by the Reid model. Professor Randy Borum, from the University of South Florida; Michael G. Gelles, Chief Psychologist of the US Navy Criminal Investigation Branch; and Steven M. Kleinman, a career intelligence officer, then provide an overview of developments in the USA including methods used by military and law enforcement agencies. The chapter starts to examine the thorny question, how far would one go with torture, if the ticking bomb scenario occurred? This chapter leads the reader nicely into Part 2 of the book, which examines current issues of interest and concern with regard to interrogation and investigative interviewing.

Part 2: Current issues in interrogation and investigative interviewing

This section of the book starts with Chapter 7, written by Professor Rod Morgan, formerly chair of the Committee for the Prevention of

Torture, Council of Europe, and Dr Tom Williamson, and it examines why and how people become torturers and then goes on to examine critically the arguments for the utilitarian case for torture, which continues to be made by some respected academics and organisations alike. On a similar vein, Chapter 8, written by Dr Ulf Holmberg, Kristianstad University College, Sweden, then explains why humane interviewing methods are more productive and how they provide a route into restorative and therapeutic models of justice.

The final two chapters of this book concern the question of whether we can detect deceit effectively. This is an integral part of interviewing within the criminal justice arena. Chapter 9, written by Professor Aldert Vrij and his colleagues, Professor Ronald Fisher, and Drs Samantha Mann and Sharon Leal, examines the research that indicates that it is difficult to detect lies and deceit. The chapter also critically evaluates guidelines for detecting lies in professional practice. The final chapter of the book, written by Dr Peter Bull, is the second chapter examining whether we can detect deceit, and it will critically analyse some of the traditional studies and their methodologies and explain new methods involving the simultaneous microanalysis of communication from verbal and non-verbal channels that may yield more useful results in this kind of analysis in the future.

No conclusion will be drawn, as our late colleague, Dr Tom Williamson, was meant to be part of the ending to this fruitful discourse. In his untimely death, Tom asked us to complete the book for him as part of his legacy. Instead what we want to say is that investigative interviewing would not be where it is today if it were not for Dr Tom Williamson. This book has been edited and written in his honour, and we hope the result lives up to his expectations. Tom's passion and determination for improving investigative interviewing practice in the UK and across the globe should be commended, and this was recently recognised at the Third International Investigative Interviewing Conference, held in Canada in 2008, where Tom was awarded a posthumous award for his work regarding human rights and investigative interviewing. We all miss him, and his drive for change, very much.

References

Holmberg, U. (2004) 'Crime Victims' Experiences of Police Interviews and Their Inclination to Provide or Omit Information', *International Journal of Police Science and Management*, 3: 155–170.

Moston, S., Stephenson, G.M. and Williamson, T. (1992) 'The Effects of Case Characteristics on Suspect Behaviour During Police Questioning', *British Journal of Criminology*, 32: 23–40.

Part 1

Investigative interviewing and interrogation around the world

Chapter I

Investigative interviewing of suspects in Australia

Stephen Moston

A matter of opinion

In Australia the criminal justice system is largely the responsibility of the states (there are six) and territories (two), with each state and territory having its own police force, laws and justice system. The Commonwealth, in the form of the Australian Federal Police, which was established in 1979, only takes responsibility for a limited range of offences, including national and international operations, and peacekeeping (Fleming 2004).

Surprisingly little primary research has been conducted in this country on investigative interviews with suspects. Instead, research has tended to focus on perceptions of the investigative process, with studies exploring the views of judges, prosecutors, defence lawyers, police officers, the public and even defendants (e.g. Dixon 2006; Moston and Fisher 2006; Kebbell *et al.* 2006). The reasons for this particular focus are complex, but centre on a deep-seated distrust (in both directions) between academics and police officers. This chapter will explore what we currently objectively know about investigative interviewing practices in Australia, with data mainly coming from a series of thorough (but narrowly focused) audit commissions, and also how the various players in the criminal justice system see the legislation, technology and operational practice of interviewing. It focuses on the investigative interviewing of suspects in criminal investigations, and thus excludes some interesting and innovative work on the interviewing of children who have witnessed criminal activity (e.g. Wilson and Powell 2001; Powell *et al.* 2002; Powell and Thomson 2003).

A bad beginning

According to the latest public opinion survey by the Queensland Crime and Misconduct Commission (2006), about a quarter of respondents (26.7 per cent) stated that they believed that the 'Police have a bad image in Queensland'. The percentage of respondents agreeing with this statement has shown a fairly steady decline since the survey was first conducted in 1991, when the majority (59.3 per cent) agreed with that same statement. This particular series of public opinion surveys were introduced after the public release of the final report in 1989 of the *Commission of Inquiry into Possible Illegal Activities and Associated Police Misconduct* (now commonly referred to as the 'Fitzgerald Report').

The Fitzgerald Report was a judicial inquiry into allegations of police corruption in Queensland that had initially been voiced in a series of newspaper articles, and later in a television documentary (for an investigative journalist's perspective, see Dickie 1988). Initially expected to last about six weeks, the inquiry lasted for nearly two years, directly resulting in the fall of the state government and the conviction of the Police Commissioner on charges of corruption. According to the report (p. 200),

> The Queensland Police Force is debilitated by misconduct, inefficiency, incompetence, and deficient leadership. The situation is compounded by poor organization and administration, inadequate resources, and insufficiently developed techniques and skills for the task of law enforcement in a modem complex society. Lack of discipline, cynicism, disinterest, frustration, anger and low esteem are the result. The culture which shares responsibility for and is supported by this grossly unsatisfactory situation includes contempt for the criminal justice system, disdain for the law and rejection of its application to police, disregard for the truth, and abuse of authority.

One of the most pervasive forms of police misconduct identified in the Fitzgerald Report was the process of 'verballing' (where a confession or other damaging statement is fabricated by the police), which was seen as arising from a sense of frustration and contempt for the criminal justice system. Verballing was used for two main reasons: to attack the enemies of the police force, and as a form of defence to protect officers who were the subject of charges. The practice of verballing has a long and curious history. Long, in that as early as 1893 (in the UK), Justice Cave, in *R* v. *Thompson*, had expressed doubts over the reliability of claims by police officers that suspects had spontaneously confessed and then subsequently changed their minds (Findlay *et al.* 2005). Curious, in that unless a verbal was absurd, or in contradiction of conclusive evidence, Australian courts appeared only too willing to give such evidence credence. Further, even when verbals were recognised as outright lies, police officers were rarely punished for attempting to fabricate such evidence.

According to Dixon (2006), the widespread practice of verballing reflects a legal system which placed a heavy dependence on confession evidence. For example, according to archival research by Stevenson (1980), a staggering 96.6 per cent of cases seen in Australian criminal courts included confession evidence.

Even though the courts are notionally relied on to control police malpractice through the exclusion of evidence, such controls are rarely ever observed. In fact, the limited amount of control on interviews with suspects was reflected in the fact that until 1997 Australian police officers did not have any statutory power to detain a suspect for investigative purposes between arrest and charging (Dixon 2006).

The dialogue of the deaf

In their review of the relationship between police research and practice, Perez and Shtull (2002: 169) wrote, 'The historical reluctance of the police in America to analyze, to accept, and to apply research findings to their daily tasks has been slowly exiting the stage for a quarter of a century now.' That very same sentiment might equally be applied to Australia, with senior policing figures, such as Victoria Police Research Fellow David Bradley (2005), acknowledging some progress, but lamenting the lack of improvement in linking research, evaluation and policy in policing.

To put matters in perspective, in the UK in the last 25 years, there have been several large-scale studies of police interviewing procedures and suspect behaviour (e.g. Moston *et al.* 1992; Baldwin 1993; Moston and Stephenson 1993b; Bucke and Brown 1997; Phillips and Brown 1998). In addition, there have also been several smaller- scale studies focusing on specific populations (e.g. juveniles, by Evans 1993) or specific research issues (e.g. the impact of psychological vulnerabilities on confessions, by Pearse *et al.* 1998).

During this same period, there has only been a single study of police interrogation in Australia (Dixon and Travis 2004, 2007). For many years Stevenson's (1980) study of criminal cases in the NSW District Court stood as the only published study on confessions. Stevenson (p. 106) had hoped that her study would 'inject some empirical data into a debate characterized by speculation and pontification' and also that the tentative conclusions should be reviewed in subsequent research. Regrettably, no such study was undertaken. A possible reason for this may be that it is difficult even to discuss measures that could be interpreted, or even misinterpreted, as favouring suspects (Dixon 2006).

When studies have been undertaken, they have tended to focus on objectively verifiable concerns rather than more subjective or harder to quantify measures such as interviewing competency. For example, in audit studies in Queensland by the Criminal Justice Commission (1999) and the Crime and Misconduct Commission (2004), researchers analysed taped records of interviews ($n = 136$ and $n = 125$ randomly sampled cases respectively) to determine (among other objectives) the percentage of suspects who were advised of the right to silence (95.6 and 93.6 per cent respectively). While these were important data, since all suspects should be advised of their right to silence, neither study reported how many suspects actually exercised this right. While such data were beyond the parameters set for these studies, an opportunity was clearly missed.

In part, this reflects a long-standing antagonism between the police and academic researchers (mainly criminologists). Two key problems exist, the first of which has been a general disdain for research, a situation which is only slowly being resolved. For example, Commissioner Mick Keelty, of the Australian Federal Police, was interviewed as part of a series of interviews with senior police officers, published in the journal *Police Practice and Research* (Fleming 2004). Commissioner Keelty stated (p. 322), 'We recognise the value of theory in our work and have begun to work closely with academics in recent years… It's a strong policing organisation that can expose itself to research and to academics, to look at what it's doing, to measure what its doing, and to critically analyse its efforts.'

Chief Commissioner Christine Nixon (Victoria Police), who was also interviewed as part of the *Police Practice and Research* special issue (Prenzler 2004), expressed similar sentiments, saying, 'For me, academic studies have affected my view of policing. Access to research has underpinned the way I try to think about what we're going to do in policing and overcome the opinion-based, "this is what I feel," stuff.'

To readers outside Australia, such statements may seem somewhat obvious. Of course, research and practice should go hand-in-hand. The fact that they clearly do not reflects the second key problem, namely a history of animosity between police and criminologists, described by Chief Commissioner Christine Nixon as follows:

> There's a famous publication in the NSW Police called 'The Dialogue of the Deaf,' on relations between police and criminologists and how they come from different perspectives. One says, 'Why is it they only ever want to publish things we've done wrong?' The other says, 'Why do they always want to cover up what they've done wrong?' (Prenzler 2004: 310)

Notwithstanding the fact that the paper referred to was actually describing the relationship between the police and criminologists *in the UK* (the original paper was prepared for the Police Foundation of England and Wales in 1987 by Barry MacDonald), it is evident that the situation in Australia is an ongoing cause for concern. Chief Commissioner Nixon commented on the police-bashing industry among criminologists, suggesting, 'That hasn't done a lot of good. Some make a reasonably good living out of it. But policing is just as responsible for not having opened up to research. Although, it would be good to see criminologists take a more positive perspective on researching policing' (Fleming 2004: 310).

It is not only in the policing area that such antagonism exists. Many forensic research issues in Australia are effectively off-limits, as organisations retreat behind ever increasingly rigorous ethics restrictions. For example, in order to conduct primary research on police interviewing practices, such as analysing videotaped records of interviews, the records of interviews must first be de-identified. This process means that a videotaped record must first have the image of the suspect removed (thereby negating the value of analysing the video rather than the audio record), and any identifying details of the suspect and offence must be similarly removed from the soundtrack. This is not to say that primary research is impossible, but it is often extremely difficult. In some criminal justice organisations, research ethics boards have come to see their role as stifling independent research, often imposing tight quotas on the number of studies that can be approved each year. Consequently, much of what we know about police practice in investigative interviewing comes directly from the police services themselves, as well as the many investigatory bodies that oversee police conduct. These studies typically seek to investigate compliance with legislation, such as those reviewed in the following section,

Legislation and the practice of investigative interviewing

ERISP

The Electronic Recording of Interviews with Suspected Persons (ERISP) was first introduced in New South Wales in 1991, although it was not until 1995 that the law of evidence was changed (for example, in New South Wales, Tasmania and South Australia) to make electronic recording of interviews a prerequisite for the admissibility of confessional evidence (Dixon 2006), albeit only in serious cases. Nevertheless, police routinely use ERISP (noting that the terminology differs from state to state) to record all formal interviews. The reason for the widespread adoption of video-recording appears to have been an attempt by the police to dispel accusations of verballing, as opposed to it being a control on police questioning practices.

Under the 1995 laws, evidence of a confession or admission by the accused 'in the course of normal questioning' is not admissible unless 'there is available to the court a videotape of an interview with the accused person in the course of which the confession or admission was made' (s8 of the Tasmania Criminal Law (Detention and Interrogation) Act 1995), or there is a reasonable explanation as to why a videotape could not be made and the accused explains on videotape the circumstances of their earlier (non-recorded) admission.

When a suspect makes a 'confession, admission or statement' in non-ERISP interviews, the police officer is required to record the interview in full in a notebook. The suspect should be asked to sign the notebook. In any subsequent ERISP, the notebook entries should be read to the suspect who should be asked to comment on them (see NSW Police 2005, *Code of Practice for Custody, Rights, Investigation, Management and Evidence*, p. 26). This particular practice may be seen as condoning the use of preparatory interviewing, that is, informal interviews conducted away from recording equipment. In fact, data from a survey of police officers by Dixon (2006) suggest that the majority of officers (63 per cent) reported having questioned their most recent suspect before the beginning of ERISP. Similarly, a survey involving 1,005 defendants appearing before magistrates' courts in Queensland by the Criminal Justice Commission (2000) found that 49 per cent of defendants claimed that they had been interviewed at the point of first contact with police, and also that 33 per cent had been questioned informally at the police station. The same study found that 48 per cent of suspects recalled being formally interviewed at the police station.

Dixon (2006) suggests that while pre-ERISP interviewing may be alarming, most of the cases featuring such questioning are probably innocuous, with officers asking suspects how they will respond (admit or deny) during formal questioning and also as part of the preparation for a formal interview.

Given the concerns about pre-ERISP interviews, it is not surprising to learn that, in common with official and unofficial practice in other countries, many Australian police officers now carry personal recording devices. The Criminal Justice Commission (2000) defendant study reports that about 33 per cent of 'in the field' questioning was audio-recorded with another 2 per cent being video-recorded.

Australian courts will often grant police officers considerable leeway to report on interviews conducted away from ERISP facilities (or in fact any recording equipment). The limits of the legislation were illustrated in the High Court of Australia case of *R* v. *Kelly* (2004). During a videotaped interview, Shane Kelly accepted that he had told the police in an earlier unrecorded interview that he had confessed to the murder of a police informant. However, in the recorded interview, Kelly claimed that the earlier confession had been false. Some 30 minutes to an hour after the recorded interview had concluded, Kelly was escorted out of the police building to be taken to a hospital in order to obtain a blood sample. In the car park, Kelly then allegedly made the following statement: 'Sorry about the interview – no hard feelings, I was just playing the game. I suppose I shouldn't have said that, I suppose you will make notes of that as well.' The police officers did not respond, nor did they return him to an interview room. Nevertheless, this 'admission' was declared admissible in court, a decision which Dixon (2006) suggests invites process corruption.

The actual impact of ERISP on observable behaviours (such as convictions, confessions and use of the right to silence) is unknown, since there are no pre-ERISP data to permit any comparisons. In the absence of empirical data, opinion will have to suffice. Dixon (2006) conducted a survey in which police officers ($n = 123$), prosecutors ($n = 71$), defence lawyers and public defenders ($n = 77$), and judges ($n = 49$) were asked a series of questions about ERISP. The survey

9

found that the majority of police officers (62 per cent) and prosecutors (73 per cent) felt that ERISP had increased the number of guilty pleas in NSW, with about half of defence lawyers and judges (49 per cent in both samples) expressing the same opinion. Interestingly, in response to a question about the effect of ERISP on confessions, the police (41 per cent) and prosecutors (48 per cent) felt that the number of confessions had decreased.

The presence of legal advisers during interviews

Suspects have a right to legal advice while being questioned, although no legal aid or duty solicitor schemes are provided. Not surprisingly, then, it is rare that suspects see a lawyer before being charged or have one present during questioning, Dixon and Travis (2004) reporting that from a sample of 262 interviews that they observed, lawyers were present on only two occasions (just under 1 per cent). Similarly, the Criminal Justice Commission (2000) defendant study featured 385 cases in which defendants were formally interviewed in the police station. In only one case was a lawyer present, and in another two the defendant had spoken to a solicitor. Thus lawyers were contacted in less than 1 per cent of all formal interviews.

Stevenson (1980) had reported that from her sample, data indicated that a lawyer was contacted during or prior to interrogation in 10 out of 147 cases (almost 7 per cent). Interestingly, all suspects who made contact with a lawyer confessed. Together, these studies show that in Australia lawyers rarely ever play a part in the questioning of suspects. In addition, although the Stevenson (1980) and Dixon and Travis (2004) studies both have limited sample sizes, and Stevenson's and the Criminal Justice Commission data may be skewed, by virtue of being cases already at court (Stevenson) and because of the exclusion of suspects remanded in custody (Criminal Justice Commission), it appears that the use of lawyers may have declined over time.

The presence of other support persons in questioning

Dixon and Travis (2004) also report that it is more common to find support persons other than lawyers present during questioning, including family members (observed in 41 interviews, or about 16 per cent of the sample), and even members of the Salvation Army, or other religious affiliations (seen in five interviews; about 2 per cent). A similar picture emerged in an audit study conducted by the Crime and Misconduct Commission (2004) in Queensland, the purpose of which was to ascertain the extent to which the legal requirements of police officers during interviews with suspects were being adhered to. In this study, 16 per cent of suspects exercised their right to have a friend present at interview.

Support persons typically play little if any role in the interview itself, a situation that appears to owe much to the seating arrangements in the interview room, where police officers typically seat the support person behind the suspect (Dixon and Travis 2004). The limited activity of support persons suggests that they are not fulfilling the roles expected of them. For example, according to the NSW Police (2005: 17),

> When a support person arrives tell them they are there to assist and support the person during an interview; observe whether the interview is being conducted properly and fairly; and to identify any communication problems. Where possible allow the support person and person in custody to consult privately at any time, but within view of the police.

Identifying the vulnerable

In most states there is legislation (e.g. NSW Police 2005, Clause 24 of the Law Enforcement (Powers and Responsibilities) Regulation) that a person who falls within one or more of the following categories is a 'vulnerable person':

(a) children
(b) people who have impaired intellectual functioning
(c) people who have impaired physical functioning
(d) people who are Aboriginal or Torres Strait Islanders
(e) people who are of non-English-speaking background.

In most of the above cases, the interview should not proceed unless there is a support person present. In the Northern Territory, special rules, known as the Anunga Rules, exist for the interviewing of Aboriginals and Torres Strait Islanders. For example, there should be a 'prisoner's friend' present, the caution should be read back by the accused, questions should not be leading, and the custody manager should contact Aboriginal legal aid. Such instructions reflect awareness that interviews with indigenous persons may be complicated by a number of factors, including potential miscommunication arising from differing uses of language and the wider socio-cultural contexts of events (Powell 2000).

Police officers are advised, and in some states *required*, to ask the suspect questions to determine whether they might be vulnerable. Sample questions (NSW Police 2005) include:

- Do you use drugs (prohibited or prescribed)?
- Have you had any alcohol today?
- Do you have any mental illness?
- Are you taking medication?

The motives for determining the vulnerability of suspects are clearly specified in the NSW Police (2005) *Code of Practice for CRIME* (p. 114):

> In many offences the suspect's drug or alcohol dependency or mental illness might become an issue in court proceedings. For example, the suspect might claim in mitigation their dependency on heroin as a reason why they committed the offence. It might be appropriate for you to ask the suspect questions about drug/ alcohol use or mental illness.

The Queensland Crime and Misconduct Commission (2004) audit study found that less than half (45 per cent) of suspects who were identified as having special needs were asked questions (during taped interviews) in order to assess ability to understand their rights and ability to participate in a formal interview.

The right to silence

Suspects in Australia have a common law right to silence, except in specific circumstances where the law requires them to provide information (NSW Police 2005). In New South Wales the initial caution is as follows:

> I am going to ask you some questions. You do not have to say or do anything if you do not want to. Do you understand that? We will record what you say or do. We can use this recording in court. Do you understand that? (NSW Police 2005: 46.)

Despite legislative requirements, the Crime and Misconduct Commission (2004) audit study found that about 12 per cent of suspects were not informed (on tape) of their right to silence and of the fact that anything they said could be used in evidence. Further,

18 per cent were not informed of their right to a lawyer, and the same percentage were not advised of their right to have a friend or relative attend the interview.

Approach to interviewing

CSI Australia

Until recently, Australian police officers rarely received training in interviewing skills, even within specialist crime investigation units. Training initiatives (supplied by external consultants) are only gradually being introduced. To date, there has been very little critical thought on the topic of the effectiveness of interviewing techniques. This reflects a growing trend in which investigative skills have become increasingly replaced by a reliance on technology. It is a popular fallacy that most criminal investigations are solved through the use of scientifically verifiable evidence (such as fingerprints and DNA). In fact, the majority of cases are solved through evidence obtained in interviews with witnesses, or interrogation of suspects. Nevertheless, instead of training in interviewing skills, there is a common assumption that cases are solved through objective (mainly scientific) evidence rather than subjective evidence, such as information from witnesses or suspects. This is popularly referred to as the 'CSI effect' (Goodman-Delahunty and Newell 2004; Mirsky 2005).

The CSI effect is observable in a number of different forensic arenas. For example, Horvath and Meesig (1996), from a review of empirical findings, argued that the majority of criminal cases do not involve the use of any physical evidence. Further, even when it is available, it is not always used. The same authors (Horvath and Meesig 1998) subsequently argued that textbooks on criminal investigation perpetuated the same myth by overemphasising the role of forensic evidence relative to its actual use.

'Schlock psychology'

It should be noted that the current ERISP system involves simultaneous video- and audio-recording of interviews. It was initially expected that audiotaped records of interview would be relied on by the police, lawyers and courts. The purpose of the videotape was expected to be restricted to confirming the authenticity of the audiotape. However, according to Dixon (2006: 333) courts have routinely come to rely on the videotaped record. The reasons for this are noteworthy.

NSW judges have shown considerable interest in interpreting the ERISP image, particularly for the detection of deception. A disturbing encounter early in our research was with a judge who confidently claimed to be able to assess the veracity of witnesses by observing whether they glanced to left or right. Judges' interest in detecting deception provided much of the pressure for the showing of ERISPs in court.

Further support for this suggestion comes from the survey by Dixon (2006), where over half of the prosecutors and judges (56 and 57 per cent respectively) agreed with the statement, 'A suspect's demeanour during the interview indicates whether he or she is telling the truth.' Only about a quarter of police officers and defence lawyers (28 and 26 per cent respectively) agreed with that same statement.

While the Dixon (2006) survey suggests that police officers may not believe that they can detect deception, the NSW Police (2005: 25) document *Code of Practice for CRIME* does contain the following suggestion:

If the co-suspect has made an admission or confession on video, there is nothing prohibiting the showing of that admission to the suspect, albeit with an appropriate caution. Consider putting a television/video recorder above the electronic recording device and play the relevant parts of the co-suspect's admission to the suspect during your interview. This might result in some significant body language from the suspect.

Dixon (2006) is particularly scathing of the pervasive views concerning the value of reading body language, arguing that the existence of beliefs such as the ability to detect deception necessitates a programme of education and training for criminal justice professionals (including judges), to counter the 'widespread dissemination of schlock psychology through magazine articles or brief professional education courses' (p. 334). While the debate over whether or not it is possible to detect deception continues (e.g. Colwell *et al.* 2006), Australian police officers are making good use of the fact that observers frequently think that they can detect deception, regardless of their actual abilities. Confidence in a skill does not equal to competence (e.g. Colwell *et al.* 2006). It appears that Australian police officers are aware of this fact, and equally aware that many other professionals in the criminal justice system are not!

The use of evidence

Studies have shown that the strength of evidence against the suspect is the strongest predictor of the outcome of an interview, namely the decision to confess, deny or say nothing (e.g. Gudjonsson and Petursson 1991; Moston, *et al.* 1992).

Moston *et al.* (1992) suggested that the objective amount of evidence against a suspect is possibly of less importance than the suspect's perception of that evidence. That is, if evidence is strong (such as a video recording of a theft) but the suspect believes that it is weak (the suspect believes he/she was not seen), a confession is probably unlikely. Conversely, if the evidence is weak but the suspect perceives it as strong, then a confession may be more likely. This point has subsequently been borne out in a mock-suspect study by Kebbell *et al.* (2006), in which suspects were less likely to confess when confronted with a statement containing some inaccurate eyewitness evidence, compared to another comparable statement without any such inaccuracies.

Having strong evidence should make a confession more likely, provided the suspect perceives that evidence as confirming their guilt. When evidence is used prematurely in an interview, it gives the suspect an opportunity to offer an alternative explanation for the discovery of the evidence, often confounding the interviewer who had expected a confession (Moston and Stephenson 1993a; Moston *et al.* 2006). Police officers in New South Wales (NSW Police 2005) are specifically warned about the problems of evidence (such as fingerprints).

> If the suspect admits the offence after the allegation is put then proceed with normal questioning. However, if the suspect denies the offence do not introduce the fingerprint allegation 'upfront' as it gives the suspect opportunity to offer an explanation as to why their prints are where they are. (p. 56)

The Code of Practice then suggests that if the suspect claims to know nothing about the offence under investigation, then the officer should continue questioning in the following way. The suspect could be asked,

> Do you know where … is located? If the suspect claims not to know where the premises are then show the suspect a photograph of the premises. I show you a photograph of … Do

you recognise the house (shop etc) in the photograph? Have you ever been to that house (shop etc)? If 'yes' EXPLORE – when, where, did you go inside, what rooms did you go in, what did you do in them? Do you know the occupants? Please sign, date and place the time on the rear of the photograph. What is your current occupation? On the (date of offence) were you employed? Do you know the occupants of …? Do you know anybody by the name of (name of victims)? Do you have any knowledge of this break, enter and steal offence? Did you commit this break and enter? Do you know who did? Once the suspect's denials are complete then it is time to introduce the questions about the fingerprint evidence. (NSW Police 2005: 56)

This approach to interviewing is very different from the approaches seen in some other countries (e.g. the USA, where the ever popular 'Reid technique' holds that denials by the suspect are to be avoided; see Inbau *et al*. 2004). This approach is closer to that seen in countries such as The Netherlands (van der Sleen 2006), an approach described by Moston *et al*. (2006) as the 'anticipated denial interview'. In such an approach, the emphasis is on getting the suspect to give a detailed statement that would prevent a guilty suspect from rejecting the implication of the evidence in the case, while allowing innocent suspects the opportunity to explain how they have come to be under suspicion. However, before concluding that Australian police officers are actually conducting interviews of this type, primary research on current questioning practices is required. It may well be that NSW police officers do not conduct structured interviews, a conclusion that is borne out in the observations of Dixon and Travis (2004), which suggested low levels of skill and planning.

Legislative developments

Perhaps the most significant piece of legislation to be introduced in the last few years was the Police Powers and Responsibilities Act 2000 in Queensland, the purpose of which was to consolidate the vast majority of police powers into a single Act, the first of its kind in the country. Jim O'Sullivan, the Commissioner of Police in Queensland at the time the Act was introduced, said that 'it was clear from the Fitzgerald experience that support for broadening the powers to investigate crime would not be supported by the Queensland community or the State Government unless there was confidence in police to use the powers to further protect the community' (O'Sullivan 2000: 4). The public opinion surveys cited earlier would seem to suggest that the Australian public do now have (relatively) high levels of confidence in the police. This is in many ways quite surprising, as claims, and indeed proof, of corruption are frequently aired in the media. For example, in January 2007, the former judge Don Stewart accused the Victoria Police of corruption, an issue which will be returned to later in this chapter (see 'Video nasty').

There have also been other significant developments in policing in several states with the creation of special investigatory bodies (frequently dubbed 'Star Chambers' in the local media). For example, the Crime and Misconduct Commission in Queensland (see http://www.cmc.qld.gov.au/) is an independent law enforcement agency set up to combat organized crime, paedophilia, and corruption in the public sector. Normally, under Australian law, information from a detained person must be given voluntarily. Suspects have the right to refuse to answer and they cannot be coerced into answering (NSW Police 2005). However, one of the most striking aspects of these new bodies is that they acknowledge that major crime and corruption are often characterized by a 'wall of silence', and thus the commission has the power to conduct 'coercive hearings'. That is, suspects have to answer questions; the right to silence is not an option. Public opinion on these new bodies does not yet appear to have been assessed, and there is some disturbing evidence that the public may be developing an increasing tolerance of police misconduct, as is illustrated in the following case.

Video nasty

In September 2006, the Office of Police Integrity (OPI) in Victoria conducted hearings into allegations of brutality towards suspects in custody by the Armed Offenders Squad. During the hearings, the members of this unit were accused of assaulting several suspects, charges that squad members denied, although in one case the defendant (Detective Senior Constable Darren Paxton) said that he could not recall any acts of brutality (much to the disbelief of Judge Hartog Berkeley, who said, 'This is not the sort of thing one would forget'). As one officer took the stand to deny accusations of brutality, the OPI offered some remarkable new evidence. The OPI had secretly placed video cameras into the interview rooms used by Armed Offenders Squad officers, and the video record of an assault on one suspect (referred to as A100) was played to the court. This video was remarkable not only in terms of the evidence it offered, but as illustration of police and public reactions to allegations of police misconduct. Here are some of the 'highlights' of the tape (*Herald Sun* 2006).

May 10 2006 18:01.05

POLICE: Well, what are you going to do? How are you going to play it?

A100: Can I sit down?

POLICE: No, tell me now. You going to be all friendly and co-operative and tell us everything, look after your girlfriend? You going to do it that way or are you going to do it the f… hard, hard, hard way? Which way do you want to do it? Well (A100)?

(Appears to be thrown across the room)

POLICE: Welcome to the armed robbery squad.

A100: I'm thinking, I'm thinking man.

POLICE: Think faster, think faster, think faster.

A100: I'm thinking man.

POLICE: Think faster.

A100: I'm trying, I'm thinking.

POLICE: Alright. Where's the gun? Where's the gun?

A100: I'll tell you, I'll tell you, I'll tell you, I sold it.

(Comes back into the picture and sits down)

POLICE: When did you sell it? Don't shake your head.

(Appears to be assaulted again)

POLICE: F… dirty piece of sh.. running around shooting people.

A100: You don't understand, it wasn't …

POLICE: No, you don't understand.

A100: I haven't told you the full story yet …

POLICE: Don't sit there and shake your f… head in disgust at me. Sit down, I didn't tell you to get up. Sit down like the dirty piece of sh.. that you are. Are you beginning to get an understand of what's going on? We don't take too kindly to f…. c… like you pointing shotguns into people's heads. You think about what it was and I'll come back in a better mood hopefully and then we'll talk about it.

Finishes at 18:04.30

Resumes at 18:05.57

POLICE: Sit down now, the inspector wants to talk to you.

POLICE: It's going to be a long old day for you … It's going to be a long day for you alright. I suggest you listen to some

> of the advice that the boys are going to give you, it might be a lot less painful and a lot easier for you alright.

Finishes at 18:06.35

Resumes at 18:17.04

POLICE: Where's the gun?

A100:   I don't have it.

POLICE: I know you don't have it, where is it? Don't shake your f... head at me cos when I get up you're going to be in f... agony.

A100:   What do you want me to say?

POLICE: Tell us where it is, simple.

A100:   Can I at least have a cigarette.

POLICE: Tell us where the gun is first.

A100:   I've given you that much information already ... I just want to speak to my girlfriend, make sure my girlfriend is alright.

(Assault appears to take place, inaudible yelling and screaming)

POLICE: You f... piece of sh.. Make an ar... of me in my f... office.

A100:   I'm sorry boss, I'm sorry, I'm sorry I tell ya. (Assault seems to continue)

POLICE: Where is it?

POLICE: Start showing us some f... respect here – f... armed ... robbery ... squad.

Perhaps not surprisingly, the officer on the stand at the time the video was revealed (Detective Senior Constable Robert Dabb) actually fainted after seeing the tape. The official response to this evidence was that the Armed Offenders Squad would be immediately disbanded, although just over a week later Chief Commissioner Nixon agreed to restore the unit, albeit with a new name, 'the Armed Offenders Taskforce', a move which was seen as a significant back down in some parts of the media (e.g. Hughes 2006), while others seemed less surprised. For example, an article in *The Australian* (Rintoul 2006) included the following commentary on the case: 'Yes, the film looks bad, but what is the big picture here? Would a jury ever convict a detective for violently extracting evidence from a violent criminal about the location of a shotgun?'

This case is a telling reflection on the status of investigative interviewing in Australia. While efforts are being made to eliminate corruption and increase investigative competency, all too often the police, judiciary and public appear to have developed a not inconsiderable degree of tolerance of corruption and even incompetence. Confirmed cases of miscarriages of justice fail to ignite public outrage. One notable example is the case of the West Australian Andrew Mallard, who was convicted of murder in 1995. The main evidence against Mallard was a 20-minute, videotaped confession in which Mallard was shown theorising on how the killer of Pamela Lawrence might have committed the act. The remaining eight hours of Mallard's interview were not recorded. It took several appeals over nearly 12 years for the true details of this case to come to light.

What eventually emerged was that the police hid evidence that would have invalidated Mallard's theory (police tests showed that the murder weapon Mallard suggested had been used, could not have caused the injuries to Pamela Lawrence), and similarly also hid evidence from witnesses that contradicted the case against him (for example, one witness described the likely killer as having a beard but no moustache, while Mallard had a moustache but no beard). When Mallard was finally released from prison, the Director of Public Prosecutions, Robert Cock, was far from apologetic, publicly stating that Mallard remained a prime suspect for the murder. Nevertheless, police involved in the case stated that a new 'person of interest' had been identified (based on a new analysis of a palm print that had been found at the crime scene back in 1995). Shortly after being named as the new suspect, Simon Rochford, who was serving a life sentence for the murder of his girlfriend, committed suicide in his prison cell.

It is very likely that similar cases will come to light in the next few years. It will be interesting to see how the police services react to such developments, and, perhaps most importantly, how this will affect public perceptions. At the moment, a climate of indifference prevails, and thus any new initiatives are likely to come from within the police services themselves, rather than being imposed from the outside by state governments.

References

Baldwin, J. (1993) 'Police Interviewing Techniques: Establishing Truth or Proof?', *British Journal of Criminology*, 33: 325–352.

Bradley, D. (2005) 'Tackling the Knowledge Deficit in Policing: Strategic Change Versus Ad Hocery and Paint Jobs'. Paper presented at the conference 'Safety, Crime and Justice: From Data to Policy', Australian Institute of Criminology, ABS House, Canberra, 6–7 June.

Bucke, T. and Brown, D. (1997) *In Police Custody: Police Powers and Suspects' Rights Under the Revised Pace Codes of Practice*. A Research and Statistics Directorate Report. London: Home Office.

Colwell, L.H., Miller, H.A., Miller, R.S. and Lyons, P.M. (2006) 'US Police Officers' Knowledge Regarding Behaviors Indicative of Deception: Implications for Eradicating Erroneous Beliefs Through Training', *Psychology, Crime and Law*, 12: 489–503.

Crime and Misconduct Commission (2004) *Listening in: Results from a CMC Audit of Police Interview Tapes*. Monitoring Integrity in the Queensland Police Service, No. 1: April, Brisbane: Crime and Misconduct Commission Queensland.

Criminal Justice Commission (1999) *Analysis of Interview Tapes: Police Powers Review Briefing Paper*. Brisbane: Criminal Justice Commission, Research and Prevention Division.

Criminal Justice Commission (2000) *Police Powers in Queensland: Findings from the 1999 Defendants Survey*. Brisbane: Criminal Justice Commission, Research and Prevention Division.

Dickie, P. (1988) *The Road to Fitzgerald and Beyond*. St. Lucia: University of Queensland Press.

Dixon, D. (2006) '"A Window into the Interviewing Process?" The Audio-Visual Recording of Police Interrogation in New South Wales, Australia', *Policing and Society*, 16: 323–348.

Dixon, D. and Travis, G. (2004) Questioning Suspects and ERISP. Draft Report. Sydney: University of New South Wales.

Dixon, D. and Travis. G. (2007) *Interrogating Images: Audio-Visually Recorded Police Questioning of Suspects*. Sydney: Sydney Institute of Criminology.

Evans, R. (1993) *The Conduct of Police Interviews with Juveniles*. Royal Commission on Criminal Justice Research Study No. 8. London: HMSO.

Findlay, M., Odgers, S. and Yeo, S. (2005) *Australian Criminal Justice* (3rd edn). Oxford: Oxford University Press.

Fleming, J. (2004) 'Commissioner Mick Keelty, Australian Federal Police', *Police Practice and Research*, 5: 317–326.

Goodman-Delahunty, J. and Newell, B. (2004) 'One in How Many Trillion?', *Australian Science*, August: 14–17.

Gudjonsson, G.H. and Petursson, H. (1991) 'Custodial Interrogation: Why Do Suspects Confess and How Does it Relate to Their Crime, Attitude and Personality', *Personality and Individual Differences*, 12: 295–306.

Herald Sun (2006) 'Armed Offenders Squad Video Nasty', 19 September. Retrieved online on 20 September 2006 from: http://www.news.com.au/heraldsun/story/0,21985,20439385-2862,00.html.

Horvath, F. and Meesig, R. (1996) 'The Criminal Investigation Process and the Role of Forensic Evidence: A Review of the Empirical Findings', *Journal of Forensic Science*, 41: 963–969.

Horvath, F. and Meesig, R. (1998) 'A Content Analysis of Textbooks on Criminal Investigation: An Evaluative Comparison to Empirical Research

Findings on the Investigative Process and the Role of Forensic Evidence', *Journal of Forensic Science*, 43: 133–140.

Hughes, G. (2006) 'Backflip on elite squad', *The Australian*, 'Gotcha with Gary Hughes', (29 September 2006). Retrieved online on 29 September 2006 from: http://blogs.theaustralian.news.com.au/garyhughes/index.php/theaustralian/comments/backflip_on_elite_squad/.

Inbau, F.E., Reid, J.E., Buckley, J.P. and Jayne, B.C. (2004) *Criminal Interrogations and Confessions* (4th edn). London: Jones & Bartlett.

Kebbell, M.R., Hurren, E.J. and Mazerolle, P. (2006) 'An Investigation into the Effective and Ethical Interviewing of Suspected Sex Offenders', *Trends and Issues in Crime and Criminal Justice*, No. 327. Canberra: Australian Institute of Criminology.

Kebbell, M.R., Hurren, E.J. and Roberts, S. (2006) 'Mock-Suspects' Decision to Confess: The Accuracy of Eyewitness Evidence is Critical', *Applied Cognitive Psychology*, 20: 477–486.

Mirsky, S. (2005) 'Crime Scene Instigation', *Scientific American*, 25 April. Retrieved from www.sciam.com.

Moston, S. and Fisher, M. (2006) 'Defining the Limits of Police Interrogation Techniques with Criminal Suspects', in M. Ioannou and D. Youngs (eds), *Explorations in Investigative Psychology and Contemporary Offender Profiling*. London: IA-IP Publishing.

Moston, S. and Stephenson, G.M. (1993a) 'The Changing Face of Police Interrogation', *Community and Applied Social Psychology*, 3: 101–115.

Moston, S. and Stephenson, G.M. (1993b) *The Questioning and Interviewing of Suspects Outside the Police Station*. London: Royal Commission on Criminal Justice/HMSO.

Moston, S., Stephenson, G.M. and Williamson, T.M. (1992) 'The Effects of Case Characteristics on Suspect Behaviour During Police Questioning', *British Journal of Criminology*, 32: 23–40.

Moston, S., Fisher, M. and Engelberg, T. (2006) '"It Was My Evil Twin": Plausible and Implausible Denial Strategies in the Interview Room'. Paper presented at 2nd International Investigative Interviewing Conference, University of Portsmouth, 6 July.

NSW Police (2005) *Code of Practice for Custody, Rights, Investigation, Management and Evidence (CRIME)*. Sydney: NSW Police.

O'Sullivan, J.P. (2000) 'Police Powers Legislation a First in Australia', *Vedette*, 178: 4–5.

Pearse, J., Gudjonsson, G.H., Clare, I.C.H. and Rutter, S. (1998) 'Police Interviewing and Psychological Vulnerabilities: Predicting the Likelihood of a Confession', *Journal of Community and Applied Social Psychology*, 8: 1–21.

Perez, D.W. and Shtull, P.R. (2002) 'Police Research and Practice: An American Perspective', *Police Practice and Research*, 3: 169–187.

Phillips, C. and Brown, D. (1998) *Entry into the Criminal Justice System: A Survey of Police Arrests and their Outcomes*. Home Office Research Study No. 185. London: HMSO.

Powell, M.B. (2000) 'PRIDE: The Essential Elements of a Forensic Interview with an Aboriginal Person', *Australian Psychologist*, 35: 186–192.

Powell, M.B. and Thomson, D.M. (2003) 'Improving Children's Recall of an Occurrence of a Repeated Event: Is It a Matter of Helping Them to Generate Options?', *Law and Human Behavior*, 27: 365–384.

Powell, M., Wilson, C. and Hasty, M. (2002) 'Evaluation of the Usefulness of "Marvin", a Computerized Assessment Tool for Investigative Interviewers of Children', *Computers in Human Behavior*, 18: 577–592.

Prenzler, T. (2004) 'Chief Commissioner Christine Nixon, Victoria: Australia's First Female Police Chief', *Police Practice and Research*, 5: 301–315.

Queensland Government (2000) *Police Powers and Responsibilities Act 2000*. Brisbane: Queensland Government.

Rintoul, S. (2006) 'Judge Rejects Detective's Tale', *The Australian*, 21 September. Retrieved online on 21 September 2006 from: http://www.theaustralian. news.com.au/story/0,20867,20448757-2702,00.html.

Stevenson, N. (1980) 'Criminal cases in the NSW District Court: A Pilot Study', in J. Basten, M. Richardson, C. Ronalds and G. Zdenkowski (eds), *The Criminal Injustice System*. Sydney: Australian Legal Workers Group (NSW) and Legal Services Bulletin.

van der Sleen, J. (2006) 'A Structured Model for Investigative Interviewing of Suspects'. Paper presented at 2nd International Investigative Interviewing Conference, University of Portsmouth, 6 July.

Wilson, J.C. and Powell, M.B. (2001) *A Guide to Interviewing Children*. Sydney: Allen and Unwin.

Chapter 2

Investigative interviewing in the UK

Andrea Shawyer, Becky Milne and Ray Bull

Introduction

Investigative interviewing by police in the UK has changed dramatically over the last few decades. The aim of the interview has evolved from a confession-seeking exercise to a process that seeks to gather high-quality information to aid the investigation in a fair and ethical manner. Even the labels applied to such interviews have evolved from 'interrogation' (persuasion) to 'investigative interviewing' (enquiry), suggesting a less confrontational and aggressive approach (Rabon 1992). The importance of the interviewing of suspects, witnesses and victims in the investigation process cannot be underestimated, as it forms an essential and core element of crime investigation (Milne and Bull 1999).

Changes in the format and process of interviewing in the UK came about partly due to a number of miscarriages of justice (for example the Guildford Four, the Birmingham Six) that led to legislative change (Police and Criminal Evidence (PACE) Act 1984), and to related guidance resulting in the development of new interviewing policy and training. In addition, research concerning behaviour in the interview room (e.g. Moston *et al.* 1992; Baldwin 1993) highlighted the fact that, for suspects, witnesses and victims, the interviewer can have a significant impact on the quality and quantity of information gathered from the interviewee. This chapter will discuss the evolution of investigative interviewing of both suspects and witnesses/victims in England and Wales (though the majority of these changes are reflected across the UK). This chapter will begin by considering suspect interviews, with a brief history of pertinent cases and relevant legislation. The chapter will then go on to discuss the interviewing of witnesses and victims. Finally, new developments in interviewing within the UK will be presented.

Interviewing of suspects

The interviewing of suspects is a key stage of the investigation process, and provides essential information for the development of the case, informing future directions of enquiry and providing crucial evidence to support the case (Schollum 2005). Consequently, it is vital that this evidence be gathered in a manner which ensures that it is accurate and thorough. In the 1970s, the UK police were being pressurised to address increasing public concern over the tactics that they were employing during interviews with suspects, as more and more miscarriages of justice came to light (Savage and Milne 2007). These miscarriages highlighted the issues of corrupt police practices leading to false confessions (Gudjonsson 1992) and the problems associated with poor interviewing techniques (Bull and Cherryman 1995). At that time, interviews with suspects were still not being electronically recorded, and thus the interview room was not open to outside scrutiny, although research such as Irving and Hilgendorf's (1980) observational study for the Royal Commission on Criminal Procedures (1981) offered some insight into police interviewing practice. They reported that the interviewers were using manipulative tactics to gain confessions from the suspects. It was not until the mandatory taping of suspect interviews following the implementation of PACE in 1984 that the interviewing process became more widely accessible. This in turn resulted in a substantial body of research examining behaviour and practice in the police interview room (for example, Baldwin 1992).

The associated codes of practice offered guidance on the questioning of suspects in police custody (for example, tape recording of interviews and access to free legal advice), highlighting the need to avoid oppressive tactics during interviews, with an aim to gather information rather than gain a confession per se (Williamson 2006). This change in focus aimed to reduce the risk of 'noble cause corruption', the practice of using unethical tactics to gain a confession at all costs. However, despite the legislation protecting the 'suspect' (PACE) and a move towards a culture of 'fairness', there were still cases coming to light about miscarriages of justice arising from inappropriate interview techniques – for example, the 'Cardiff Three' case, in which the murder in 1988 of the prostitute Lynette White led to the conviction of three men, all of whom were freed two years later at appeal. The handling of this case is currently still under investigation by South Wales Police, and so far four witnesses from the original trial have been charged with perjury, with 14 more people still under investigation (Crown Prosecution Service 2007). In addition, the interviewing of one of the men in particular was criticised at the Court of Appeal: 'Delivering his ruling, Lord Justice Taylor said that short of physical abuse, it was hard to conceive of a more hostile and intimidatory approach by police officers to a suspect, during the interview of Steve Miller' (BBC 2003).

Furthermore, despite PACE recommendations, Baldwin's critical report in 1992 highlighted serious issues in police interviewing, including poor technique and assumptions of guilt (Milne and Bull 1999). These criticisms and miscarriages of justice cases highlighted the underlying issues with using unethical interviewing techniques in an investigation, in terms both of human rights concerns regarding the innocent being incarcerated and of the actual perpetrators still being free to reoffend. Simply put, oppressive and biased interviewing is not an 'intelligent' way in which to inform the investigation and gather good-quality information resulting in successful case solutions.

Thus, it was clear that a move towards more ethical interviewing practices was needed, and the concept of investigative interviewing and associated values of fairness, openness and accountability began to emerge. Far from being a 'soft option', this model of interviewing should be viewed as the rational choice for any investigation. The seven principles of investigative interviewing approved by the (England and Wales) Association of Chief Police Officers (ACPO) and the Home Office (i.e. government) Steering Group on Investigative Interviewing in 1992 included open-mindedness, fairness, and con-sideration of vulnerable interviewees, as well as the right to ask questions, even persistently, if relevant (National Crime Faculty 1996). These principles indicated a more neutral role for the interviewer, with the emphasis on gathering information rather than merely seeking a confession (Williamson 1994). Subsequently, these principles and associated techniques were developed into a standardised framework for ethical interviewing known as PEACE (see below) involving a five-day training course, and outlined in two booklets issued to all 127,000 police officers in England and Wales by the Central Planning and Training Unit (CPTU) in 1992: *A Guide to Interviewing* (CPTU 1992a) and *The Interviewer's Rule Book* (CPTU 1992b).

The PEACE model of investigative interviewing is a mnemonic for *P*lanning and preparation; *E*ngage and explain; *A*ccount; *C*losure; and *E*valuation. The framework encourages an open-minded and ethical approach to interviewing suspects, and the aim at each stage is to increase the quality and quantity of information gathered from the interviewee (Shaw 1996). The model is based on psychological principles and theory (e.g. regarding non-verbal behaviour, vulnerability and memory) and in turn derives further influence from practice. The planning and preparation stage prior to the interview requires that the interviewer gather all the necessary evidence and information about the event, and prepare topics, questions and points to prove. The next three stages (engage and explain, account, and closure) occur during the interview and help the process to flow in a logical manner, and at each phase, the interviewer is encouraged to use open questions, and to develop the topics logically, summarising along the way. During the account stage of PEACE, two techniques can be used by the interviewer to encourage the interviewee to talk: conversation management (CM) or the cognitive interview (CI). CM can be used for uncooperative interviewees (who will largely be suspects, but may also include witnesses) and involves techniques for maximising the information gathered and facilitating communication between interviewer and interviewee (Shepherd 1986). In this stage, skills in active listening, rapport building and conversational turn-taking are key in encouraging the interviewee to talk, and in gathering an accurate and thorough account. The other technique is the cognitive interview (CI) (Fisher and Geiselman 1992).

The enhanced cognitive interview (ECI) (see Milne and Bull 1999 for details) uses psychological theories on memory to gather a high-quality, comprehensive account from the cooperative interviewee (mostly witnesses and victims but also suspects). This technique will be discussed in more detail in the section on witness interviewing. The final stage (evaluation) refers to both the content and the quality of the interview, whereby the interviewer can consider good and poor practice, and to the evaluation of the information generated from the interview.

The overriding ethos of PEACE is related to fairness and openness, and does not advocate such practices as trickery and deception in order to obtain a confession. PEACE encourages the interviewer to avoid assumptions of guilt, to keep an open mind, and to seek the 'truth'. Kassin *et al.* (2003), among others, consider that such assumptions of guilt made prior to the interview can lead to 'confirmation bias' during the interview, whereby interviewers are looking for behaviour and information that supports their prior beliefs, even if these beliefs may be faulty (Ede and Shepherd 2000). This practice is more likely to result in a judgemental attitude and a closed mind, which in turn could mean that vital new information is missed or ignored. Closed-mindedness is also likely to lead to coercive questioning as the interviewer attempts to 'break' the interviewee and get a confession.

In addition to the behaviour described above, if interviewers are also looking for supposed signs of deception to support their assumptions, then inaccurate beliefs about the types of non-verbal behaviours that might indicate deception can further compound the problem (Vrij 2000). This increases the risk of the interview disintegrating into a defective 'cycle of confirmation' whereby interviewers are actively looking for behaviours that they believe indicate deception (such as fidgeting and lack of eye contact), but these behaviours may be more indicative of nervousness unrelated to deception and/or of a reaction to the interviewer's own behaviour (Vrij 2000). Figure 2.1 illustrates the cycle of confirmation that can occur in an interview, given the relevant conditions. The risk of this cycle of interviewer assumptions and behaviour is that the interviewer could become aggressive or oppressive during the questioning of the suspect, in an attempt to confirm potentially incorrect beliefs (which could well result in causing the suspect to behave in ways (incorrectly) believed to indicate deception).

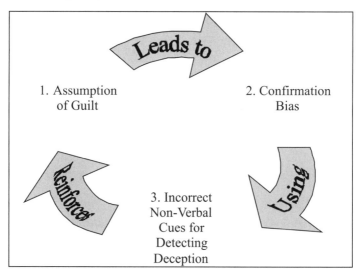

Figure 2.1 Interview cycle
(taken from Shawyer, in preparation)

The intention of the PEACE philosophy is to move away from the 'questions-and-answer' format previously employed in interviews with suspects, and to use a more interviewee-led format. In this way, interviewees are given an opportunity to put across their version of events, and the information gathered is likely to be much more useful in terms of points to prove. The use of open questions ('Tell me everything that you did on that day') is more likely than a closed question to lead to more detailed answers (if the interviewee is not interrupted by the interviewer), with information being in the interviewee's own words (Griffiths and Milne 2006). The interviewee is challenged at a later stage in the interview when appropriate. As well as encouraging the use of open questions and appropriate closed probing questions (why, what, where, when and how types of questions that aim to probe further into issues already raised by the interviewee), it is also important to avoid leading questions, as these can not only increase the risk of false confessions with vulnerable interviewees but also taint any subsequent information given by the interviewee.

The taping of suspect interviews has opened the police to close scrutiny and greater accountability, meaning that evidence collected in an interview can be assessed in terms of its authenticity and quality at any subsequent stage in the criminal justice system. In addition, many other agencies have adopted a similar approach in their investigations and interviews, and some of these will be discussed in the next section.

Gudjonsson (2003) suggests that false confessions are a potential risk in interviews which have the characteristics shown in Figure 2.1. If an interviewee faces coercive questioning, he or she may resist the pressure to confess or, conversely (and in particular if vulnerable – young, or with mental health issues), may falsely confess to the crime. This confession may occur despite the suspect's still believing in his or her own innocence (coerced-compliant), or even more worryingly, he or she may even internalise the beliefs of the interviewer and start to accept his or her own guilt (coerced-internal) (see Gudjonsson 2003 for examples). A third category of false confession is termed 'voluntary' and does not involve issues of unscrupulous police practice or external pressures (Gudjonsson 1992; Kassin 1997). If individuals are particularly suggestible or compliant, it is more likely that they will be influenced by leading questions and oppressive interviewing techniques. Both the interview situation and the interviewee's disposition (suggestible, compliant, and tendency to conform or obey authority figures) can influence the likelihood

29

of a 'coerced' false confession. The PEACE model therefore aims to address the first of these issues (the situation), and knowledge of vulnerable groups (i.e. the second issue) will help interviewers to optimise the interview.

The PEACE technique and associated principles therefore aim to minimise the risks of false confessions. Although knowledge of the conditions that might lead to a true confession should be understood and maximised, this should not prevent the interviewer from seeking further information after a confession has been made, (i) to help assess whether the confession is genuine, and (ii) to reduce the likelihood of later retraction of the confession (Centre for Investigative Skills 2004). PEACE, therefore, far from being the 'soft option' that it may be perceived as, offers instead an intelligent approach to interviewing suspects.

It might be assumed that a PEACE-based interview would be more likely to result in reliable confessions, as interviewees are treated with respect and have a fair opportunity to tell their story. Similarly, false confessions would appear to be a less likely outcome of the PEACE interview process, as there should be no coercion or undue pressure put on the interviewee. Did PEACE work? Did the new philosophy of investigative interviewing change the behaviour of the interviewers? Research conducted since PEACE was adopted (by all forces in England and Wales in 1993) suggests general improvement but that some aspects of interviewing still need attention (for example, see Clarke and Milne 2001), although it appears that the taping of interviews has at least minimised the unscrupulous practices and oppressive tactics used in earlier years (Bull and Milne 2004). Recent guidance from Centrex (a government-funded body involved in the training and development of best practice in the police, and, since April 2007, part of the National Policing Improvement Agency (NPIA)) has suggested that certain core interviewer skills need to be developed for successful interviewing, such as good planning, listening skills and rapport building (National Crime Faculty 2004), adding to the debate about whether good interviewing is a natural skill or can be taught to any individual (Shepherd and Kite 1989; Williamson 1994; Milne and Bull 1999; Cherryman and Bull 2001). Questioning skills are still an issue (Griffiths and Milne 2006), with an unacceptable level of leading and inappropriate questions still being asked during the interview, and, as discussed earlier, these can increase the risk of false confessions with certain vulnerable individuals. Issues have also been highlighted about the transference of skills from the training course to the workplace, and the necessity of adequate evaluation and supervision for full effectiveness of training to take place (Clarke and Milne 2001). Griffiths and Milne (2006) highlight the overall decline in interviewer performance after time compared to 'end of training' assessment, but suggest that this may be due to the very different nature of post-training tests to real-life interviews, and is not necessarily an indication that skills are deteriorating. Recent developments in investigative interviewing aim to address these issues. Some of these developments, including the new 'five-tier' initiative (Griffiths and Milne 2006) focusing on the training of police officers, will be discussed later in this chapter. The next section will briefly consider the adoption of PEACE by agencies other than the police.

PEACE and public sector agencies

In the UK, the PEACE model of interviewing has also been adapted for use in many different spheres of investigation, in both the public and private sectors. The Department for Work and Pensions (DWP, which investigates cases relating to various unemployment benefit frauds) and other government departments, has developed a training programme for fraud investigators aiming to standardise investigation techniques, including surveillance, expert witness practices, and interviewing. Known as PinS (Professionalism in Security), this training package aims to generate a professional body of counter-fraud investigators using techniques that are considered to be successful in police investigations. The critical question is whether techniques such as PEACE can be successfully adapted to fit public sector fraud interviews. Findings from the small amount of research that has focused on this issue, specifically in the DWP, suggest that some aspects of PEACE are applied more successfully than others in the interviews (Shawyer and Milne 2006; Walsh and Milne 2007, 2008). The use of open questions seems to present a particular problem to public-sector counter-fraud investigators, with interviews shown to be peppered with closed or, more worryingly, leading questions (Shawyer and Milne 2006; Walsh and Milne 2007). The investigators themselves, when surveyed, found the model to be particularly cumbersome for *some* fraud interviews; 'a sledgehammer to crack a nut' was how one fraud investigators described PEACE when used in public-sector fraud interviews (Shawyer, in preparation). This may be an issue of supervision, and transference to the workplace, whereby the skills learnt and practised in the training are not sufficiently supported later in the workplace.

The next section will focus on use of the enhanced cognitive interview to gather information from willing suspects, victims, and witnesses.

Witness interviews

Interviews with witnesses have historically received relatively less scrutiny from police researchers and practitioners than interviews with suspects, possibly due to the high profile of cases of miscarriage of justice that involved unscrupulous suspect interviewing practices, and due to the importance placed on confessions as evidence. However, the information generated by witness interviews can be considered to be the most important aspect of the investigation (Milne and Bull 2003). Inadequately collected witness evidence will have a negative effect on the future direction of the investigation, or may lead to false convictions (Savage and Milne 2007). Consequently, it is essential to ensure that the interview generates a large quantity of high-quality information that can be effectively used in the investigation. More recently, since the 1980s, researchers have focused on methods for obtaining such large-volume, high-quality information from interviewees, and have turned to psychological theory to support this endeavour (Milne and Bull 1999).

The cognitive interview (CI) was developed by using psychological theories of memory to extract as much accurate information as possible from the 'willing' interviewee. Based on the principle that memory is vulnerable and fallible (many factors may actually affect the accuracy and quantity of what is remembered), the CI uses a range of techniques that have been found to enhance memory and that support the communication of accurate recall of information about an incident. The use of this approach for witnesses and victims, generating, as it does, more accurate information (Koehnken *et al.* 1999), will clearly aid the investigation of the incident. The enhanced CI (Fisher and Geiselman 1992) advocates an interviewee-led approach to the interview, giving interviewees the space and time to provide their version of the events. Questions asked must be open and neutral, to avoid any bias that the interviewer may bring to the interview. The key objective of a witness interview should be to increase recall quantity, without jeopardising the accuracy of that information.

There is no PACE equivalent for witnesses and victims; however, there are two important pieces of relevant legislation in the UK to be considered. The first is the Criminal Justice Act 1991 that allowed the videotaping of interviews with children in certain serious cases to be admitted as their evidence-in-chief in court proceedings. The *Memorandum of Good Practice for Video Recorded Interviews with Child Witnesses for Criminal Proceedings*, produced in 1992 (Home Office and Department of Health 1992), aimed to give guidance to police officers and social workers on the conduct of such interviews, as interviews conducted in an inappropriate manner (e.g. using predominantly leading questions) could cause the video interview to be deemed inadmissible. In child abuse cases (where there often is limited forensic evidence), the child's account is pivotal to the case. If this account is not obtained properly, a conviction is most unlikely. Using psychological knowledge and research, the guidance outlined the best ways to interview children to gather the most complete and accurate account without putting words into their mouths. But why should only children be allowed such special measures? The Youth Justice and Criminal Evidence Act 1999 widened the scope of these measures, extending the potential for videotaping interviews with 'vulnerable' or 'intimidated' adult witnesses or victims. This includes those that qualify due to some form of physical or mental incapacity or to the level of fear or distress experienced by them. As a result, the *Memorandum of Good Practice* was expanded and updated in 2001 in a document entitled *Achieving Best Evidence in Criminal Proceedings: Guidance for Vulnerable and Intimidated Witnesses Including Children* (Home Office and Department of Health 2001), which provided comprehensive guidance on the interviewing of wider groups deemed vulnerable (including not only children but also vulnerable adults). It should also be noted that the videotaping of witnesses has additional benefits such as having a record of the interview for subsequent investigations if the witness becomes a suspect.

The ethical interviewing of witnesses is thus as crucial as in those interviews involving suspects; not only can witnesses disclose essential information in the investigation – which therefore needs to be accurate and thorough – but they also need to be treated in a manner that will maximise the likelihood of witnesses coming forward for future investigations and ensure that their experience is not a negative one. The witnessing of a crime can be a very stressful event for most people; then to become involved in the Criminal Justice System because of this is an extra burden on the individual, and this pressure needs to be recognised.

The next section will consider recent changes in the training and nature of investigative interviewing in England and Wales, with respect to suspects, witnesses and victims.

Recent developments in investigative interviewing

The advent of PEACE training has had some positive impact on the quality of interviews with suspects, but this is not universal or consistent (Clarke and Milne 2001). A more appropriate and comprehensive system of training police officers to interview suspects, witnesses and victims was required to bring the standard of interviewing to a higher level. In 2004, the police began a new initiative, developed from recommendations made by Clarke and Milne in 2001, to put the training that was given to police officers into five tiers (Table 2.1). This has had the effect of focusing the training in a more appropriate and relevant fashion, considering the experience, skills and previous training of each officer and the likely complexity of various types of interview. Police officers should be equipped with the most useful tools to suit their needs in any specific situation and relevant to their level or position.

The five-tier strategy involves extensive training (one to three weeks) at each level, with continual workplace assessment and support (see Griffiths and Milne 2006; Milne *et al.* 2007 for more detail). In addition, guidance from the national police Centre for Investigative Skills (CFIS) (2004) recommends strategies for gathering robust, accurate and full accounts from interviews, and discourages a reliance on confessions as an interview outcome.

In addition to this initiative, the Professionalising Investigation Programme (PIP) has been implemented by the police in England and Wales to improve police performance in investigations more generally, by providing adequate training to all investigators, who are assessed and accredited to ensure that a high standard is maintained at all levels of policing. The five-tier strategy will work alongside this national initiative, and provide a structure to the training and

Table 2.1 Five tier interview training

Tier	Interviewing training
1	Introductory interview training for new recruits (up to two years of service)
2	Extension and development of tier 1 for more experienced officers
3	Interviewing suspects and witnesses in serious/complex crime investigations
4	Supervision of interviews in the workplace
5	Coordinating of interviews in serious/complex crime investigations

assessment needed to achieve an acceptable standard of interviewing within any investigation.

So with the UK moving towards more ethical and fair interviewing techniques, the system being one of due process, respect of the interviewee, and the seeking of information rather than just a confession, the treatment of people in police custody has improved, and the likelihood of false confessions minimised.

The development of the PEACE model highlights the benefits of sharing information between academic researchers and investigators. Not only can the findings from academic research inform practical applications, but the experiences and problems encountered by practitioners can guide and inform the direction of research. The intention of a recent investigative interviewing conference was to facilitate such an exchange of views, issues and solutions. This conference in Portsmouth (July 2006) enabled UK researchers and practitioners to present and explain current practice in the UK to delegates from around the world. This resulted in lively debates on the use of methods for detecting deception (this issue is dealt with in Chapter 9 and 10), and the use of tactics in investigative interviews to gain a confession. Such tactics are used across the USA and in many other countries. However, due to the Police and Criminal Evidence Act 1984, restrictions and guidelines have been put in place to protect people in police custody and during subsequent interviews, resulting in the use of some tactics being almost defunct in the UK. In addition, the use of trickery and deception to encourage a suspect to confess would undermine the ethos of PEACE, in terms of fairness, open-mindedness and ethical questioning. The use of minimisation techniques, whereby the seriousness of the crime is played down, and suggesting that a lesser sanction is possible with a confession, are designed to increase the possibility of a confession. Unfortunately, they may also increase the risk of a false confession (Gudjonsson 1992). Consequently, such tactics are avoided in the UK. In addition, confessions or evidence obtained in an oppressive or deceptive manner seriously risks being rejected by the courts, as the quality of the evidence and the authenticity of the confession may be deemed unacceptable due to the way in which they were gathered.

Williamson (2006) highlighted one of the conundrums for Criminal Justice Systems across the globe: 'there are considerable difficulties in balancing the needs of the state for achieving security for its people and simultaneously respecting human rights' (p. 3), but it is suggested here that the UK is beginning to achieve this balance. Investigative interviewing in the UK has developed to become a transparent and fair framework for interviewing, and the development and use of the PEACE model and related techniques render police (and public sector) interviewing open to public scrutiny as never before. This has the additional benefit of building the reputation of the UK police, which has suffered in past decades due to well-publicised miscarriages of justice, and should improve public confidence in the police. Indeed, investigations rely on witnesses and victims coming forward in the first place, so an added bonus of this is the increased likelihood that witnesses and victims will be more willing to come forward and testify and suspects will be more likely to cooperate. The knock-on effect in terms of improved human rights for suspects, witnesses and victims within the UK criminal justice system is inevitable, and this should be the ultimate aim of any investigation in order to minimise the risks of miscarriages of justice and maximise the opportunity for a fair trial.

References

Association of Chief Police Officers (ACPO) (2005) *Investigative Interviewing Strategy Document.* Bramshill: Centrex.

Baldwin, J. (1992) *Videotaping of Police Interviews with Suspects – An Evaluation.* Police Research Series Paper No. 1. London: Home Office.

Baldwin, J. (1993) 'Police Interview Techniques: Establishing Truth of Proof', *British Journal of Criminology*, 33: 325–352.

BBC (2003) 'Killing Led to Miscarriage of Justice'. Retrieved on 5 December 2006 from http://news.bbc.co.uk/1/hi/wales/3038672.stm.

Bull, R. and Cherryman, J. (1995) *Helping to Identify Skills Gaps in Specialist Investigative Interviewing: Literature Review.* London: Home Office.

Bull, R. and Cherryman, J. (1996) *Helping to Identify Skills Gaps in Specialist Investigative Interviewing: Enhancement of Professional Skills.* London: Home Office Police Department.

Bull, R. and Milne, R. (2004) 'Attempts to Improve the Police Interviewing of Suspects', in G.D. Lassiter (ed.), *Interrogations, Confessions and Entrapment* (pp. 181–196). New York: Kluwer.

Centre for Investigative Skills (CFIS) (2004) *Practical Guide to Investigative Interviewing.* England: Central Police Training and Development Authority.

Cherryman, J. and Bull, R. (2001) 'Police Officers' Perceptions of Specialist Interviewing Skills', *International Journal of Police Science and Management*, 3: 199–212.

Clarke, C. and Milne, R. (2001) *National Evaluation of the PEACE Investigative Interviewing Course.* Police Research Award Scheme, Report No: PRAS/149.

Crown Prosecution Service (2007) *CPS Authorises Police to Charge Four People with Perjury in Lynette White Case.* Press release, retrieved on 2 April 2007 from www.cps.gov.uk/news/pressreleases/113_07.html.

CPTU (Central Planning and Training Unit) (1992a) *A Guide to Interviewing.* Harrogate: Home Office.

CPTU (Central Planning and Training Unit) (1992b) *The Interviewer's Rule Book.* Harrogate: Home Office.

Ede, R. and Shepherd, E. (2000) *Active Defence* (2nd edn). London: Law Society Publishing.

Fisher, R.P. and Geiselman, R.E. (1992) *Memory Enhancing Techniques for Investigative Interviewing: The Cognitive Interview.* Springfield, IL: Charles C. Thomas.

Griffiths, A. and Milne, R. (2006) 'Will it All End in Tiers? Police Interviews with Suspects in Britain', in T. Williamson (ed.), *Investigative Interviewing: Rights, Research and Regulation* (pp. 167–189). Cullompton: Willan.

Gudjonsson, G. (1992) *The Psychology of Interrogations, Confessions and Testimony.* Chichester: Wiley.

Gudjonsson, G. (2003) *The Psychology of Interrogation and Confessions: A Handbook.* Chichester: Wiley.

Holmberg, U. (2004) 'Police Officers' Attitudes in Interviewing Victims and Suspects of Violent and Sexual Crimes: Consequences for Interview Outcomes'. Unpublished PhD thesis: Stockholm University.

Home Office and Department of Health (1992) *The Memorandum of Good Practice for Video Recorded Interviews with Child Witnesses for Criminal Proceedings.* London: HMSO.

Home Office and Department of Health (2001) *Achieving Best Evidence in Criminal Proceedings: Guidance for Vulnerable and Intimidated Witnesses Including Children.* London: HMSO.

Inbau, F.E., Reid, J.E., Buckley, J.P. and Jayne, B.P. (2001) *Criminal Interrogation and Confession.* Gaithersburg, MD: Aspen.

Irving, B.L. and Hilgendorf, L. (1980) *Police Interrogation: The Psychological Approach.* Royal Commission on Criminal Procedure, Research Study No. 1. London: HMSO.

Kassin, S.M. (1997) 'The Psychology of Confession Evidence', *American Psychologist*, 52: 221–223.

Kassin, S.M., Goldstein, C.C. and Savitsky, K. (2003) 'Behavioral Confirmation in the Interrogation Room: On the Dangers of Presuming Guilt', *Law and Human Behavior*, 27: 187–203.

Koehnken, G., Milne, R., Memon, A. and Bull, R. (1999) 'The Cognitive Interview: A Meta-analysis', *Psychology, Crime and Law*, 5: 3–28.

Milne, R. and Bull, R. (1999) *Investigative Interviewing: Psychology and Practice.* Chichester: Wiley.

Milne, R. and Bull, R. (2003) 'Interviewing by the Police', in D. Carson and R. Bull (eds), *Handbook of Psychology in Legal Contexts.* Chichester: Wiley, 111–125.

Milne, R., Shaw, G. and Bull, R. (2007) 'Investigative Interviewing: the role of research', in D. Carson, R. Milne, F. Pakes, K. Shalev and A. Shawyer (eds), *Applying Psychology to Criminal Justice*. Chichester: Wiley.

Moston, S., Stephenson, G. and Williamson, T. (1992) 'The Effects of Case Characteristics on Suspect Behaviour During Police Questioning', *British Journal of Criminology*, 32: 23–40.

National Centre for Police Excellence (2005) *Professionalising Investigation Programme, Levels 1, 2, and 3*. Bramshill: Centrex.

National Crime Faculty (1996) *Investigative Interviewing: A Practical Guide*. Bramshill: National Crime Faculty.

National Crime Faculty (2004) *Investigative Interviewing: Training Material*. Bramshill: National Crime Faculty.

Rabon, D. (1992) *Interviewing and Interrogation*. Durham, NC: Carolina Academic Press.

Savage, S. and Milne, R. (2007) 'Miscarriages of Justice – the Role of the Investigative Process', in T. Newburn, T. Williamson and A. Wright (eds), *Handbook of Criminal Investigations*. Cullompton: Willan, 610–627.

Schollum, M. (2005) 'Investigative Interviewing: The Literature'. New Zealand Police. Retrieved on 8 January 2007 from http://www.police.govt.nz/resources/2005/investigative-interviewing/investigative-interviewing.pdf.

Shaw, G. (1996) 'Investigative Interviewing: Supervision', *Police Review*, February.

Shawyer, A. (in preparation) Investigative Interviewing: Investigation, Counter Fraud and Behaviour. Unpublished PhD thesis. University of Portsmouth.

Shawyer, A. and Milne, R. (2006) 'Investigative Interviewing and Fraud'. Paper presented at the 2nd International Investigative Interviewing Conference, Portsmouth.

Shepherd, E. (1986) 'The Conversational Core of Policing', *Policing*, 2: 294–303.

Shepherd, E. and Kite, F. (1989) 'Teach 'em to Talk', *Policing*, 5: 33–47.

Vrij, A. (2000) *Detecting Lies and Deceit: The Psychology of Lying and Its Implications for Professional Practice*. Chichester: Wiley.

Walsh, D.W. and Milne, R. (2007) 'Perceptions of benefit fraud staff in the UK: Giving P.E.A.C.E. a chance?', *Public Administration*, 85(2): 525–540.

Walsh, D.W. and Milne, R. (2008) 'Keeping the P.E.A.C.E.? A study of investigative interviewing practices in the public sector', *Legal and Criminological Psychology*, 13: 39–57.

Williamson, T. (1994) 'Reflections on Current Police Practice', in D. Morgan and G. Stephenson (eds), *Suspicion and Silence: The Right to Silence in Criminal Investigations*. London: Blackstone Press, 107–116..

Williamson, T. (2006) 'Towards Greater Professionalism: Minimising Miscarriages of Justice', in T. Williamson (ed.), *Investigative Interviewing: Rights, Research and Regulation*. Cullompton: Willan Publishing, 147–166.

Chapter 3

Investigative interviewing in the Nordic region

Ivar A. Fahsing and Asbjørn Rachlew

Introduction

The Nordic region consists of the five countries, Denmark, Finland, Iceland, Norway and Sweden (Figure 3.1). The region is normally associated with small, stable and tranquil societies. However, several high-profile cases of miscarriage of justice, directly linked to the

Figure 3.1 Map of the Nordic region

way the police conduct their investigative interviews, have recently brought about a need for change. Our aim is to provide the reader with a brief description of regional trends and national differences within the field of investigative interviewing in the Nordic region. The description includes a few case reviews, demonstrating the importance of research and training. Finally, a tactical model, conceived and continually developed through close cooperation between patricians and academics, is presented.

The system of government in Scandinavia (Denmark, Norway and Sweden) is constitutional monarchy, while Finland and Iceland are republics. All the countries have unilateral national police forces. The criminal procedures are fairly similar and all court systems are accusatorial. In Denmark and Norway, the local functions of the prosecution system are an integrated part of the police service. The basic police training in the region is typically of three years' duration, of which approximately one year consists of practical training within the police service. Criminal law procedure and fundamental investigation techniques are taught as part of the basic training in all of the countries. There are, however, no further requirements to become a police detective in the Nordic region. Nonetheless, all of the national police training institutions in the region offer various voluntary specialist detective training courses. Traditionally, little time has been specifically directed towards the vital task of investigative interviewing. However, all the Nordic countries, except Finland, have developed, or are about to develop, designated training courses in investigative interviewing. These are influenced by the British PEACE model and the body of research within the field of investigative interviewing, including the cognitive interview. However, there seems to be a significant difference in the process concerning the methodological and ethical foundation of the interviewing of suspects. Our data were gathered through questionnaires and semi-structured interviews with central contributors in each country,[1] and a thorough search through the relatively extensive information provided by the European Committee for the Prevention of Torture and Inhuman or Degrading Treatment or Punishment (CPT) in relation to their, total of 17 visits to the Nordic region.

Each time the CPT visits a country, it provides a general description of how the European regulations against torture or inhuman or degrading treatment or punishment are respected, including how persons held in police establishments are treated. In general, countries in the Nordic region are receiving positive feedback from the committee. Apart from a few allegations of excessive use of force at the time of apprehension, there has been no allegation of such malpractice in relation to police interviews. However, the CPT has constantly (and repeatedly) encouraged governments in the region to draw up a more detailed code of practice on police interrogations and recommended that the authorities explore the possibility of making electronic recording of police interviews a standard practice. The CPT has also expressed concern regarding the delayed presentation of suspects' rights. A few additional comments from CPT to individual countries in the region will be addressed in the sections below.

Because of limitations of space, this chapter will only cover the matter of general police interviews. The interesting and related development within the field of child interviews is consequently not included.

Norway

- constitutional monarchy
- population: 4.6 million
- police force: 11,000
- prison population rate (per 100,000 of national population): 59.

The Norwegian police force suffered a major setback in 1997. A young man was acquitted by the Crown Court for a murder to which he had confessed. The disputed confession was elicited by a detective who, at the time, was regarded as one of the best interviewers in Norway. He worked as a homicide detective at the National Norwegian Criminal Investigation Service, a unit whose professionalism had never been challenged in any serious way. As described in more detail below, the court-appointed forensic experts concluded that the style of interviewing seemed heavily influenced by the philosophy that underlies the style in the North American literature on interrogation (Inbau et al. 2001), where manipulation and various tricks are employed with one goal in mind: to obtain a confession.

The case revealed that Norway had little formal expertise within the field of forensic psychology. As a consequence, the Norwegian police offered full sponsorship for two detectives (the authors) to undertake forensic MSc courses in the UK. The first dissertation (Rachlew 1999) was specifically designed as a White Paper, facilitating the first, national investigative interviewing training programme (KREATIV). Rachlew's dissertation documented that Norwegian police officers had little or no training in investigative interviewing. Their skills were based on experience and observational learning, placing them at 'survival level',[2] identified in England and Wales approximately 10 years earlier (Shepherd and Kite 1988). Furthermore, the majority of the few texts available in Norwegian regarding investigative interviewing were written by police officers, classified as 'police only' material. A subsequent review of these texts (Rachlew 2003a) confirmed the discouraging picture drawn up by the forensic experts in the murder trial. The texts, all written in an advisory form by experienced police officers, at the time recognised as the most skilful interviewers in the nation, were dominated by a manipulative, confession-focused approach:

> You use your influence to 'soften him up' from the very beginning. Your goal is to become the only one providing him with comfort and support in his difficult situation. You control who he is allowed to have contact with, and in that way prevent him receiving psychological support from others. (Rachlew 2003a: 4)

It seems evident that CPT never had access to these 'secret' documents. Nevertheless, in the 1990s, CPT repeatedly expressed concern with interviews with suspects in Norway. It was reported that 'officers routinely seek to put pressure upon inmates subject to restrictions, by suggesting to them, that restrictions could be eased or lifted if they began to provide information which would assist the police investigation. A number of police officers with whom the delegation spoke indicated that these allegations were not unfounded' (CPT 2000: 22). Detained persons met by CPT expressed the belief that 'the purpose of restrictions was to exert psychological pressure on them, that restrictions were most common when the police had a weak case and that, even if it had not been explicitly stated by the police, restrictions would be eased or lifted in response to co-operation with the police' (CPT 1997: 12).

Based upon the work in conjunction with the authors' MSc degrees from UK universities, a turnaround operation was initiated from within the Norwegian police force. With support from the Oslo police district, the National Norwegian Criminal Investigation Service and the Director of Public Prosecutions, a national, investigative interviewing training course was commissioned by the National University College in 2002, based on a pilot training programme (KREATIV), heavily influenced by the British PEACE course. Professor Ray Bull and Detective Chief Inspector (DCI) David Murthwaite (Merseyside Police) were brought to Norway to train the trainers and initiate the programme. The trainers were recruited from within the police force, and since 2001, approximately 50 officers have completed the 6-week trainers' course, covering topics such as pedagogy, human rights, ethical communication skills (the PEACE model), eyewitness memory, cognitive interviewing, interview strategy and false confessions.

In an attempt to prevent the problems identified by Milne and Bull (1999), who reported that some of the trainers in England and Wales had to train others in the model, having only just completed a training course themselves, scholars were brought in. Fortunately, the Department of Psychology at the University of Oslo was also starting to increase its research on forensic psychology (Magnussen 2004; Wessel *et al.* 2005) and as a result could cooperate with the police force. However, the scientific practice in the field is still new in Norway. Hence, international scholars, predominately from Sweden, have assisted the training of the trainers in Norway.

The trainers are encouraged to improvise and exemplify their lessons when delivering the course in the field. However, to ensure consistency and prevent another problem identified in England and Wales, where some areas were downplayed while others were over-emphasised (Shaw 2001), the Norwegian trainers are provided with a presentation package of 22 short, but mandatory PowerPoint lessons. These are on a yearly basis evaluated by the trainers and updated by scholars in an attempt to keep KREATIV up to date with the scientific development within the field. The KREATIV course is, in line with Baldwin's conclusions (1993), pitched at a 'down to earth' level, free from any psychologically advanced techniques, and has now been delivered to almost a thousand detectives, senior officers and members of the prosecution service. The course is, like the original PEACE course, a 5-day, intensive training programme with mandatory reading of literature in advance.

Electronic recording of police interviews is becoming increasingly common in Norway. The Director of Public Prosecutions (Prosecutor General) has encouraged the police to tape interviews of suspects and key witnesses in serious cases. A pilot programme, initiated by the Ministry of Justice (1998–2003), confirmed the positive effects already documented in the international literature (Milne and Bull 1999; Kassin 2006). The Norwegian pilot study included 598 taped interviews. No claims of malpractice were reported. Witnesses (n = 169) and suspects (n = 419) confirmed their recorded police statement in court. Police officers appreciated the enhanced possibility to evaluate their performance and reported that tape recording enhanced the communication and made them plan their interviews better (Rachlew 2003b). As a result, a wider, more permanent programme is in progress. Custom-made, digital software, especially designed for audio and video documentation of police interviews (Indico),[3] was developed and refined during the pilot study. The software is running smoothly and is already an integrated part of the national training programme, a combination that has led to an increasingly enthusiastic use of recordings by the police and courts. This is an encouraging development in the cause of fair justice, improved communication, and more effective interview training, and it represents an important information source for further research and development.

The Birgitte Tengs case

In May 1995, a 17-year-old girl, Birgitte Tengs, was found murdered on Karmoy Island in Norway. The case had remained unsolved for 18 months when her (then) 19-year-old cousin was arrested for the murder. The cousin was remanded in custody and isolated. In spite of repeated recommendations by CPT to Norwegian authorities to explore the possibility of making electronic recording of police interviews a standard practice, recordings were unfortunately, but perhaps quite typically, not a common practice prior to this notorious case. However, through the interviewer's personal notebooks it eventually became evident that the young man had been subjected to advanced manipulative interrogation techniques during the extensive interviews. Initially, the suspect maintained his innocence and was isolated from social contact. Upon request by the interviewing officer, the cousin drafted a 'movie script' in his cell. The script dealt with a murder he maintained he had no memory of – the very same murder that the police told him they could prove he had committed. That turned out to be a bluff. During the subsequent 180 hours of interviews and 'informal talks' between the interviewer and the suspect, the movie script was gradually transformed into a sort of confession. The main character, who, in the original script was referred to as a neutral third person, was replaced with the much more personal (and incriminating) character 'I'. The interviewer had promised the suspect that his memories of the actual event would gradually reveal themselves. According to the cousin, this never happened. As a consequence, he felt obliged to retract his 'confession'. The police, however, felt that the revised version of the movie script confirmed their suspicion, and one of Norway's most problematic criminal cases headed into the court system. The criminal court shared the police interpretation of the written statements and convicted the cousin of the murder. The Crown Court, subsequently, acquitted the cousin, evidently sharing the views of the two court-appointed forensic experts, Gisli Gudjonsson and Barrie Irving, regarding the reliability of the information retrieved through the lengthy police interviews. As pointed out by Gudjonsson (2004: 606), the fundamental problem with the interviews was the extreme use of isolation, combined with an instrumental-like, therapeutic rapport building, solely designed to obtain a confession from someone presumed, in the eyes of the interviewing officer, to be guilty. Another essential flaw was the total absence of any reliable method of documentation of the information obtained. The problems identified by the forensic experts were later confirmed by the Norwegian Supreme Court (2003) and Rachlew's (2003a) review of previously confidential police manuals, issued by the National Norwegian Criminal Investigation Service.

The Fritz Moen case

In September 1976, Sigrid Heggheim (aged 20) was found strangled after attempted rape in the northwestern city of Trondheim, Norway. Eleven months later, Torunn Finstad (aged 20) was found raped and strangled in the same community. They were both students at the Norwegian Institute of Technology in Trondheim. The vulnerable Fritz Moen subsequently confessed to the murders. Although Moen was vulnerable in many ways, including the obvious handicap of a missing arm, the courts felt confident that the confessions elicited by Norwegian police were genuine, even though his blood group was not the same as the semen found inside one of the sexually abused victims. Fritz Moen was sentenced to 21 years of imprisonment – a sentence he served to its full extent. Moen had retracted his confessions prior to his trial, claiming that the police had pressured him to confess to the murders of the young women. He maintained his innocence until he died on 1 May 2005, awaiting his appeal to the newly established Criminal Cases Review Commission. The sad fact is that his innocence became public knowledge just months after Moen passed away when another man confessed to the murders. The Norwegian Minister of Justice has ordered an independent inquiry to determine why Fritz Moen confessed to crimes he never committed. Fritz Moen was deaf and unable to speak, and we already know that his first confession was elicited by detectives from the National

Norwegian Criminal Investigation Service at a time when the detectives were alone in the interview room with him – the sign-language interpreter took a break. The independent inquiry was meant to clarify why such a seemingly unreliable practice was not challenged by the Norwegian court system.[4]

Denmark

- constitutional monarchy
- population: 5.4 million
- police force: 13,600
- prison rate: 59.

The Danish police have not yet had a case that has led to an embarrassing public exposure of their interview methods. Although CPT has reported some problems associated with delayed information to suspects of their rights (CPT 1997b), allegations of inappropriate psychological pressure have not been reported. Consequently, the Danish police have not in any way been directly or indirectly forced to make any changes in their interview concept. Their interview skills are primarily developed through personal experience and supervision by senior colleagues. There has, nonetheless, been a noteworthy development within the field in Denmark in recent years. The Danish Police College has, in close cooperation with the National Commissioner and scientific personnel, introduced a 1-week national investigative interview training course. The course has been running since 2005. Approximately 150 detectives have so far received the training. Consequently, the Danish concept is based on the cognitive interview technique and the recent research and development in northern Europe. Their training programme is building on the Norwegian KREATIV model, which is described above. However, regarding the interview of suspects, there is one significant difference between the Norwegian and the Danish progress. While the Norwegian training programme advocates an approach that minimises the differences between the interviews of suspects and other interviewees, the Danish Police are planning a separate training course directed solely towards the interviewing of suspects. Hence, the Danish Police contrast to their colleagues in Norway, who are focusing on a change from traditional confession-focused techniques. Nor is the use of recording equipment widespread in Denmark. We argue that an explanation may be found in the fact that Denmark has not yet experienced any major judicial scandals linked to poor documentation and/or confession-focused police interviews, like their neighbours in the north. Suspect interview techniques have never been a subject of systematic research in Denmark and are arguably facilitating the continued belief that interviewing suspects requires a different set of skills, a belief thoroughly downplayed in the scientific literature on investigative interviewing (Shepherd 1991, Alison 1998, Sear and Williamson 1999).

Sweden

- constitutional monarchy
- population: 9 million
- police force: 22,000
- prison rate: 68.

Sweden is, in many ways, a pioneer within the field of forensic psychology (Granhag 2001). This is a heritage very much kept alive today by the significant research conducted by Sven Åke Christianson, Pär Anders Granhag and their colleagues at the universities of Gothenburg and Stockholm. These academics, in many ways, represent the establishment in the Nordic Network for research on Psychology and Law (NNPL), which was founded in 2004. Thus, the Swedish police were the first in the Nordic region to offer any formal education in investigative interviewing. The first programme began in 1994. It was called 'Advanced Interview Management Training', and the 3-week course comprised law, social and forensic psychology, communication skills, interview strategy, and practical lessons. This programme was developed and administered by experienced police detectives in cooperation with scholars from the represented academic disciplines. Although the course focused on ethical communication and principles based on forensic research, it did not focus on interview structure (e.g. as the PEACE model does), nor the dangers associated with confession-oriented interview styles. The latter is perhaps not surprising, as, until recently, the Swedish Police had not been embarrassed by any public scandals directly linked to their interview methods. Nevertheless, in 2004, a new concept based on the PEACE model replaced the former training. This is a 5-week programme delivered at the National Police Academy in Stockholm. The main components in the study are as follows:

- the terms of investigative interviewing and the dilemmas involved
- the meaning of a professional and ethical approach
- interview and communication skills
- the psychology of witness evidence
- the psychology of lies and deception
- memory-enhancing techniques for investigative interviewing
- the PEACE model
- methods for further development.

The course is developed and administered by Harriet Jacobson Öhrn, a social scientist with a PhD in real-life police interviews, working in close cooperation with experienced police detectives and psychologists. So far, a mere 110 officers have received the new, extensive training programme. A somewhat unique characteristic within the region is that Sweden has a multitude of regional interview courses, in addition to the training offered by the Police Academy. These are operated by the individual regions and commercial entrepreneurs. As a result, the variety of interview training around the country may arguably lead to considerable variations in interview practice There are also local differences in electronic recording of police interviews in Sweden. Some of the forces do routinely record all interviews in the more serious enquiries, and others do not. However, there seems to be an increasing tendency towards a more widespread use, in line with CPTs recommendations to Swedish authorities (CPT 1992).

Unfortunately, in 2005, Sweden saw a public scandal revealing tactics clearly not in line with the principles of ethical interviewing, but more commonly associated with the philosophy behind Inbau *et al.*'s version of an effective interrogation, including manipulative techniques employed to obtain a confession from someone already presumed, in the eyes of the interviewing officer, to be guilty (Kalbfleisch 1994). However, unlike the Norwegian case described above, these interviews were tape recorded, making it possible to evaluate the highly questionable police behaviour.

Tommie Karim

One morning in March 2005, the police in the city of Gävle in central Sweden received a telephone call from a young man, Tommie Karim, who was living in a five-storey block of flats with his girlfriend Anna and their 3-month-old son. He reported that he had just woken up to find an unidentified man in their kitchen stabbing Anna. In panic,

Karim rushed out and downstairs to his father's flat, from where he made the call. The police arrived at the scene a few minutes later and found Anna dead on the kitchen floor, suffering from some 30 stab wounds to her body. Tommie and his two half-sisters were able to give a brief description of the killer, who had fled the scene just before the police arrived. Tommie was brought to the police station where he was charged with the murder and immediately interrogated. The term 'interrogation' is deliberately chosen, as nothing else would describe the interviews of Tommie Karim. Below follows Tommie's own perception of the situation as he gave it to a local newspaper. Subsequently, tapes from the interview were broadcast on national television, confirming Tommie's version of events (documentary on *Kalla Fakta*, 15 February 2006):

> It was obvious that the police did not believe me. They did all they could to make me break down and confess. I was questioned by two officers. One of them played good to me and the other was bad. Later on they changed the roles, says Tommie Karim.

> He lost count of how many hours he was interrogated, but estimates that he claimed his innocence 'at least a hundred times'.

> Since Tommie Karim only observed the killer, in the checked shirt, for a few seconds he slowly started to lose confidence in his own recollection of the event.

> In the end I thought that I was mentally ill and that I actually did it. Despite my innocence I was worrying about what the DNA tests would reveal.

Tommie should have had no reason to worry. Three weeks later, DNA from blood, found inside the flat, proved another man's presence, and this person's blood was mixed with the victim's blood. Nevertheless, the police went on with their tactics, which involved showing him close-up pictures of the body of his extremely mutilated girlfriend. The police told Tommie that they knew he was the murderer and argued forcefully that he killed his girlfriend because she did not love him and that she thought of him as 'a shit' and a lousy father. Tommie cried and begged them to stop, but the police went on with increasing pressure for more than two months, claiming that no one else could reveal the truth. Seven months later, another woman was killed in her home nearby. DNA samples from this investigation linked the two murders. The killer, a former acquaintance of the victims, subsequently confessed.

Interestingly, high-ranking officials from both the local police and prosecution service later repeatedly endorsed the way Tommie Karim was interrogated. A more ethical approach to the interviews of Tommie Karim would undeniably have saved him the torture and humiliation he had to endure. We are left to speculate whether a more open-minded approach to the initial investigation, including the interviews of Tommie Karim, who in fact was a prime witness, also could have saved the life of the second victim.

Finland

- republic
- population: 5.2 million
- police force: 11,000
- prison rate: 59.

Academics and police personnel at the National Police School in Finland, responsible for the training within the field of crime prevention and investigation, report that there has been no public concern regarding Finnish police interviews in general. Although investigative interviewing, including a presentation of the cognitive interview, is taught by psychologists both at basic and advanced levels, limited time is spent on training. Finland does not have a special course on investigative interviewing. The topic is, however, integrated in the general crime prevention/investigation training, including university-level courses at the Finnish Police College.

An academic book on 'interrogation tactics' was published in Finland in 1996 (Ellonen *et al.* 1996). The book (286 pages) was written in Finnish and Swedish (the two official languages in Finland) and has sold 2,000 copies. It draws on international eyewitness research, including a detailed review and presentation of cognitive interview techniques. However, the advocated techniques in relation to suspect interviews seem to drift more towards police-based manuals, including that of Inbau *et al.* (1986).

Apart from child interviews, recordings of police interviews are not common practice in Finland. In its response to CPT's recommendation to consider the possibility of making electronic recording a standard practice (CPT 1993a), Finnish authorities hesitated, arguing that: 'In most cases, recording makes the person to be interrogated (and, occasionally, also the interrogator) freeze and therefore results in the loss of a confidential atmosphere which police officers always try to create' (CPT 1993b: 21). An analysis of the Finnish response to CPT provides a few interesting questions. Reports from around the globe provide a clear indication that the police, certainly after having tried it for a while, endorse the practice of recording interviews (Schollum 2005: 84–93), recognising that not only is recording of police interviews a useful safeguard against ill-treatment but it also has advantages for the police. Thus, the Finnish hesitant response indicates that Finnish police officers had not, or did not wish to, record their interviews at that time. However, in murder investigations and other major crime investigations where the identity of the perpetrator is in doubt, the use of recordings has increased.

Finnish scholars are actively involved in the Nordic Network for Psychology and Law (NNPL), and hosted last year's successful meeting at the University of Turku. Forensic psychology continues to be a research topic in Finland. However, studies of how Finish police interview their suspects have not yet been published.

Iceland

- republic
- population: 304,400
- police force: 700
- prison rate: 38.

One of the most senior researchers within the field of investigative interviewing, Professor Gisli Gudjonsson, is Icelandic. Although he has predominantly worked in the UK, forensic psychology is on the rise in Iceland (Sigurdsson and Gudjonsson 2004). However, the Icelandic police do not have a formal training programme in investigative interviewing; in fact, it is just about to start up. Although there has been no recent judicial scandal linked to general police interviewing in recent years, the courts have harshly criticised the interview practice in a child abuse case in 2005. Consequently, there is a clear understanding of the need to strengthen the evidential value of information obtained in police interviews. Hence, the Icelandic police have initiated a project to develop a national training programme based on PEACE. Representatives from the higher prosecution service in Iceland have attended the Norwegian KREATIV programme.

Since 1997, the Reykjavik police department has had equipment to record interrogations via video and audio. However, this equipment has only been used sporadically, as there has been a shortage of procedures and training. There are plans to implement new procedures and the computer software Indico has already been translated from Norwegian into Icelandic. The Icelandic congress appropriated funds for the necessary equipment, and by 2009 all police districts in Iceland had received video recording equipment.

Tactical use of potential evidence in suspect interviews

The recent development of KREATIV is, as described above, based on research on investigative interviewing. The information-gathering techniques are advocated in an attempt to eliminate the use of confrontational or manipulative, 'confession-electing techniques', identified in Norway by Gudjonsson and Irving in 1998, as described above. In 1993, Moston and Engleberg found that 43 per cent of the studied officers opened their suspect interviews with a question containing a direct accusation, a question seeking a confession, or a question describing evidence signifying the person's guilt together with a direct accusation (Figure 3.2). Moston and Engleberg argued that such a tactic is particularly unhelpful, as many suspects completely deny any knowledge or involvement, and as a result it leaves the interviewer and the interviewee with little room to manoeuvre (Baldwin 1992) and, as explained earlier, will seldom lead to the suspect's changing his or her story.

Although the British PEACE-training course has received international recognition, several scholars have expressed concern, pointing out problems associated with the 'new' approach. It has been argued that the training programme failed to provide the British police service with an effective alternative to interview uncooperative suspects; thus, Alison (1998) stated that 'the general theme is defensive in its tone' and that it 'provides little positive guidance or assistance in formulating strategies to improve information retrieval from suspects'. Although Ede and Shepherd (2000: 85) describe a three-stage approach taken by police forces in England and Wales when interviewing suspects, the Norwegian Police University College has critically addressed these concerns and implemented a tactical model in the PEACE structured interview. The model, which, in our view, is

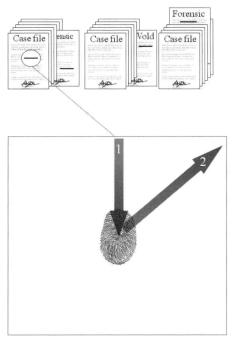

Figure 3.2 Approaching a suspect interview with a direct accusation (arrow 1) may facilitate a false, unchallenged denial (arrow 2).

a defined illustration of the philosophy behind information-gathering interview techniques (Baldwin 1992; Shepherd 1993; NCF 1998), is described below.

The feedback from the first officers who received the training in Norway was remarkably positive. Unfortunately, the lack of systematic audio and video recordings of Norwegian police interviews hampers research of satisfactory ecological validity. However, in 2006, a questionnaire was sent from the Norwegian Police College to the first 464 detectives who had completed the training programme (Fahsing and Rachlew 2006). Forty-nine (49) detectives were unable to answer (new job, on leave, etc.). A total of 241 detectives (32 per cent female) returned the anonymous questionnaire, providing a response rate of 58 per cent. The average respondent was 38.8 years old with nearly 9 years of experience of detective work.

The participants were initially asked whether or not, prior to the training programme, they had used elements of confession-focused interrogation techniques. Seventy-five per cent stated they had used such techniques 'often' or 'sometimes', and 14.2 per cent stated that they 'usually' or 'always' had used confession-orientated techniques.

The remaining 10.8 per cent stated that they had 'never' used, or were 'unsure' whether they had used such techniques.

The majority (96 per cent) of the Norwegian detectives claimed that the training programme had made them more aware of the potential dangers of manipulative techniques, and 88.8 per cent reported that the training programme had, in some way or another, altered their interviews of suspects. Ninety-eight per cent reported that the tactical model was 'useful' (52 per cent) or 'very useful' (48 per cent) in real-life interviews. Of the 241 participating detectives, 239 (99 per cent) claimed that, upon completing the training, they 'sometimes' (19 per cent), 'often' (32 per cent), usually (33 per cent) or 'always' (15 per cent) applied the tactical model in their interviews of suspects.

The tactical interview model (TIM) provides the police officers with a strategy that eliminates conceivable manoeuvres for the guilty suspect by sustaining evidence in early stages of the interview. A well-executed interview will secure and, in some cases, enhance the potential evidence inherent in any inquiry. Furthermore, the approach stimulates open-mindedness and prevents officers from falling into the pitfalls associated with premature decisions (Ask and Granhag 2005), identified as a critical component in ethical interviewing (Shepherd 1991). The tactical model has been experimentally tested by Maria Hartwig and her colleagues at the University of Gothenburg with very encouraging results (Hartwig 2005).

The tactical interview model (TIM)

Prior to the introduction of the tactical interview model, Norwegian police officers (including the authors) had a hard time explaining exactly what characterises a successful interview strategy. We could not describe what essential components, or constituent parts, would separate a well-conducted interview from a well-conducted *tactical* interview.

We believe the main reason we found this difficult to articulate was the depressing fact that the only resources available for interview strategy were one of the following:

(a) published police manuals, predominantly North American, written for legal systems promoting lie detection, pressure, manipulation, tricks and deceit

(b) unpublished police manuals, written for internal use only, including tricks that were not appropriate if exposed in court

(c) unwritten police practice, passed on by experienced police officers, also including tricks inappropriate if exposed in court

(d) published material containing information on how to read the suspect's thoughts and lies through various unfounded techniques, mainly by reading the suspect's body language.

In fact, if we ignore the unethical and/or illegal tricks and manipulative tactics advocated through these sources, no text, of either academic or police origin has, in our opinion, successfully managed to create a normative model describing how to conduct a tactical investigative interview. Our view is supported by Kornkvist's extensive review of 20 international investigative interview manuals (Kronkvist 2006). A review of the international literature regarding investigative interviewing (e.g. Shepherd 1991; Baldwin 1993; Williamson 1993; Milne and Bull 1999; Clarke and Milne 2001) provides a clear indication that Norwegian police officers were not the only detectives around without a clear strategy of how they were to make the most out of the potential evidence available in the case files.

Consequently, in cooperation with Royne Nilsson (former detective superintendent and lecturer at the Swedish Police Academy), an illustrative model of tactical interviewing was developed and refined. The refined TIM (see Figures 3.2–3.4) was first presented to Norwegian homicide detectives in 2001, and implemented in real-life interviews the same year. The ideas behind the model, namely to delay the presentation of evidence, were presented by Royne Nilsson to Swedish police officers in the mid-1990s and are currently undergoing further empirical testing (Vrij and Granhag 2007).

TIM – step 1 (planning stage)
1 Identify all potential evidence in the case files.

The first step of any effective interview is solid preparation (Baldwin 1992; McGurk *et al.* 1993; Stockdale 1993). The TIM is obviously in line with this view. It would be naive to expect an effective and tactical interview if one does not have a clear view of the information that forms the case against the suspect. Before the interviewer enters the interview room, he or she must be able to answer the question, what information are you planning to handle in a tactical way?

Consequently, every piece of information that has the potential of forming evidence should be treated in a tactical way. At this stage, it is irrelevant whether the information is apt to clear or tie the suspect to the crime.

TIM – step 2 (preparation stage)
2. For all potential evidence, identify all possible explanations of its origin.

If the suspect is guilty and wants to get away with it, he or she must provide a plausible false explanation for each potential piece of evidence indicating guilt. Hence, to stay on top of the situation, the tactical interviewer will, as far as possible, identify these explanations in the planning phase of the interview. This is deduction – classical detective work. How good the interviewer is depends on the information and creativity on hand.

Shepherd (1991) and Ask and Granhag (2005) point out the dangers of going into an interview with a fixed view on the available evidence. Therefore, if the suspect is innocent, or took part in the event with another role than first anticipated, the process of trying to identify all possible explanations should stimulate an open mind and, hence, reduce the risk of premature conclusions.

Failing to comply in accordance with the tactical steps outlined here – for instance, through a direct and positive challenge before completing step 3 – will provide guilty suspects with an opportunity to construct a deceitful but nevertheless plausible explanation that may be impossible to disprove. As shown in Figure 3.2, arrow no. 1 illustrates a premature challenge, and arrow no. 2 illustrates an unchallenged, true or deceitful response. Detectives with a clear understanding of the tactical model will immediately sense a feeling of possible failure, realising that if the suspect is guilty, potential evidence may be insubstantial or lost forever.

In order to avoid tactical blunders as illustrated in Figure 3.2, detectives must carefully complete steps 2 and 3 before any challenge is considered (step 4).

TIM – step 3 (the information-gathering interview)
3. Seek to eliminate all possible explanations identified in step 2 and follow up any response from the suspect by exploring, in detail, all accounts presented by the suspect before you move on to the next topic.

Given that ethical and non-confrontational communication secures the most reliable information (Holmberg and Christianson 2002; Hartwig

2005), the tactical interviewer should, at this stage of the interview, start all topics by asking open-ended questions and, when necessary, proceed with probing questions designed to elicit information that will eliminate all plausible alternative explanations. Any explanation (true or false) provided by the suspect before the challenge (step 4), must be explored in detail immediately (Figure 3.3). The interviewer is, in fact, searching for alternative explanations. The procedure stimulates open-mindness, but requires planning and flexibility.

As illustrated in Figure 3.3, it is of utmost importance at this stage of the interview that the interviewer starts his/her questioning with the questions that are the least likely to unveil the interviewer's knowledge of the potential evidence. If the question reveals the nature of the potential evidence, the bright suspect might grasp the strategy and then use the information to design a false plausible explanation before the interviewer is able to eliminate it.

Hence, a well-executed tactical interview is both effective and ethical, since it has the potential to encircle the guilty, whereas the open-minded approach will facilitate a fair and sound interview of

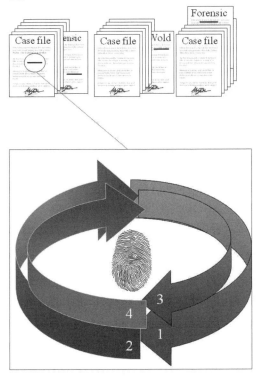

Figure 3.3 Approaching potential evidence, with a tactical consideration

an innocent suspect. It may be argued that delayed disclosure of evidence, represents a breach of one of Eric Shepherd's (1991) six principles of investigative interviewing, namely 'The disclosure principle'. However, the disclosure principle has to be balanced against the need for a sensible administration of the available evidence in a criminal case. In our view, only a deceitful, guilty suspect would benefit from a premature disclosure.

TIM – step 4 (the challenge)

It is probably best to illustrate step 4 by an example. Imagine the case of a missing person in which a forensic team have searched a car belonging to the suspect. In the boot, they located a strand of hair, and a DNA analysis tied this to the missing victim. In steps 1 and 2, the interviewer has identified the evidence and all possible explanations of how the hair might have ended up in the car. The interviewer produces a tactical interview plan allowing for all of the explanations. In the subsequent interview, the plan is followed and the suspect cannot produce any alternative explanations.

Hence, the interviewer feels confident that all plausible explanations are positively eliminated by the suspect himself. Before leaving step 3 and entering step 4, the tactical and systematic interviewer should by now have established (for example) that the suspect bought his car before the victim disappeared (arrow no. 1 in Figure 3.4), and he is the only one that has used the car in the last month (arrow no. 2 in Figure 3.4, etc.). The suspect has not lost his car keys, his car has never been stolen, it has not been broken into, and he has not transported any luggage for anyone else. In fact, the suspect has stated that he has not picked up any passengers, except his wife, within the last month, etc.

Now, when the interviewer feels confident that every plausible explanation seems to have been eliminated, the interviewer should start the challenge by first summing up the suspects explanation regarding his car and make him reconfirm this. It is at this stage that the interviewer should clarify and correct eventual misunderstandings and prevent the guilty suspects from claiming misunderstandings at a later stage. The interviewer should now confront the suspect with the potential evidence (Figure 3.4, arrow no. 6). This is best done in a calm tone and with a clear statement that actively invites a question: for example, 'Sir, our forensic team has examined your premises. Can you please explain how a strand of hair, belonging to the missing girl, ended up in your car?'

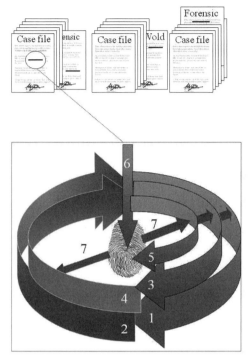

Figure 3.4 Confronting the suspect with potential evidence, after the alternative explanations have been eliminated

At this point, the interviewer shows that he is prepared to disclose his sources so that the suspect is able to make a fair judgement on the reliability of the interviewer's sources and the existence of biases and prejudices. After delivering the question, the interviewer should give the suspect plenty of time and silence to produce an answer. If the suspect is guilty, the preceding elimination process makes it likely that any answer at this stage is a contradiction of at least one of his earlier accounts (Figure 3.4, arrow no. 7). The interviewer should, depending on the suspect's response, repeat the question and be prepared to explain clearly how the evidence has been secured and analysed. One should, however, not go into detail concerning the nature of the evidence, since these details must be held back to serve as control information if the suspect later decides to provide an explanation. If the suspect is not able to produce such an explanation, the interviewer must ensure that this fact is unmistakably documented. This is, in our view, best done on a video recording.

A case file will often include more than one potential piece of evidence, and thus normally necessitate a postponement of the challenging questions (step 4) until all potential evidence is treated in accordance with the step 3 procedure. An early confrontation will usually have a negative effect on the communication and the suspect's ability to remember (Hartwig 2005). Furthermore, it will reveal the strategy before all of the points to prove are covered.

The tactical model outlined above requires thorough planning and preparations. If the suspect chooses to exercise his right to remain silent, or limits his answers to 'no comment', the creative work laid down in steps 1 and 2 is by no means a waste of time for the police. Every plausible explanation identified constitutes an important line of inquiry that should be addressed to secure an open-minded investigation and simultaneously eliminate the guilty suspect's chances of a successful 'ambush defence'. There is nothing revolutionary in this approach to a suspect interview, and, as the alert reader may have already noticed, it is certainly not bulletproof. Nevertheless, we believe the ideas are in line with modern and ethical principles. The Norwegian survey (Fahsing and Rachlew 2006) shows that experienced detectives value its usefulness in real-life interviews. Some of the underlying theories behind the model; *the psychology of guilt* and *the psychology of innocence*, are currently being addressed by researchers from the University of Gothenburg.

The way forward

As outlined above, the development of investigative interviewing in the Nordic region is to some extent comparable to the process in England and Wales, which led to the development of a new ethical and scientific foundation for investigative interviewing. The extent, speed and depth of the Nordic process seems to vary depending on (a) the motivation and capacity of the personnel involved and (b) the number and size of judicial scandals in the countries. Norway seems to have adopted most of the ideas of their British colleagues, while other countries, such as Iceland, are now about to start a similar process. However, except for the launching of the Norwegian Criminal Cases Review Commission in 2004, which was not directly linked to failing police interviews, none of the countries have so far made any structural changes. Nor have any of the countries developed any official, standardised code of conduct for investigative interviewing. This clearly indicates that executives within the police services and governmental offices in the region still have not fully realised the need for national guidelines reflecting the body of knowledge within the field. The above mentioned case from Sweden indicates ignorance of the literature on ethical interviewing. Ironically, the demonstrated view within the police and prosecution service is in sharp contrast to the more emphatic approach supported in a groundbreaking Swedish study by Holmberg[5] and Christianson (2004). Hence, a more humble attitude to the importance of updated knowledge is needed. Another key issue is the need for a more widespread use of electronic documentation tools in line with the recommendations of researchers (e.g. Milne and Bull 1999) as well as the European Parliament (CPT Standards, article 36).

Relevant research is a central component for development. Detectives seem to have an inbuilt scepticism of ideas originated outside the force, especially when change is required. Some theories are arguably more applicable than others. However, scepticism seems to have undermined important points and hampered real-life application. A strong link between police and research environments is therefore essential. A plausible explanation of why Norway seems to have made progress towards understanding that the ideas derived through psychological research are applicable to not only witness interviews but also suspect interviews, might be that the authors (two relatively experienced detectives) were given the opportunity to earn the MSc in forensic psychology and later given the positions needed to make changes from within. The establishment of a Criminal Cases Review Commission in Norway indicates a need for change not only within the police; thus, all actors within the juridical systems should take in new knowledge. Recently, the National Courts Administration in Sweden initiated a 2-day mandatory seminar for all judges in the country. Experienced scholars, such as Sven Åke Christianson, were brought in to facilitate the use of forensic psychology in court proceedings to enhance the knowledge of investigative interviewing. As mentioned above, an important contribution to the development of investigative interviewing in the Nordic region is the establishment of the Nordic Network for Research on Psychology and Law (NNPL). Since its establishment in 2004, scholars have met annually. The aims of the network can be summarized as follows:

- to stimulate exchange between Nordic institutes and research teams
- to provide opportunity for researchers to present their work to Nordic colleagues

- to initiate larger research projects
- to pool resources in order to be able to invite and host international researchers
- to initiate joint PhD courses and research schools.

In addition to the more established research on forensic psychology and memory, there are a multitude of highly interesting research projects going on, focusing directly on investigative interviewing in Sweden, Denmark and Norway. Interestingly, several of these projects are run by researchers, either police officers themselves or employed by the police service. A concluding remark would therefore be that, in total, the Nordic region has the experience and capacity needed to create a sound and common approach to an even more fruitful future for both research in and the practice of investigative interviewing.

Notes

1 Many thanks to: Denmark – Kurt Kragh and Kristina Kepinska Jakobsen; Finland – Erkki Ellonen and Kiimmo Kiiski; Iceland – Bjarni Bogason and Olafur Bragason; Sweden – Harriet Jakobsson Öhrn, Royne Nilsson and Pär Anders Granhag.
2 'Survival level' – achieving a seemingly acceptable outcome most of the time (Shepherd and Kite 1988).
3 For further details of the development and a description of the software see, www.indicosystems.no.
4 The report (492 pages) was published on 25 June 2007 (Fritz Moen og norsk strafferettspleie, NOU 2007: 7; available online at www.regjeringen.no/pages/1989602/PDFS/NOU200720070007000DDDPDFS.pdf (Norwegian). It is highly critical of a number of aspects of the extensive and coercive interrogations of Fritz Moen. In sum, he was subjected to more than 150 hours of interrogation, including sessions lasting more than 15 hours, in which his interrogators shouted accusations and 'we know you did it!', and pounded the table with their fists. The report is also highly critical of the coercive interviews of witnesses, including suggestive interviews conducted in 2001, when Fritz Moen tried to reopen the case(s).
5 Also a former detective in the Swedish police.

References

Alison, L. (1998) Criminal Rhetoric and Investigative Manipulation. Doctoral thesis, University of Liverpool.

Ask, K. and Granhag, P.A. (2005) 'Motivational Sources of Confirmation Bias in Criminal Investigations: The Need for Cognitive Closure', *Journal of Investigative Psychology and Offender Profiling*, 2: 43–63.

Baldwin, J. (1992) *Video-taping of Police Interviews with Suspects – an Evaluation*. Police Research Series: Paper No. 1. London: Home Office.

Baldwin, J. (1993) 'Police Interview Techniques – Establishing Truth or Proof?', *British Journal of Criminology*, 33: 325–351.

Clarke, C. and Milne, R. (2001) *National Evaluation of the PEACE Investigative Interviewing Course*. Research Award Scheme, Report No. PRSA 149, Home Office.

CPT (1992) Report to the Swedish Government on the Visit to Sweden Carried out by the European Committee for the Prevention of Torture and Inhuman or Degrading Treatment or Punishment (CPT) from 5 to 14 May 1991.

CPT (1993a) Report to the Finnish Government on the Visit to Finland Carried out by the European Committee for the Prevention of Torture and Inhuman or Degrading Treatment or Punishment (CPT) from 10 to 20 May 1992.

CPT (1993b) Response of the Finnish Government to the Report of the European Committee for the Prevention of Torture and Inhuman or Degrading Treatment or Punishment (CPT) on its visit to Finland from 10 to 20 May 1992.

CPT (1997a) Report to the Norwegian Government on the Visit to Norway Carried out by the European Committee for the Prevention of Torture and Inhuman or Degrading Treatment or Punishment (CPT) from 17 to 21 March 1997.

CPT (1997b). Report to the Danish Government on the Visit to Denmark carried out by the European Committee for the Prevention of Torture and Inhuman or Degrading Treatment or Punishment (CPT) from 29 September to 9 October 1996.

CPT (2000) Report to the Norwegian Government on the visit to Norway carried out by the European Committee for the Prevention of Torture and Inhuman or Degrading Treatment or Punishment (CPT) from 13 to 23 September 1999.

CPT (2002) European Committee for the Prevention of Torture and Inhuman or Degrading Treatment or Punishment. Paragraph 34, 12th General Report [CPT/Inf (2002)15].

Ede, R. and Shepherd, E. (2000) *Active Defence* (2nd edn). London: Law Society Publishing.

Ellonen, E., Karstinen, E. and Nykänen, V.E. (1996) *Förhörstaktik*. Polisens läroboksserie. Inrikesministeriet, Polisavdelningen, Finland.

Fahsing, I.A and Rachlew. A. (2006a) 'Effective and Ethical Interviews of Suspects; a Utopian Idea?' Paper presented at International Investigative Interviewing 2nd Conference, Portsmouth. Published in Norwegian as in following reference.

Fahsing, I.A. and Rachlew, A. (2006b) Etiske og effektive avhør. *Politiforum, Juni /juli 06/07/2006. Retrieved from http://www.phs.no/bibliotek/phsbibl/prosjekt/ artikler/fulltekst/avhor8.pdf.*

Granhag, P.A. (2001) *Vittnespsykologi.* Lund: Studentlitteratur.

Gudjonsson, G.H. (2003) *The Psychology of Interrogations and Confessions: A Handbook.* Chichester: Wiley.

Hartwig, M. (2005) Interrogating to Detect Deception and Truth: Effects of Strategic Use of Evidence. Unpublished PhD thesis. Department of Psychology, Göteborg University.

Holmberg, U. and Christianson, S.A. (2002) 'Murderers' and Sexual Offenders' Experiences of Police Interviews and Their Inclination to Admit or Deny Crimes', *Behavioural Sciences and the Law,* 20: 31–45.

Inbau, F.E., Reid, J.E. and Buckley, J.P. (1986) *Criminal Interrogation and Confessions* (3rd edn). Baltimore, MD: Williams & Wilkins.

Inbau, F.E., Reid, J.E., Buckley, J.P. and Jayne, B.C. (2001) *Criminal Interrogation and Confessions* (4th edn). Gaithersburg, MD: Aspen.

Kalbfleisch, P.J. (1994) 'The Language of Detecting Deceit', *Journal of Language and Social Psychology,* 13: 469–496.

Kassin, S.M. and Gudjonsson, G. (2004) 'The Psychology of Confessions', *Psychological Science in the Public Interest,* 5: 33–67.

Kassin, S. (2006) 'A Critical Appraisal of Modern Police Interrogations', in T. Williamson (ed.), *Investigative Interviewing. Rights, Research, Regulation.* Cullompton: Willan Publishing.

Kaufmann, G., Drevland, G., Wessel, E., Overskeid, G. and Magnussen, S. (2003) 'The Importance of Being Earnest: Displayed Emotion and Witness Credibility', *Applied Cognitive Psychology,* 17: 21–34.

Kronkvist, O. (2006) Strategisk bevisanvändning i manualer och handböcker om polisiär förhörsteknik. Unpublished master's thesis, University of Vaksjo, Sweden.

Magnussen, S. (2004) *Vitnepsykologi.* Troverdighet og pålitelighet i dagligliv og rettssal. Oslo: Abstrakt Forlag.

McGurk, B.J., Carr, M.J. and McGurk, D. (1993) *Investigative Interviewing Courses for Police Officers: An Evaluation.* Police Research Series: Paper No. 4. London: Home Office.

Milne, R. and Bull, R. (1999) *Investigative Interviewing: Psychology and Practice.* Chichester: Wiley.

Moston, S. and Engleberg, T. (1993) 'Police Questioning Techniques in Tape Recorded Interviews with Criminal Suspects', *Policing and Society,* 3: 223–237.

NCF (National Crime Faculty) (1998) *A Practical Guide to Investigative Interviewing* (2nd edn). Bramshill: Training and Development Unit, NCF.

Rachlew, A. (1999) Norwegian Police Officers' Perception of Investigative Interviewing – Implications for Training. Unpublished MSc, University of Liverpool.

Rachlew, A. (2003a) 'Norske politiavhør i et internasjonalt perspektiv', *Tidsskrift for Strafferett,* No. 4/2003.

Rachlew, A. (2003b) *Evalueringsrapport.* Justisdepartementets Lydopptaksprosjekt 1998 – 2003. Retrived from http://www.regjeringen.no/upload/kilde/jd/prm/2003/0070/ddd/pdfv/188187-lydbandopptak.pdf.

Scollum, M. (2005) *Investigative Interviewing: The Literature.* Office of the Commissioner of Police, New Zealand.

Sear, L. and Williamson, T. (1999) *British and American Interrogation Strategies.* 'Interviewing and Deception', D.V. Canter and L. Alison (eds), vol. 1, Aldershot: Dartmouth, 65–82.

Shaw, G. (2001) 'Current State of Force Interview Training', in J. Burbeck 'New ACPO Investigative Interviewing Strategy', Warwickshire Police: England.

Shepherd, E. (1991) 'Ethical Interviewing', *Policing*, 7: 42–60.

Shepherd, E. (ed.) (1993) *Aspects of Police Interviewing.* Issues in Criminological and Legal Psychology, No. 18, Leicester: British Psychological Society.

Shepherd, E. (1996) 'The Trouble with PEACE', *Police Review*. 26 July: 14–16.

Shepherd, E. and Kite, F. (1988) 'Training to Interview', *Policing*, 4: 264–280.

Sigurdsson, J.F. and Gudjonsson, G.H. (2004) 'Forensic Psychology in Iceland: A Survey of Members of the Icelandic Psychological Society', *Scandinavian Journal of Psychology*, 45: 325–329.

Stockdale, J.E. (1993) *Management and Supervision of Police Interviews.* Police Research Group. London: Home Office.

Vrij, A. and Granhag, P.A. (2007) 'Interviewing to Detect Deception in Suspects', in S.Å. Christianson (ed.), *Offenders' Memories of Violent Crimes* (pp. 279–304). Chichester: Wiley.

Wessel, E., Drevland, G., Eilertsen, D.E. and Magnussen, S. (2006) 'Credibility of the Emotional Witness: A Study of Ratings by Court Judges', *Law and Human Behavior*, 30: 221–230.

Williamson, T. (1993) 'Review and Prospect', in Eric Shepherd (ed.), *Aspects of Police Interviewing* (pp. 57–59). Issues in Criminological and Legal Psychology, 18.

Chapter 4

Police interviewing in France, Belgium and The Netherlands: something is moving

Sylvie Clément, Marc van de Plas,
Paul van den Eshof and Nicole Nierop

In recent years, we can see a heightened interest in police interviewing in these three countries. However, we can still distinguish some differences in evolution in each country. While France and Belgium are still developing a methodological, well-structured training programme, The Netherlands has already taken some organisational measures to enhance police interviewing in the field. The following chapter will outline the existing provisions made in each of these countries and will then conclude with a discussion regarding what the future holds.

Training in interview techniques: the case of the French gendarmerie

Sylvie Clément

Implementing a training course is time-consuming and complicated. Firstly, it has its origins in a social, economic or political background that forces the professional group to think deeply about its practices and its training policy in this field. As soon as this is established, several training courses must be developed (including creation of course content, recruiting and training teachers, and so on) to answer previously and correctly identified internal needs. The French national gendarmerie, a police force with a military status, has undergone these different phases in the field of training in hearings and interrogations. In 2002, a huge project was set up in order to implement training units on hearings and interrogations. The following concerns a historical discussion regarding this initiative.

A social background suitable to questioning the work of the investigators

Because they have powers which largely exceed common law, police forces are the object of many controls. However, police officers and gendarmes have recently seen their professional practice strongly questioned, notably in the field of criminal investigation. The affirmation presumption of innocence, the ever-restricting evolution of the rules of criminal law procedure,[1] the growing importance of victims, but also the burst of interest of the media in judicial investigations[2] have been a suitable field for critics, especially regarding investigation methods.

Moreover, it is obvious that some cases, known as miscarriages of justice, have discredited the work of criminal investigators and the administration of justice in general: the cases of Outreau in 2000, of Toulouse in 2003, and of Dils in 1987 and 2002. These cases have in common the fact that they failed partly because of the interviews and interrogations. The work of the investigator has been pointed at highlighting a lack of neutrality, giving pressure during police custody, having a lack of technique as far as interview of children are concerned. These cases have also in common that they were based on statements rather than on hard evidence. Interestingly, this also coincides with the development of crime scene, forensic investigators, where audiovisual recording has become the shield against such malfunctions.

Emotion arising from public opinion, especially in the case of Outreau because it involved children, has firmly established the need for the police to reconsider the interview and interrogation techniques of investigators.[3] The weakness which has crept in has strengthened the need of protection. Thus, one positive outcome is that it has speeded up the need of training courses in this field.

Empiricism could not last

Professional culture in the police world strongly promotes learning on the job (experience on the spot) contrary to learning through training courses (Monjardet 1996). This is especially the case as far as interviews and interrogations are concerned, which until recently were only based on this purely practical learning. One would frequently hear that either you have talent for interrogating, or you do not. Furthermore, this attitude does not fit the new, ever-demanding social context, where the work of the investigator had to be professionalised.

Empiricism within the police has clearly been identified through two exploratory studies[4] carried out within the framework of a working group on interview and interrogation methodology set up in 2002. The outcome of this research demonstrated that there was a consensus on the need to organise training courses in this field because conducting an interview or an interrogation is unanimously considered to be a technically arduous, intellectually demanding, and humanly difficult situation. Didactic and procedure learning prevailing in school is not completed with practical cases. Advanced education does not leave more time for a dynamic approach to the subject. This can be easily understood if we take into consideration the growing complexity of the initial training, whose key word is 'polyvalence' (Clément 2006).

Observing practical cases has shown that hearings and interrogations are complex acts whose execution is not restricted to the procedure application. In addition, succeeding in conducting a hearing or interrogation depends on two other factors: (i) the person who is asking questions and (ii) the environment where the communication takes place. To conclude, problems and needs are different depending on whether the questioner is a gendarme or an investigator belonging to a specialised unit (investigation unit).

One last element completed this review – the importance of the interview and the interrogation in the inquiry process. Despite the lack of statistics on the subject, the investigators we met all stressed that it is an important stage of the inquiry and that questioning a witness or a victim can prove as difficult as questioning an offender.

Identifying needs

Beyond this review of practical cases, the need of training courses has also been clearly identified where 85 per cent of investigators questioned noted it to be important. However, it does not have to take the form of one sole framework that would signify a stronger control of practice. Moreover, discussions and answers to questionnaires have revealed basic needs (behaviour, assessment, how to establish contact) and more technical needs (directed to specific offences). In addition, requests for specialisation in training remain high.

Other proposals have been submitted during the discussions which concerned the developing of training initiatives with universities or specialised institutes, optimising existing resources (internal training courses with specialised units with regard to minors), creating handbooks, developing exchanges between judicial units (self-training), and setting up of a literature structure dedicated to the judicial field (selection of documents, follow-up and dissemination of information).

In summary, there are needs. They sometimes deal with basic demands and sometimes with very narrowly targeted skills. As a consequence, the approach of training conducted in several stages is required. A set of complementary stipulations can be added in order to complete initial or continuing education. In the light of what has been mentioned, it is obvious that professional practice must evolve and that it is complicated. As a consequence, a training plan must meet those needs.

A supply in training to be developed

The observation and consideration phases have lasted quite a long time, that is, about two years. But the phase regarding the development of training courses was even longer. It is not over yet. In November 2004, an experimental seminar of training in interviewing had been organised in order to test hypotheses regarding the pedagogical world (focus on practical experience and exchange) and interview methods to be taught. Intended for a small group of 15 investigators experienced in the judicial field, it lasted one week and gathered teachers coming from various areas (such as psychologists, judges and prosecutors, academics, and gendarmes). Subsequently, there was an assessment which proved to be positive and which really launched the project.

Now that the basic principle had been established, one had to convert it into a coherent training module. Two main training poles have been distinguished: (i) initial education (for officers and junior officers) and (ii) advanced education (for all staff). A cadre of teachers was also required in addition to the two above-mentioned systems. A training intended for experienced investigators is being studied. So, schools had to adapt by setting up training modules for the officer school as well as for the junior officer school. Within this framework, the network of teachers had to be set up and existing training courses had to be adapted. Teaching material was also needed: a film intended for participants in training courses was shot in 2007 in order to make them aware of the difficulty of the exercise.

All these projects required a lot of preparatory work in order to give the necessary shape to the project: defining pedagogical goals, drawing pedagogical sheets, etc. In summary, the supply in training courses relied on two major principles: (i) common bases for all modules and (ii) similar educational methods (practical situations and feedback of experience). This common basis is required to ensure equality between training, which is profitable to all.

There is still much work to do and many other projects are being finalised. This approach is a complete success in its methodology (audits to establish the facts and identify training needs, defining a supply in training at several levels, and setting up an experimental seminar to approve hypotheses) as well as in the success it has with the staff dealing with it. It required substantial human and financial means, showing the importance the institution wants to attach to this professional practice. The future looks rosy with much work to do.

The police interview in Belgium

Marc van de Plas

1. Miscarriages of justice

As far as we know in Belgium, no miscarriages of justice cases have been revealed in which innocent people were convicted or investigators were shown to make an obvious mistake when conducting an interview. Nevertheless, one of the most discussed cases is probably the so-called X-files that were opened as a result of the Dutroux case in 1996.[5]

After this case came to light, several 'victims' turned up who claimed to have been sexually abused and to have witnessed murder. A conspiracy theory was rampant, and there was talk of an organised network up to the highest level in Belgian society. Several victims/witnesses were interviewed under hypnosis. However, the statements proved to be unverifiable and in the end the whole investigation was suspended. The way the interviews were conducted and hypnosis as a technique were questioned, in particular with regard to suggestibility and prejudice. Indeed, Savage and Milne (2007) have noted that one definition of a miscarriage of justice is ineffective investigations.

2. Applied interviewing techniques

2.1. Legal framework

The Belgian Code of Criminal Procedure stipulates that the police interview is part of the criminal or judicial preliminary investigation.

This preliminary investigation is secret and written and is conducted by a magistrate. This has two consequences. Firstly, the investigator does not act independently. The magistrate supervises the correct performance of the investigative actions. Secondly, the investigation file always contains a written report of the interview in the form of a statement.

The same code, however, provides for the recording of police interviews on videotape or audiotape. If the victim or the witness is under the age of 18, video interviewing is advisable. This facility is also open to adults. The decision to tape the interview lies with the magistrate, and he or she appoints the investigator by name to conduct the interview. The legislation on child interviewing, understandably, is more stringent and was fuelled by the promulgation of a ministerial circular letter that lays down the procedure to conduct such interviews. This circular letter also mentions the basic principles that have to be met with regard to the execution of the interview. It is laid down that video interviews of a minor should be conducted in a stepwise, respectful and non-suggestive way.[6]

In addition to the legislation on the interview in general and the interviewing of children in particular, Belgium has legislation on the use of the polygraph in criminal cases. This procedure is regulated in detail in a ministerial circular letter of 2003. A polygraph test is considered as a special form of police interviewing to orient an investigation. Stringent demands are imposed on the use of this technique. It is only allowed when principals of proportionality and subsidiarity are applied. The first principle means that the polygraph is not used in minor cases; the second means that all 'classic' investigation methods must have been applied but failed to get sufficient material proof. The circumstances in which a magistrate is allowed to order a polygraph test, the information and the voluntary participation of the person who has to be heard, and the working method that has to be followed are clearly stated. In addition, the polygraph test has to be filmed entirely.

2.2. What actually occurs in Belgium?
2.2.1. General findings
Video interviewing is more optional for adults, and as a result considerably fewer video interviews in practice are being conducted. On the one hand, this makes it harder for the magistrate to supervise this investigative action. S/he can only rely on the contents of the written report of the interview and much research has shown the problems with accurately recording an interview in written form (see

Milne and Bull 2006 for more on this). In addition, this haphazard policy limits the scientific research on this matter in Belgium. Only three known studies on the interviewing of adults, all based on the investigators' self-report (and in one case also from the interviewees) exist to help inform policy and practice. Each will be examined in turn.

Ponsaers *et al.* (2001) conducted a survey of 360 investigators on the use of interrogation techniques and found that the primary aim of the interrogation was not so much confession-oriented as intended to gather verifiable information. The investigators concerned were presented with 105 interrogation tactics and were asked to what extent they used each of these. It was reported that most tactics were not or very rarely used. There were nevertheless some striking findings. For example, 23.8 per cent of all respondents frequently referred to evidence about which the investigator had reached no certainty. In 9.1 per cent of the cases, evidence is referred to which the investigator is sure does not exist. Consciously showing one's conviction of the suspect's guilt was frequently used as a strategy by 37 per cent of the investigators. Minimising the facts was a strategy used by 1 out of 10 investigators, attributing the blame to the circumstances by 5.9 per cent, and attributing it to the victim by 2 per cent. The researchers concluded that the use of interrogation tactics in Belgium is going well on the whole, but at the same time they pointed out that social desirability may have played a role (that is, what officers say they do and what they actually practise may not be one and the same; Ponsaers *et al.* 2001).

In another study, De Fruyt *et al.* (2006) asked 230 investigators to characterise themselves with regard to 66 interviewing competences. The results could be grouped into five independent components in which the different police interviewers were placed. They were then presented with 20 interrogation situations, so that interview competences could be linked with interview situations. The five competency clusters obtained significantly different scores depending on the type of person who was to be interviewed, in particular whether it was a victim, witness or suspect. With regard to the interviewing of victims, a positive connection was found between the clusters 'kindness'[7], 'sensitivity'[8] and 'non-reactivity'.[9] A significant negative connection was found with the cluster 'dominance'.[10] With regard to the interviewing of witnesses, a significant positive connection was found with the clusters 'kindness', 'sensitivity' and 'carefulness'.[11] With regard to the interrogation of suspects, significant positive connections were found with 'sensitivity', 'carefulness' and 'dominance'. Another striking finding was that there was a negative connection with the competence 'kindness'. As a result, the researchers developed a 'police interview competency inventory' (PICI), which could be a useful tool to train interrogators and to optimise the interrogation process. At the same time, the authors point out the possible limits of self-report, as noted above (De Fruyt *et al.* 2006). Indeed, what strikes us most in this research is the perception of many police officers that the approach to victims, witnesses and suspects differs in practice. The majority of the investigators questioned noted that suspects should be interrogated in a more offensive and authoritarian way in order to achieve results.

The final and most recent study conducted by Vanderhallen (2007) inquired into the interview style by questioning both police officers and interviewees right after 126 real victim, witness, or suspect interviews. Whereas the investigator did not see a difference in his/her approach to victims, witnesses and suspects, the perceptions of victims and witnesses on the one hand and of suspects on the other hand were clearly different. Suspects felt that they were treated more assertively and with less humanity than the victims and witnesses questioned. The interview situation was less clear for them, and they felt that they were treated with less respect and more hostility. Suspects reported significantly more fear. This finding showed a negative correlation with the amount of information delivered by the interviewee. They considered the interviewer to be less competent and less reliable.

The research findings of De Fruyt *et al.* (2006) and Vanderhallen (2007) suggest that a large number of Belgian investigators still start from a guilt hypothesis when conducting a suspect interrogation and follow the controlling interrogation style rather than the humanitarian style. Research, however, demonstrates that the controlling interrogation style has a negative impact on a good working relationship and understanding (Holmberg 2004a, 2004b) and that the willingness of guilty suspects to make a complete statement is actually stimulated by a respectful approach and good relations (Milne and Bull 1999).

The work of Vanderhallen (2007) confirms the idea of the chain reaction in which the prepossession of the interviewer of the guilt of the suspect (Moston *et al.* 1992) promotes the mechanisms of confirmation bias and belief perseverance that will in turn make him or her look predominantly for a confession and the gathering of inculpatory evidence (Mortimer and Shepherd 1999; Kassin *et al.* 2003; Kassin 2005). This tendency influences the interviewing style, which becomes more controlling and accusatory. This style produces less clarity, more fear, and more defensive behaviour from the interviewee (Vanderhallen 2007). Furthermore, the research suggests that the investigators themselves are not aware of this or do not want to report it. More research is therefore warranted on this issue.

2.2.2. The interviewing of minors

Every year, more than 1,000 interviews of minors are videotaped. In a recent scientific study, 57 interviews were analysed at the microlevel (Dommicent et al. 2006). All interviewers had followed a specialised training in child interviewing. A third of them received an individual follow-up, a third received a collective follow-up, and a third had no follow-up. A grid was developed, composed of 127 observation scales, taking into account the main insights and aptitudes taught in the specialised training programme in child interviewing. The study showed that the three basic principles (stepwise approach, respect and non-suggestibility) are applied in general, but investigators who received an individual follow-up were significantly more respectful. Interviewers who received a collective follow-up demonstrated no significant differences from interviewers without any follow-up. The study demonstrated also that the time dedicated to free recall was positively correlated with non-suggestibility (Dommicent et al. 2006).

2.2.3. With regard to polygraphy

Since the start of polygraph training for Belgian investigators, more than 1,500 tests have been conducted, mainly with suspects. The 'demand' still increases every year.[12] The polygraph operators are trained at the Canadian Police College and basically apply the control-question technique. The research examining the validity of this technique differs greatly, and its usefulness has been questioned by many academics.[13]

Due to Belgian legislation, the polygraph test is mainly applied in investigations that contain few or no elements of proof and in which a presumption of guilt remains, as, for instance, on account of statements. In more than 85 per cent of the cases, the test result was found to be 'truthful'. For many suspects, this means that they can close a chapter, sometimes after years of 'labelling' without sufficient material proof.

Despite the clear intention of the Belgian Minister of Justice to use the polygraph only as a means of orientation during the preliminary investigation, the actual practice differs. Because evidence in criminal cases is free in Belgium, the deceptive polygraph result is in fact used as an element of proof before the court. Because 'false positives' are a typical risk when using a control-question technique, this use of the 'untruthful' test in Belgium seems to be a more alarming finding (British Psychological Society (BPS) Working Party 2004).

2.2.4. Forensic hypnosis

Forensic hypnosis is also a technique that has been strongly criticised by academics. Crombag and van Koppen (1997) state that hypnosis will deteriorate memory, due to the higher sensitivity to suggestion. So the risk for pseudo-memories increases when one uses hypnosis as an investigative tool (Crombag and Van Koppen 1997).

   Although it is not used by the police and although it does not fall under the legislation of police interviewing, this technique should also be mentioned. Every year, dozens of interviews using forensic hypnosis are carried out by psychologists or physicians in Belgium. A magistrate can take this initiative in the form of an expert assessment. These interviews always take place after one or more 'classic/traditional' interviews have been conducted, and only when witnesses or victims claim that they cannot remember specific details, such as, the number on a number plate or the detailed description of a perpetrator. Despite the scientific criticism, we have to state that some investigations have been helped by the information that was gathered in such interviews. In two cases, for instance, the photofit picture that was drawn up in a hypnosis interview led to the identification of the perpetrator. In another case, the victim could describe a phone call she did not remember in normal interviewing conditions. Of course, what we do not know is the degree of profoundness by which the former 'classic' interviews were done.

3. Policy and training

Front-line police officers are trained in 10 provincial police schools in Belgium. The second-line police (non-uniformed investigators) are trained in one central criminal investigation school. In 2006, a study group, made up of 'interview' instructors, behavioural scientists and magistrates, investigated to what extent the existing 'interview' training corresponded to the needs of officers in the field, whether the necessary coherence exists between the first- and second-line training, and to what extent the taught techniques are legally and scientifically acceptable.[14] The study group concluded that a great effort has been made in Belgium in police interview training over the last decade. Twenty years ago, the training was mainly theoretical, whereas now it is more practice-based. However, insufficient attention is given to the acquisition of the basic skills (communication and basic interview technique) and the achievement of sufficient depth, both with respect to the preparation and to the questioning during the interview.

A comparative study of the provincial police schools showed that there are big differences between the basic training, as far as the content of the material goes, and the number of practical exercises given. In the basic training of each police officer, only 22 hours is provided for the module 'interviewing' (Volckaert 2005). The responsible services are currently paying special attention to this problem.

As far as the acceptability of the interrogation techniques goes, it was found that elements of the Reid technique (Inbau *et al.* 2001) are mainly taught in the second-line police officers' interview training class. Such training concerns, among other things, minimisation, projection of guilt, offering themes, and asking behaviour observation questions, linked with the interpretation of truthfulness and deception. An alarming finding is that some instructors walk into the trap of the 'recognisability in practice' of these techniques and the corresponding behaviour of 'guilty suspects'. In their opinion, 'waiting for scientific proof' is tantamount to loss of time and stagnation. This is worrying, because, as has already been mentioned, this technique has been heavily criticised by the academic world as unethical (Gudjonsson 2003), because it may lead to false confessions (Kassin and Kiechel 1996), and because the instructors use rather naive ideas to interpret behaviour with respect to guilt or innocence (Mann *et al.* in press).

Besides the before-mentioned training efforts and the follow-up of the child interviewers, there are as yet no other organisational measures taken in Belgium. Measures such as follow-up sessions, workplace supervision and coaching are not systematically applied. After all, this requires the reservation of a considerable capacity and is also complicated by the scarcity of video interviews. In the meantime, the emphasis is on the harmonisation of the existing training programmes.

Interrogation of suspects in The Netherlands

Paul van den Eshof and Nicole Nierop

1. Introduction

Unlike in Belgium, in The Netherlands, miscarriage of justice cases attract considerable attention. This is particularly because these miscarriages often involve false confessions and a poor quality of interrogation. Relatively recently, it has been established that in two murder cases, the Putten case (Blaauw 2002) and the Schiedam Park murder (van Koppen 2003), innocent people were convicted. A committee specifically set up for the purpose investigated the convictions in three other criminal cases, the Enschede sexual abuse case (van Es 2003), the case of Ina Post (Israëls 2004), and that of Lucia de B. (Derksen 2006). In response to their conclusions, requests for the review of these cases are now before the Supreme Court, the highest court of justice in The Netherlands. In the following paragraphs, we will first give an overview of the interrogation methods used in The Netherlands, and then go on to discuss the two cases of miscarriage of justice referred to above. New policies to prevent miscarriage of justice in the future will be examined, and finally various other relevant developments in the field will be sketched.

2. Interrogation methods

The interrogation of suspects calls for other interviewing methods than those used in social and clinical psychology, as it is takes place within the judicial process and the most important principle on which it is based is discovering the truth. In addition, if an interrogation is to be well structured, it must be conducted by special method. In this paragraph, we discuss the standard interrogation strategy, a method devised by the Dutch Police Academy, the national police training centre (subsection 2.1), as well as some controversial methods, directly derived from applied (popular) psychology, which lack a judicial basis. An example of the latter is the so-called Zaanse verhoormethode (subsection 2.2). This chapter ends with the Public Prosecution Service's internal guideline, which prohibits certain interrogation methods (subsection 2.3).

2.1 Standard interrogation strategy

The Dutch Police Academy developed a method which serves as a blueprint for the interrogation of suspects (van Amelsvoort et al. 2006). The method, referred to as the standard interrogation strategy, is taught to all future detectives during their training and is meant for suspects who are to some extent willing to testify, but will not make an extensive statement voluntarily. In principle, this method may be applied in all cases that meet the following criteria: (i) there is sufficient tactical and/or forensic evidence to come up with an interrogation plan, (ii) the suspect must have a 'normal' tolerance for pressure, and (iii) be willing to talk about the case. The standard interrogation strategy consists of four elements: (1) minimising the suspect's resistance; (2) confronting the suspect with the evidence, in the form of circumventing questions, so that there is no denying of the facts; (3) building up pressure so that the suspect, confronted with the evidence, has no alternative but to tell the truth; and (4) rewarding the suspect if the statement is adjusted so that it reflects the truth (van Amelsvoort *et al.* 2006). The interrogation starts with subjects about which it is easy for the suspect to make a statement, and ends with subjects the suspect has more difficulty with. The interrogator prepares circumventing questions for each subject, and systematically increases the pressure in the course of the investigation. The principle behind the latter tactic is to keep the suspect's resistance low and at the same time increase the willingness to make a full statement.

Applying the standard interrogation strategy forces detectives to prepare the interrogation carefully and draw up a detailed plan. The strategy does have its disadvantages (Nierop and Mooij 2000; Nierop 2005). For instance, there are cases in which the method cannot be applied because there is no tactical evidence, and it can be difficult to determine how a suspect will respond to pressure. Also there is danger in rewarding a suspect, because this might lead to *shaping*, particularly when innocent and vulnerable suspects are involved (Nierop 2007). In addition to the standard interrogation strategy, the Police Academy teaches various other interrogation methods, such as use of the evidence matrix, individual-oriented interrogation, case-oriented interrogation, and promoting the willingness to make a statement (van Amelsvoort *et al.* 2006).

2.2 Controversial interrogation methods
One of the alternative methods used in The Netherlands, the Zaanse verhoormethode (Nierop and Mooij 2000) is not only controversial but has also given rise to a large body of legal precedents. It was developed by a communications expert, who based his method on neurolinguistic programming (Nierop and Van den Eshof 2002; Vrij and Lochun 2002) and other theories. He introduced the idea of a pool of interrogators who would all play different roles during the interrogation. These interrogators make use of mirroring (imitating the suspect's behaviour), space invasion (sitting very close to the suspect), focal points (focuses of attention based on neurolinguistic processing theories), photo collages (both of the suspect's relatives and friends and the scene of the crime), reliving the crime, and

questioning by more than one detective at the same time (De Leeuw and Hanssen 1997; Slats 1997).

After the Zaanse verhoormethode had been highlighted in the media, the Minister of Justice commissioned an investigation into the method. This investigation resulted in the recommendation not to use the method any longer. An appeal was lodged with the European Court of Human Rights in two Dutch murder cases where use had indeed been made of the Zaanse verhoormethode (*Ebbinge* v *the State of The Netherlands*; *Jager* v *the State of The Netherlands*). The European Court ruled that no psychological torture (Article 3 of the European Convention on Human Rights (ECHR)) had taken place, and that the trials had been fair (Article 6 of the ECHR) in view of the fact that the judges in The Netherlands had justly disregarded the confessions (Myjer 2000). However, Nierop and van den Eshof (2003) have pointed out that the following passage from the ruling is remarkable: 'The Court considers that it [the Zaanse verhoormethode] is a sophisticated method from a psychological point of view and therefore objectionable in the context of a criminal investigation in that it is apparently aimed at attaining, by seeking to create an atmosphere of intimacy between the suspect and the interrogators through mental stimulation, an optimal level of communication, as a result of which the interrogated person is incited, on the basis of a perceived level of trust, to confide in the interrogators in order to seek relief from a burdensome memory'. Nierop and van den Eshof interpret this passage as an indication that the European Court is apparently of the opinion that it is objectionable that 'sophisticated psychological' instruments, such as mirroring, focal points, and photo collages, are used during an interrogation to create a perceived level of trust which renders the suspect more willing to make a statement. Nierop and van den Eshof posit that this is particularly relevant to the assessment of interrogation methods, both in concrete cases and training situations.

2.3 Prohibited methods

Under the instructions regarding 'Unorthodox investigative methods' of the Board of Procurators General (which came into force on 1 November 2003), the following instruments and methods are explicitly prohibited:

- the lie detector
- narco analysis
- questioning witnesses who are under hypnosis

- the use of a medium
- using anatomically correct dolls for the questioning of children in an interrogation studio.

The Public Prosecution Service argues that:

> In principle, the business-like and professional way in which the Public Prosecution Service follows criminal procedures does not allow for the use of investigative methods which, in the assessment of scientific thinking, do not guarantee objectively reliable results. It is the task of the scientists to discover which investigative methods produce reliable results. The discussion that this process entails does not belong in a court of law. Using the results of these investigative methods as evidence is usually not allowed (see NJ 1998/798). Even if an investigation has come to a stand-still, the use of these methods is very restricted. (...) Under very special circumstances the Board of Procurators General may give permission for the use of an unorthodox investigative method at the request of the Chief Advocate General.

For the questioning of witnesses, the Police Academy has devised a method called 'guided memory'. The idea is to have the witness relive a certain situation and get a clear picture of what happened exactly. The witness must concentrate very hard – for example, by closing his or her eyes – and then answer a series of open questions. 'This method is primarily suitable for the hearing of witnesses' (van Amelsvoort *et al.* 2006). Occasionally, guided memory is used to win over a suspect who initially denies involvement in a crime. This, however, is objectionable. The committee that assessed the Zaanse verhoormethode (see subsection 2.2) objected against the suspect's reliving the crime, arguing that 'reliving' the crime is only possible if one committed it (Recherche Adviescommissie 1996).

3. Miscarriages of justice

3.1. The Putten murder case
One of the cases in which a miscarriage of justice took place was the murder of a 23-year-old air hostess in 1994. In this case, known as the Putten murder case, four men were arrested and very soon confessed. Two of them were alleged to have raped and murdered the woman, while the other two (mentally handicapped) looked on.

The men's statements kept changing and were not in line with one another. In 1995, the two prime suspects were sentenced to 10 years' imprisonment on charges of rape and murder. The convictions were mainly based on the suspects' statements, which they had retracted in the meantime. There was no forensic evidence, and the semen found was not that of any of the men. The Courts of Appeal upheld the judgement of the earlier court, and requests for a review were denied.

The efforts of a crime journalist (De Vries 2002) and a former chief constable (Blaauw 2002) kept interest in the case alive in the media, and eventually brought about a change in public opinion. After the suspects had been sent to prison, the journalist devoted dozens of critical programmes to the case, collaborating with a former chief constable who had written a highly critical book on the subject. De Vries quoted extensively from the interrogations, expressed his doubts of the interrogation methods that had been used, and highlighted the fact that the suspects' statements deviated from one another. At the request of the defence, a forensic psychologist subjected the interrogations to renewed analyses. He agreed with the criticism and expressed this in scientific terms, pointing out the following aspects: frequent and long interrogations, on several occasions continuing long into the night; an excessive relationship of trust between the interrogators and the suspects; shaping; confirmation bias; scenario-based interrogations (what could have happened?); the assumption that the suspects had repressed the murder; guided memory; and confronting the suspects with co-suspects' statements and evidence that had been wrongly interpreted. The suspects suffered from memory distrust, compliance, suggestibility and educational subnormality. Eventually, a request for a review of the case was granted, as the Supreme Court was of the opinion that new facts had come to light. The expert who had initially suggested that the semen was not the result of the rape, but of earlier sexual intercourse, withdrew his statement. The case was then retried by the court in Leeuwarden, which gave a damning indictment of the interrogation methods used. An acquittal followed in 2002. Despite the fact that forensic psychologists have no doubt about the innocence of the two men in question, many legal experts are still of the opinion that that no false statements were made.

3.2. The Schiedam Park murder
Another case in which a miscarriage of justice took place was the Schiedam Park murder (van Koppen 2003) which involved the sexual

assault and murder of a 10-year-old girl and the attempted murder of an 11-year-old boy in Schiedam in June 2000. In 2001 (and by the Court of Appeal in 2002), a suspect was sentenced who had initially been questioned as a witness. At the time of the crime, this man was cycling through the park in question and called the police when he heard the boy crying for help. He was arrested as a suspect and was later said to have made a confession during interrogation. In 2004, it emerged that a miscarriage of justice might have occurred. The suspect of a different sex crime confessed to the Schiedam Park murder during interrogation. The investigation that was carried out in response to this confession showed that his statement was corroborated by the facts. In 2005, the Court and Special Court found the suspect guilty and sentenced him to a term of imprisonment of 18 years, followed by detention under a hospital order. The man who had been sentenced earlier was acquitted by the Supreme Court.

4. Developments in response to the miscarriages of justice

4.1. Posthumus committee

In response to the miscarriage of justice in the Schiedam Park murder, the Board of Procurators General established a committee to carry out an evaluation. In their report, this Posthumus Committee heavily criticised the police, the Public Prosecution Service, and the experts consulted by the Public Prosecution Service. The committee also made some recommendations for future interrogations of suspects:

- pay more attention to interrogation methods during the training of police personnel (including management personnel and judicial officers);
- be on the alert for confessions, even if no prohibited pressure was applied and no prohibited methods were used during the interrogation;
- do not carry out scenario-based interrogations, that is, interrogations during which suspects or witnesses are asked to imagine and tell what exactly could have happened;
- for major cases, make more frequent use of interrogation plans;
- make video recordings of the interrogation of suspects in major cases.

In response to the report and by order of the Minister of Justice, the police and Public Prosecution Service devised the 'Versterking opsporing en vervolging' programme (improving the investigation and prosecution process), in which the following goals are set out: (i) boosting public confidence in the police and the Public Prosecution Service, (ii) increasing these bodies' professionalism and the quality of their work, and (iii) guaranteeing transparency and integrity. Measures envisaged include taking police education to a higher level so that in the future at least 20 per cent of all managers will have received higher professional or university education, creating a facility for counter-arguments and review within large-scale investigations, and setting up mandatory guidelines for audiovisual registration interrogations.

4.2. Committee for the evaluation of criminal cases that have been concluded

With the conclusions of the evaluation report in mind, the Public Prosecution Service decided to investigate whether other miscarriages of justice cases had taken place. For this purpose, the 'Commissie Evaluatie Afgedane Strafzaken' (CEAS – Committee for the evaluation of criminal cases that have been concluded) was established. The committee's main task is to establish in a given case, whether in the course of the criminal investigation, the prosecution, or the presentation of the evidence in court, errors were made that prevented the judge from interpreting the facts objectively. A case can be presented to the CEAS by a former or current police or judicial officer, an employee of the Dutch Forensic Institute, or a scientist who analysed the case in question and devoted a scientific publication to his or her findings. The sentence must be irrevocable, and the crime committed must have been a grave threat to public order and/or punishable with a prison sentence of at least 12 years.

The CEAS has also been the subject of criticism:

- The criteria are too strict: sentenced persons cannot present their cases to the committee themselves.
- Cases in which the judges had been fully informed and still reached an incorrect judgement are not eligible.
- The committee advises the Board of Procurators General and is therefore not independent.
- The committee consists exclusively of judicial experts and police officers, and does not include academics who are experts in the fields of methodology and forensic psychology.
- A number of scientists are of the opinion that judicial experts are not capable of judging whether evidence is permissible or not,

and that this should be left to a jury of experts, both in ordinary criminal cases and in cases that are put to a special committee.

The CEAS is a temporary committee. The possibility of a more structural solution is now being studied. The chance is small that the authorities will opt for a committee similar to the British Criminal Cases Review Commission (CCRC). According to the highest official of the Public Prosecution Service and the Minister of Justice, such a committee would not be compatible with the Dutch legal system. It is far more probable that the existing possibility of a review by the Supreme Court will be realised in a different way; the criteria for accepting new evidence could be broadened (van Dongen 2008).

4.3. Audiovisual registration of interrogations of suspects

In the near future, The Netherlands will introduce legislation that makes the audiovisual registration of interrogations obligatory in certain cases. The legislation will come into force as soon as all police forces have an interrogation studio that contains the necessary equipment. In anticipation of the legislation, many interrogations that take place within the framework of a serious case are already being recorded in this way. The objectives of this registration are to make it possible to review interrogations at a later stage of the trial and to use the recordings as reference material when the official report is put together to guarantee the quality of interrogations of vulnerable suspects, to record emotions and other non-verbal behaviour, to direct interrogations from the director's room, to make it possible for behavioural experts to assist in the interrogations, and to use the recordings as study material for students at the police academy.

Audio recording will be mandatory in the following cases: 1) crimes that carry a prison sentence of at least 12 years; 2) crimes involving a fatality or serious injury; 3) sexual crimes that carry a prison sentence of at least eight years; 4) sexual crimes in which the victim was a dependant of the offender. The interrogations must be audiovisually recorded in the following situations:

- The interrogation is of a vulnerable person (for instance, minors under 16 and mentally handicapped persons).
- Children under 12 must be questioned in a child-friendly studio (see above).
- Special interrogation methods are used (for instance, interrogations during which the interrogator gives away knowledge only the

perpetrator can have, and interrogations using the support of a behavioural scientist).

The legislation applies to the interrogation of suspects and planned interviews of victims, people filing an official complaint, and witnesses. The support of a behavioural scientist always entails an audiovisual registration of the interrogation.

Several aspects of the proposed legislation are noteworthy. First of all, it is striking that the possibility of recording non-verbal signals is alluded to, whereas forensic psychology has pointed out that the importance of non-verbal behaviour is often overrated (Vrij and Winkel 2002). Many detectives are of the opinion that non-verbal behaviour can indicate whether or not a suspect is lying, but research has shown that this is often based on false assumptions (Vrij and Lochun 2002). Even if the detectives are aware of the scientific findings, applying this knowledge in practice remains difficult. It is also remarkable that the legislation speaks of vulnerable persons, but that it does not deal with the specific problems such interrogations bring. In the authors' experience, in practice considerable effort is required to make detectives and judges aware of socio-psychological processes that may influence these interrogations. In other words, if police officers and judges are not aware of phenomena such as compliance, suggestibility, shaping, or memory distrust, it is of little use for them to watch a recording of an interrogation in order to draw a conclusion on the vulnerability of the suspect. In practice, in most cases, an expert witness will have to be called upon to assess the interrogation and draw up a report (Nierop 2007).

5. Further developments

5.1. Presence of psychologists during interrogations

In The Netherlands, it is quite common to have a psychologist present during the interrogation of suspects. The Police Academy and The Netherlands Police Agency have psychologists available who can provide advice on interrogations, regional forces are beginning to take on psychologists, and there are an increasing number of independent psychologists who offer their services to the police. The advice usually consists of two components: suggestions for possible interrogation strategies and ideas on how to increase the pressure, and ways to deal with the need for supervision in the case of vulnerable witnesses and to avoid false confessions. This second aspect is thought to be especially important in view of the recent miscarriages of justice.

Two years ago, behaviourists came together and set up the national 'Groep Verdachtenverhoor' (interrogation of suspects group). The organisation operates on the basis of a national protocol; the members share knowledge and frequently discuss their experiences. Van den Eshof and Nierop (2008) have formulated a number of rules for the use of psychologist advisers in the interrogation progress:

(1) The psychologist operates exclusively within a criminal-judicial framework, and is not there to provide care for the suspect.

(2) The psychologist does not advise the use of techniques that might contravene The Netherlands law of criminal procedure, which has as a basic principle that a suspect does not have to cooperate (caution, right to remain silent).

(3) The psychologist has received a judicial training and keeps abreast of relevant legislation and precedents (European Court).

(4) The psychologist is familiar with the interrogation methods that are taught in police training.

(5) The psychologist does not express an opinion on the suspect's guilt or innocence with the aim of providing proof.

(6) The psychologist does not talk with the suspect directly; interventions, if any, take place through a detective.

(7) Diagnostic techniques are not applied during the interrogation. If someone is referred to a forensic psychologist or psychiatrist on medical grounds, the psychologist carries out an interview outside the interrogation environment. It is permitted to use conclusions (diagnoses) from psychological reports in drawing up a recommendation for the interrogation.

(8) The psychologist is well informed on psychological theories, concepts, and scientific results, and knows what the following phenomena entail: compliance, suggestibility, excessive trust relationship, source monitoring, amnesia, shaping, guided memory, imagining, memory distrust, confirmation bias, and non-verbal behaviour/lying.

(9) Statements made by the suspect may not be used out of context, but must be judged within the framework of the interrogation and the questions and remarks of the interrogator.

(10) The psychologist provides advice on the basis of a written order, and draws up a report of the findings.

The rules have been devised because there is a lack of clarity among psychologists regarding their formal position during interrogations, the expectations of those requesting their presence, and the use of psychological know-how in this specific judicial context.

5.2. New legislation

Until recently, the word 'confession' did not occur in the Dutch (moderately inquisitorial) Code of Criminal Procedure. A few years ago, this was changed, and now a suspect's confession can have certain procedural consequences.

On 1 January 2004, the police were given the power to settle simple shoplifting cases themselves by imposing a fine ('police transaction') on the condition that the perpetrator was caught red-handed, is an adult, and confesses to the offence (instruction regarding the out-of-court settlement with the police in the case of simple theft and embezzlement, registration number 2003A015).

On 1 January 2005, new legislation came into force regarding the way in which judges are to deal with suspects who confess. 'The conclusion that the suspect committed the crime must be supported by the evidence contained in the judgment, which furnishes the facts and circumstances on which is is based. Insofar as the suspect has confessed to the proven facts, a specification of the evidence will suffice, unless the suspect has later stated otherwise, or he or his legal representative has advocated aquittal' (Article 259 section 3, Act of 10 November 2004). The question of whether there has been a confession is of a factual nature; the question must be answered by the judge deciding questions of fact (court) and, at appeal, may only be judged on its intelligibility. The Act has a general application, and so applies to murder cases as well (see Supreme Court ruling 26 September 2006, LJN: AX5776).

6. Conclusion

In recent years, The Netherlands has seen various miscarriages of justice. Measures have been proposed to improve the quality of the criminal investigation process, and the interrogation of suspects is now more closely scrutinised than before. In the current debate, a prominent role has been played by forensic psychologists and journalists. The reason for this is probably that laymen and legal experts find it difficult to imagine that an innocent suspect might confess to a crime. It is striking that in recent years legal experts have increased the legal consequences of a confession, whereas forensic psychologists have been warning against too great a reliance on confessions. Some forensic psychologists even advocate the abolition of the suspect's statement as evidence (van Koppen 2003). It is obvious that in criminal proceedings more attention should be paid to psychological processes that may influence the suspect's freedom to make a statement. With regard to this (and the main aim of discovering the truth), it would be useful to subject the interrogation of suspects to stricter regulation.

Notes

1 In the last few years, penal justice has known a permanent reform, according to Jean Danet (2006).
2 Public opinion then becomes a substitute for justice.
3 Let's mention that it has firmly shown the weakness of oral testimony.
4 The first study was carried out by a sociologist, while the second one was conducted by a psychologist, both working for the national gendarmerie.
5 Marc Dutroux was convicted of the kidnapping, abuse and murder of children and adults.
6 The Belgian legislator used the stepwise interview of Yuille *et al.* (1993) as a basis for this.
7 Characterised by 'understanding', 'compliant' and 'empathic'.
8 Characterised by 'having feeling', 'being communicative' and 'making contact easily'.
9 Characterised by 'calm', 'self-controlled' and 'being patient'.
10 Characterised by 'offensive', 'speaking eloquently' and 'being authoritarian'.
11 Characterised by 'thorough', 'persevering' and 'passionate'.
12 See annual activity reports of the Belgian Federal Police at www.police. be.
13 See, for example, the British Psychological Society (BPS) Working Party (2004).
14 Internal Federal Police document 2007.

References

Blaauw, J.A. (2002) *De Puttense moordzaak. Reconstructie van een dubieus moordonderzoek*. Baarn: De Fontein.

British Psychololgical Society (BPS) Working Party (2004) A review of the current status and fields of application of polygraphic deception detection (6 October).

Clément, S. 2004) L'Entretien judiciaire, approche sociologique, IHESI.

Crombag, H.F.M. and van Koppen, P.J. (1997) 'Post-hoc informatie, suggestie en hypnose', in P.J. van Koppen (ed.), *Het Hart van de Zaak: psychologie van het recht*. Deventer: Gouda Quint, 314–333.

Danet, J. (2006) *Justice pénale, le tournant*. Folio Actuel, février, no. 119.

De Fruyt, F., Bockstaele, M. and De Greef, K. (2006) 'Competenties in het politieverhoor: structuur, meting en het verband met persoonlijkheid', *Panopticon*, 3: 12.

De Leeuw, D. and Hanssen, H. (1997) 'De omstreden Zaanse verhoormethode legt moordenaars en verkrachters het vuur na aan de schenen. Ondervraging of intimidatie?,' *Panorama*, 84: 48–53.

Derksen, T. (2006) *Lucia de B. Reconstructie van een gerechtelijke dwaling*. Diemen: Veen Magazines.

De Vries, P.R. (2002) *De moord die nooit mag verjaren*. Baarn: Uitgeverij De Fontein.

Dommicent, J., Vanderhallen, M., Vervaeke, G. and van de Plas, M. (2006) 'Techniek audiovisueel verhoor minderjarigen: opleiding en opvolging, een evaluatie', *Panopticon*, 3: 56–75.

Gudjonsson, G.H. (2003) *The Psychology of Interrogations, Confessions and Testimony*. Chichester: Wiley.

Holmberg, U. (2004a) Police Interviews with Victims and Suspects of Violent Sexual Crimes: Interviewees' Experiences and Outcomes. Stockholm, Stockholm University, Department of Psychology.

Holmberg, U. (2004b) 'Crime Victims' Experiences of Police Interviews and Their Inclination to Provide or Omit Information', *International Journal of Police Science and Management*, 6: 155–170.

Inbau, F.E., Reid, J.E., Buckley, J.P. and Jayne, B.C. (2001) *Criminal Interrogation and Confessions*. Gaithersburg, MD: Aspen.

Israëls, J.T. (2004) *De bekentenissen van Ina Post. Dwaalsporen*. Alphen a/d Rijn: Kluwer.

Kassin, S.M. (2005) 'On the Psychology of Confessions: Does Innocence Put Innocence at Risk?', *American Psychologist*, 60: 215–227.

Kassin, S.M. and Kiechel, K.L. (1996) 'The Psychology of False Confessions: Compliance, Internalization and Confabulation', *Psychological Science*, 7: 125–128.

Kassin, S.M., Goldstein, C.C. and Savitsky, K. (2003) 'Behavioral Confirmation in the Interrogation Room: On the Dangers of Presuming Guilt', *Law and Human Behavior*, 27: 187–203.

Mann, S., Vrij, A., Fisher, R. and Robinson, M. (in press) 'See No Lies, Hear No Lies: Watching or Listening to Police Suspect Interviews: Differences in Discriminating Accuracy and Response Bias', *Applied Cognitive Psychology*.

Milne, R. and Bull, R. (1999) *Investigative Interviewing: Psychology and Practice*. Chichester: Wiley.

Milne, R. and Bull, R. (2006) 'Interviewing Victims, Including Children and People with Intellectual Disability', in M. Kebbell and G. Davies (eds), *Practical Psychology for Forensic Investigations*. Chichester: Wiley.

Monjardet, D. (1996) *Ce que fait la police. Sociologie de la force publique*. Paris: Éditions La Découverte.

Mortimer, A. and Shepherd, E. (1999) 'Frames of the Mind: Schemata Guiding Cognition and Conduct in Interviewing of Suspected Offenders', in A. Memon and R. Bull (eds), *Handbook of the Psychology of Interviewing*. Chichester: Wiley.

Moston, S., Stephenson, G.M. and Williamson, T.M. (1992) 'The Effects of Case Characteristics on Suspect Behaviour During Police Questioning', *British Journal of Criminology*, 32: 23–40.

Myjer, B.E.P. (2000) 'De Zaanse verhoormethode in Straatsburg', *NJCM Bulletin*, 25: 989–994.

Nierop, N.M. (2005) 'Het verdachtenverhoor in Nederland. Wat wordt verhoorders geleerd?', *Nederlands Juristenblad*, 80: 887–890.

Nierop, N.M. (2007) 'Juridische en psychologische aspecten van het verdachtenverhoor', in A. Ph. van Wijk, R.A.R. Bullens and P. van den Eshof (eds), *Facetten van zedencriminalitiet*. Den Haag, Reed Business Information, 193–210.

Nierop, N.M. and Mooij, A.J.M. (2000) *Het verdachtenverhoor in bijzondere zaken: de relatie tussen opleiding en praktijk*. Onderzoeksrapport ten behoeve van de Recherche Advies Commissie, Werkgroep Verhoormethoden. Zoetermeer: KLPD, divisie Recherche.

Nierop, N.M. and van den Eshof, P. (2002) 'Analytic Interviewing: spiegelen, ankeren en andere trucs', *Recherche Magazine*, 6.

Nierop, N.M. and van den Eshof, P. (2003) 'De Zaanse verhoormethode is toch echt onrechtmatig. De implicaties van een onderbelicht Europees arrest', *Nederlands Juristenblad*, 78: 783–785.

Ponsaers, P., Mulkers, J. and Stoop, R. (2001) *De ondervraging – analyse van een politietechniek*. Antwerp: Maklu.

Recherche Adviescommissie (1996) 'De "Zaanse verhoormethode". Advies van de Recherche Adviescommissie aan de Minister van Justitie over de rechtmatigheid en doelmatigheid van de "Zaanse verhoormethode"'.

Savage, S. and Milne, R. (2007) 'Miscarriages of Justice', in T. Newburn, T. Williamson and A. Wright (eds), *Handbook of Criminal Investigation*. Cullompton: Willan.

Slats, J. (1997) 'Uitvinder Hoenderdos legt hem uit De Zaanse verhoormethode', *Vrij Nederland*, 58: 18–19.

Van Amelsvoort, A., Rispens, I. and Grolman, H. (2006) *Handleiding verhoor*. Den Haag: Elsevier Overheid.

Van den Eshof, P. and Nierop, N. (2008) 'Gedragsanalyse'. Paper presented at the conference Gedragsanalyse in het tactisch rechercheproces. Apeldoorn, 8-10-2008.

Vanderhallen, M. (2007) 'De werkalliantie in het politieverhoor'. Doctoraatsstudie, Katholieke Universiteit Leuven.

Van Dongen, M. (2008) 'Onschuldig achter tralies; een nieuw proces', *De Volkskrant*, 19 January.

Van Es, A. (2003) 'Tunneldenken in Twente. Onprofessioneel onderzoek in een megaontuchtzaak', *Skepter*, 16: 24–27.

Van Koppen, P.J. (2003) 'Rechtspsychololgie 2003; Het verhoren van verdachten', *Tijdschrift voor Criminologie*, 45: 423–432.

Van Koppen, P.J. (2003) *De Schiedammer parkmoord: Een rechtspsychologische reconstructie*. Nijmegen: Ars Aequi Libri.

Volckaert, M. (2005) '"Verhoor" in de basisopleiding voor inspecteur van politie, licentiaatsverhandeling'. Katholieke Universiteit Leuven, Faculteit Rechtsgeleerdheid.

Vrij, A. and Lochun, S.K. (2002) 'Neurolinguïstisch verhoren', in P.J. Van Koppen, D.J. Hessing, H.L.G.J. Merckelbach and H.F.M. Crombag (eds), *Het Recht van Binnen*. Deventer: Kluwer, 727–736.

Vrij, A. and F.W. Winkel (2002) 'Liegen en voorgelogen worden', in P.J. Van Koppen, D.J. Hessing, H.L.G.J. Merckelbach and H.F.M. Crombag (eds), *Het Recht van Binnen*. Deventer: Kluwer, 625–647.

Yuille, J.C., Hunter, R., Joffe, R. and Zaparniuk, J. (1993) 'Interviewing Children in Sexual Abuse Cases', in G.S. Goodman and B.L. Bottoms (eds), *Child Victims, Child Witnesses: Understanding and Improving Children's Testimony*. New York: Guilford Press, 95–115.

Chapter 5

Police interrogation in Canada: from the quest for confession to the search for the truth

Michel St-Yves

The maple leaf, Canada's emblem, symbolises for many respect for human rights. This reputation stands for the most part on the Canadian Charter of Rights and Freedom, which Canada enacted in 1982.[1] The charter gives judicial guarantees, including the right to life, freedom and security, as well as to be presumed innocent until found guilty. Such a charter makes it possible to promote respect for differences, and a humane and sane justice system. Unfortunately, such initiatives are not enough for a perfect system of justice and to prevent wrongful convictions. Miscarriages of justice are a problem without frontiers and Canada is no exception to this rule.

Even if Canada is not without wrongful convictions, it is worth noting that they are extremely rare. Furthermore, when they happen, they can be attributable to factors other than interrogation, such as mistaken eyewitness identifications, crime laboratory errors and police misconduct. Although most of the wrongful convictions that have been heavily publicised in the Canadian media in recent years – David Milgaard, Thomas Sophonow, Guy Paul Morin, Donald Marshall and Michel Dumont – were to blame on factors other than police interrogation, inquiries into the miscarriages of justice did make recommendations relating to interrogation.

This chapter's goal is to look at the development of the interrogation process in Canada – closely linked to the recommendations made at the time of public inquiries – regarding the admissibility of confessions as evidence and the prevention of wrongful convictions.

Police interrogation and wrongful conviction

We estimate that the percentage of wrongful convictions for serious crimes is less than 1 per cent (Huff *et al.* 1986). Although they exist, false confessions are not the main cause of wrongful convictions. By a wide margin, mistaken eyewitness identifications are at the very top of the list (Borchard 1932; Brandon and Davies 1973; Rattner 1988). Although it is difficult to estimate the frequency of false confessions, research on that subject and the number of cases recorded (see Innocence Project) suggest that concerns are justified (Kassin and Wrightsman 1985; Leo and Ofshe 1998; Gudjonsson 2003). However, Cassell (1999) and Buckley (2006) are sceptical regarding the extensiveness of the phenomenon of false confessions. They believe that the statistics are exaggerated. The fact that only a small number of wrongful convictions due to false confessions occur in the course of the tens of thousands of interrogations conducted each year in Canada demonstrates that it is a very marginal phenomenon.

In the USA, the Innocence Project has identified 130 cases of exoneration through post-conviction DNA testing since 1989. The vast majority of these wrongful convictions were linked to mistaken eyewitness identification; other causes included forensic-laboratory error and police misconduct, inadequate legal representation and false confessions (the last accounting for 27 per cent) (Innocence Project 2006).

In Canada, the problem of wrongful convictions due to false confessions is rare. The rare cases found seemed to be imputable to long interrogations in which questions were repetitive and very suggestive:

> In 1996, in Regina (Saskatchewan), Joel Labadie and two other accomplices were arrested for first-degree murder and spent nearly 4½ months in jail for a murder they had not committed. After an interrogation that lasted more than 15 hours, Labadie confessed to a crime he did not commit. In the end, DNA evidence convicted another man. (CBS News, 28 January 2003)

Most of the time, a confession is inadmissible because it was obtained illegally or unethically, and not necessarily because it is a false confession. That is what happened in 1981 in Manitoba in *Hicks* v. *R.* (1981), 4 C.M.A.R. 199 (C.A. C.M.), held in court martial. One of the officers who led the interrogation said to the suspect, 'You know that a denial of guilt is the same as an admission. Are you denying it?' It was only following this comment by the police officer that the accused made the statement that was admitted into evidence. The court found that the words used to induce the statement given by the military police might have a tendency to cause an innocent person to make a false confession. Accordingly, it was not admissible in court.

We often refer to 'false confessions' as soon as a statement is rejected by the court. These are generally inadmissible confessions because the way they were obtained – often on the basis of offers of promises/advantages – raises a reasonable doubt of the free and voluntary nature of the statement, and the culpability of the accused (see *R. v. Warren*, [1995] N.W.T.J. No. 7 (C.S. T.-N.-O.); *R. v. Minde*, [2003] A.J. No. 1184 (Q.B. Alb.); *R. v. Spencer* (2006) 207 C.C.C. (3d) 47 (C.A. C.-B.); *R. v. Thawer*, [1996] O.J. No. 989 (C.Prov. Ont.). Sometimes a confession has been deemed inadmissible only as evidence for questions decided in a *voir dire* hearing (see *R. v. VanEindhover*, [2006] Nu.J. No. 13 (Nun Ct.). The context can also influence the admissibility of a confession, as shown in one case involving an unconfirmed confession obtained by an undercover officer during a lengthy undercover investigation. The suspect made numerous false statements, even stating that he had killed many people, without giving any credible details about the murder he was under investigation for and that he claimed he had committed (see *R. v. C.K.R.S.*, [2005] B.C.J. No. 2917 (C.S. C.-B.).

In Quebec, the last (known) wrongful conviction imputable to police interrogation took place in 1997. This was the Simon Marshall case, in which a young man with intellectual disabilities – and who also suffered from mental illness – confessed to a series of sexual assaults that took place between 1995 and 1996. In June 1997, he pleaded guilty to 15 counts of sexual assault and was sentenced to 5 years in the penitentiary. DNA testing that could have exonerated him was only done five years later.

Risks associated with confession

The quest for a confession commonly involves recourse to strategies or methods that are controversial either because they are illegal – such as torture – or because they entail risks or ethical problems, as in the case of certain techniques known as persuasive (St-Yves and Tanguay 2009). According to Gudjonsson (1992, 2003), using these methods sometimes limits the suspect's rights and is likely to result in false confessions. But what then to do with the true offenders who, without confession, would never be convicted, because of a lack of evidence? This is a classic problem that appears in almost a third of the cases (Irving and McKenzie 1989; Moston *et al*. 1992; Leo 1996).

Two main factors determine the method of conducting a police interrogation. The first is the judicial framework in which this type of interview is conducted. The second is the need to respect constitutional rights, when they exist. In Canada, as well as in the USA, tribunals accept the use of certain persuasive strategies and methods such as the Reid technique (see *R. c. Oickle*, [2000] 2 R.C.S.3). Judge Antonio Lamer of the Supreme Court of Canada has said that a criminal inquiry and the search for criminals are not a game that has to follow the rules of the Marquis of Queensbury[2]:

> The investigation of crime and the detection of criminals is not a game to be governed by the Marquis of Queensbury rules. The authorities, in dealing with shrewd and often sophisticated criminals, must sometimes out of necessity resort to tricks or other forms of deceit and should not, through the rule, be hampered in their work. What should be repressed vigorously is conduct on their part that shocks the community. (*R. c. Rothman*, [1981] 1 R.C.S. 640)

The Reid technique

The book written by Inbau and his colleagues (2001) on the Reid technique is without a doubt the one that most influences interrogation practices in North America (St-Yves and Landry 2004). Not only is it the most used interrogation method but it is also the most debated (Kassin and Gudjonsson 2004).

Inbau and his colleagues make a very clear distinction between *interviewing* a suspect and *interrogating* him (see Buckley 2006). Interviewing – before the interrogation – is non-accusatory and has the main objective of ensuring that the suspect is really the author of the crime. Interrogating does not aim to persuade the suspect to confess a crime but to talk him into telling the truth (Buckley 2006).

The interview before the interrogation

The goal of the interview before the interrogation is to gather information on the suspect, as well as on the circumstances of the crime he is presumed to have committed. This interview also makes it possible to establish a rapport with the suspect and create an atmosphere of trust favourable to confession. The relational dimension is undoubtedly one of the greatest influences on the result of an interrogation (Holmberg 2004; St-Yves *et al.* 2004; St-Yves 2006; St-Yves and Tanguay 2009). Obviously, the goal of this interview is also to learn the suspect's version of events, a free version without contamination from the interviewer. To get such a version, the investigator has, ideally, to ask an open question, such as 'Describe to me everything you did last Saturday?' Problems frequently encountered in interviews of suspects are the use of specific or closed questions at the wrong moment, directed or suggestive questions, and storms of questions or questions with forced choices (Griffiths and Milne 2006: 183). Such attitudes are not only unproductive but also represent a high risk of contamination of the witness. In acting this way, we get farther away from the truth.

Inbau *et al.* (2001) recommend that suspects be asked probing questions after they have been given the opportunity to give their version. These questions are usually prepared in advance and personalised. They are presented gradually, going from non-accusatory generic questions up to questions where the suspect will feel more concerned. For example, 'According to you, what kind of person could do such a thing? Why would someone do such a thing? According to you, how does this person feel today when faced with his actions? Would it be important for this person to justify himself?' The objective of these questions is to create reactions, verbal and non-verbal, and then evaluate the answers so as to determine whether the suspect is the author of the crime. Even if the answers to these questions are often interesting and sometimes enable us to develop or specify themes to be used upon interrogation, reactions and answers from the suspect do not make it possible to determine objectively whether the suspect is lying or telling the truth and even less so to determine whether he committed the crime or not (St-Yves and Tanguay 2009). Numerous studies on lie detection prove that people's perception of veracity is often false and grounded on subjective indicators, without scientific foundation (Vrij 2000, 2004). Kassin and Fong (1999) observed that police officers who have had Reid technique training are less accurate in their lie detection than are uninitiated students but are more confident of their results.

Usually, the last probing question concerns the implication of the suspect in the crime for which he is being interrogated. This question, commonly called a 'bait question', improves the collection of evidence and creates a doubt in the suspect's mind about a mistake he might have made or about compromising elements. For example, 'Why would a person tell us that he saw you at this place at the time the crime was committed?' This question is presented in a strictly hypothetical manner since the use of non-existent or fabricated evidence is an element liable to render the confession inadmissible as evidence (*R. c. Oickle* above-mentioned, at para. 61). This manipulation of the collection of evidence (exaggeration or false representation) is severely criticised by certain authors, who argue that it can lead to false confessions (Kassin and Kiechel 1996; Redlich and Goodman 2003; Kassin and Gudjonsson 2004).

Confrontation: the nine steps of the Reid technique

To confront a suspect who lies or keeps on denying his implication in a crime, Inbau *et al.* (1986, 2001) have developed an interview process designed to break his resistance, give him a chance to confess while minimising the consequences, and prevent him from losing face. This technique – commonly called the Reid technique – consists of nine steps.

Step 1 – positive confrontation

This first stage consists of confronting the suspect, by accusing him of the crime for which he is being interrogated: 'The investigation clearly demonstrates that you committed this crime.' Up to this stage, the question has been not to know whether the suspect is the author of the crime but rather to learn why he committed it. The problem at this stage is that the investigator does not possess any objective element allowing him to be sure that the suspect is the author of the crime. During this confrontation, Buckley (2006) states, the investigator has to be reasonably sure the suspect is guilty. This diagnosis sometimes is essentially based on the 'gut feeling' of the investigator and his appreciation of the verbal and non-verbal signals associated with lying (St-Yves and Tanguay 2009). However, numerous studies have demonstrated that the success rate for lie detection rarely goes over 50 per cent, the equivalent of 'heads or tails' (Vrij 2000; Mann *et al.* 2004).

Step 2 – theme development

A theme is the probable or plausible reason for the crime committed by the suspect. Themes[3] give the suspect a chance to confess his crime without losing face and in the belief that he gained something. They give him a chance to morally defend or justify his behavior.

Themes are often presented as a long monologue that is not limited to the motivation of the crime but that sometimes suggests a scenario – hypothetical – of how the suspect committed the crime. This procedure has certain risks, such as contamination of the witness and suggestions that can lead to false confessions. This is particularly true if the suspect presents intellectual vulnerability (Clare and Gudjonsson 1995). These themes are supposed to reflect the reasons that led the suspect to commit the crime but often translate into the investigator's perception (St-Yves and Tanguay 2009).

Steps 3 and 4 – handling denials and overcoming objections

Inbau *et al.* (2001) suggest overcoming suspects' denials (step 3) and objections (step 4) by hand gestures or by looking away, to indicate that their arguments are useless. When acting this way, the investigator has to be careful because he can deprive himself of pertinent information and therefore become trapped in tunnel vision. As mentioned by Judge Peter Cory,

> Tunnel vision is insidious. It can affect an officer or, indeed, anyone involved in the administration of justice with sometimes tragic results. [...] Anyone, police officer, counsel or judge can become infected by this virus. (Williamson 2006a: 157)

Step 5 – obtain and retain the suspect's attention

At this point, suspects typically become distant or turn a deaf ear. Visual or physical contact with the suspect often allows investigators to maintain or regain the suspect's attention.

Step 6 – handle the suspect's passive mood

At this stage, the suspect is usually less tense, and may even be resigned. He listens to themes developed by the investigator. He may also cry. The investigator usually concentrates on a particular theme and reduces it to one or two phrases while underlining the essential elements.

Step 7 – present an alternative question

The investigator presents the suspect with two versions, one desirable and one undesirable, to explain his crime. The alternative question often serves to minimise the seriousness of the crime and make it more acceptable to the suspect. For example, 'Was it the first time [most positive alternative] or did it happen more than once?' The suspect is then encouraged by the investigator to choose the most positive alternative. This strategy is without doubt the most controversial because it only offers one possibility to the suspect, and that is to incriminate himself. The risk of false confession is thereby increased (Gudjonsson 2003). Buckley points out that there is a third option to remember: that the suspect is innocent (St-Yves and Landry 2004: 19).

Steps 8 and 9 – develop the details of the offence and convert the confession into a written statement

In Canada, as well as in the UK, investigators usually record or videotape the questioning of those suspected of major crimes (St-Yves and Lavallée 2002; St-Yves 2004). In the USA, more and more states are requiring audiovisual recording of suspects' interrogations (Buckley and Jayne 2005). The primary objective is to obtain an admission from the suspect and, following that, a confession – an authentic confession, corroborated by the investigation.

Ofshe and Leo state that there are at least three ways to determine the validity of a confession (Ofshe and Leo 1997a; Leo and Ofshe 1998):

1 *Did the confession lead to the discovery of evidence that was unknown to the police?* For example, a confession may make possible the discovery of the weapon used to commit the crime, or find stolen objects. In such cases, the facts corroborate the confession.

2 *Does the confession include unusual details of the crime that are unknown to the general public?* For example, in confessing his crime, the suspect tells how and why he carved a Star of David on the stomach of the victim.

3 *Did the suspect describe details of the crime scene that were not publicised?* For example, the suspect is able to describe the type of clothing the victim was wearing or the room (which he had never visited before the crime) where the crime took place.

The investigator must ensure that the confession is not due to contamination; that is to say, that the suspect was not told of the details of the scene by another source (media, police, photographs of the scene, or a third party, including the real author of the crime) (Ofshe and Leo 1997a; Leo and Ofshe 1998). As mentioned by Cassell (1999), to prove someone's innocence can be as hard as to prove their guilt.

Usefulness of persuasive methods

In spite of all the efforts put into obtaining them, the rates of confession remain modest. The average is about 60 per cent for the UK (Clark and Milne 2001) and about 50 per cent in North America (St-Yves 2004). Some authors state that persuasive methods have little influence on the decision to confess or not, and some even claim that they are pretty much useless, or at least not essential to obtaining a confession (Irving and McKenzie 1989; Moston *et al.* 1992; Baldwin 1993; Evans 1993; Pearse and Gudjonsson 1996; Pearse *et al.* 1998; Bull 2006). Inbau *et al.* (2001) believe that the vast majority of suspects first intend to deny their implication in the crime and then, during the interrogation, thanks to the techniques used by the investigators, a large percentage of them change their mind and confess. Deslauriers-Varin and St-Yves (2006) observed that 25 per cent of convicted people stated that they changed their initial position during the interrogation. However, of that number, almost half (46 per cent) said they intended to confess their crime and that they changed their mind. This shows that the decision process can be influenced in either direction. Deslauriers-Varin (2006) also noted that 43.5 per cent of the people who confessed their crime to the police said that they had been entirely ready to do so at the beginning of the interrogation. As for the others who confessed, 31.5 per cent stated that they had not been ready to do so at the beginning of the interrogation. Why did they change their mind? The quality of evidence? Remorse? The investigator's attitude? Interrogation techniques?

Effective methods to prevent false confessions

In Canada, wrongful convictions have led to public inquiries that led to the adoption of positive changes. Among the main recommendations made by the FTP Committee's working group of prosecutors (2004), we find:

(1) Record interrogations on videotapes or audiotapes if possible – otherwise, the judge may make a negative inference (*R.* v. *Moore-McFarlane*, [2001] O.J. No. 4646 (C.A. Ont.).

(2) Offer training in interview techniques for more reliability.

(3) Give special attention to certain categories of suspects (intellectual disabilities).

(4) Sensitise police officers to the phenomenon of methods of avoiding tunnel vision and these traps.

Audiovisual recording of interrogations

In Canada, audiovisual recordings of interrogations are not limited to the suspect's final statement (recapitulation of the confession on video) but include the whole interrogation, from the reading of the rights to the end of the confession. Not only has this technology had no negative effect on the rate of confession but video recording seems to generate a greater number of answers and more incriminating information than do written statements (Grant 1987; Geller 1992). In addition to preserving the exact words of the interrogation, the audiovisual recording stimulates investigators to conduct better interrogations and protects them from unjustified blame (Pitt *et al.* 1999). Many tribunals have pointed out that 'recording provides an objective file on which the judge can base their decision about the free and voluntary nature of a confession, the circumstances in which it was made, as well as its contents, rather than rely on subjective and self-serving assertions made by the protagonists' (*L'enregistrement audiovisuel des interrogatoires des suspects ou des accusés: Rapport d'étape* 1996: 51). The audiovisual recording also makes it possible to form an opinion about the atmosphere in which the interrogation took place, as well as the attitudes and non-verbal language of the protagonists. It is also an effective means of preventing wrongful convictions. It is the most faithful witness of the unfolding of the interrogation (St-Yves 2004c: 122).

Training in police interrogation

Police training in interrogation is essential to make sure that the methods used are legal and that they have a positive influence on the investigation's results. In Quebec, a passing grade in specialised training in interrogation and interviewing is necessary to be allowed to conduct audiovisually recorded interrogations of major crimes. Moreover training can convey ethical principles and a philosophy focused on the quest for the truth rather than the quest for confession.

Whatever techniques are taught – Reid's or adaptation – it is essential to inform police officers of the limits and risks associated with the use of certain tactics and stratagems used in police interrogations. It is also very important to inform them about the psychological aspects of the interrogation – e.g. the confession process and false confessions – and about certain vulnerabilities (mental or intellectual problems) that can influence suspects' understanding of their rights, and generate false confessions (see Kassin and Wrightsman 1985; Gudjonsson 2003).

Sensitising police officers to the phenomenon of tunnel vision

Tunnel vision has been defined as 'the single-minded and overly narrow focus on an investigation or persecutorial theory so as to unreasonably colour the evaluation of information received and one's conduct in response to the information'. Tunnel vision has been identified as a leading cause of wrongful convictions in Canada and elsewhere (FTP Heads of Prosecutions Committee Working Group 2004). This is exactly what happened in the cases of Morin and Sophonow (Savage and Milne 2007).

Beyond *savoir faire* ('how to do'), often associated with the use of interrogation more or less sophisticated methods, it is important to put more emphasis on the development of relational competence, also called *savoir être* ('how to be)' which plays an essential role in the results of an interrogation (Mucchielli and Clément 2006; St-Yves 2006). To pay attention to others, to manifest empathy, to develop a relationship with them and build rapport are attitudes that translate well the essence of *savoir être*. In criminal investigations, *savoir être* also means being open-minded and having an impartial attitude. It is waiting to have all elements on hand before forming an opinion in which we risk reconstructing reality. *Savoir être* is probably the best protection against tunnel vision.

Establishing rules and principles

Police interrogation policies differ across cultures and judicial systems, sometimes even from one police department to another. Thus, it is very difficult, if not impossible, to standardise the proceedings of interrogation on an international basis. However, it seems easier and more realistic to agree on the establishment of rules and principles that to respect human rights and promote effective procedures (see Williamson 2006b). In England, a set of ethical principles for investigative interviewing was developed by a committee of police practitioners, psychologists, lawyers and policymakers under the aegis of the Home Office, and circulated to all police forces in England and Wales. These Principles for Investigative Interviewing encouraged officers to see their role as searching for the truth, and are set out below (see the Home Office, circular 22/1992).

- The role of investigative interviewing is to obtain accurate and reliable information from suspects, witnesses or victims in order to discover the truth about matters under police investigation.

- Investigative interviewing should be approached with an open mind. Information obtained from the person who is being interviewed should always be tested against what the interviewing officer already knows or what can reasonably be established.

- When questioning anyone, a police officer must act fairly in the circumstances of each individual case. The police interviewer is not bound to accept the first answer given. Questioning is not unfair merely because it is persistent. Even when the right of silence is exercised by a suspect, the police still have a right to put questions.

- When conducting an interview, police officers are free to ask questions in order to establish the truth, except for interviews with child victims of sexual or violent abuse which are to be used in criminal proceedings; they are not constrained by the rules applied to lawyers in court.

- Vulnerable people, whether victims, witnesses or suspects, must be treated with particular consideration at all times.

In Quebec, the practice and teaching of investigation interviews helped us identify five essential rules for the better management of the risks associated with police interrogation: (1) keeping an open mind and remaining objective; (2) building rapport; (3) paying attention; (4) keeping a professional attitude; (5) knowing how to conclude (St-Yves *et al.* 2004; St-Yves 2006).

Rule 1: keeping an open mind and remaining objective
Research by Asch (1987) shows that we quickly form an opinion of others from the first elements perceived, and that afterwards we have difficulty in getting rid of it, especially when it is mistaken. The tendency is rather to try to validate our perception, instead of staying receptive and open to one another. That is what we call the Pygmalion effect, better known as the Rosenthal effect (Rosenthal and Jacobson 1968). Lack of objectivity can also be translated into suggestive questions or what we call 'scotomisation', which means eliminating shameful information from our field of analysis (Abric 2003). To enter into an in-depth conversation with a suspect, we must break the scripts constructed from our personal and professional experiences, erase stereotypes, and put aside our prejudices. We must protect our perception as we do a crime scene, because once it is contaminated, it is often too late. Between the investigator and the

person being interrogated, only one was present at the commission of the crime and knows the truth (St-Yves and Tanguay 2009).

Rule 2: building rapport

To build rapport is to pay attention to the needs and concerns of others. It is also to take the necessary time to establish an atmosphere of trust favourable to the divulgation of confidences, and to be open to others' feelings and beliefs. Rapport is the heart of the interview, and techniques that are taught are only complementary. A rapport can be built without techniques, but techniques need a rapport to be effective (St-Yves 2006).

Rule 3: paying attention

A study in France revealed that more than 85 per cent of police officers quickly interrupt the statements of witnesses (Ginet and Py 2001). On average, these interruptions occur 7.5 seconds after the start of the narration (Fisher and Geiselman 1992: 21). These interruptions disturb the concentration of the person being interviewed, who becomes increasingly passive and unmotivated in parallel with the number of interruptions and proportionally reduce the quality of the narrative (Jou and Harris 1992; Py *et al.* 2004). Paying attention makes it possible to understand what really happened, not what we think happened (St-Yves 2006).

Rule 4: keeping a professional attitude

Holmberg and Christianson (2002) have observed that interviewers with a *dominating* style are associated with denial whereas interviewers with a *humane* style are associated with confession. A humane attitude, characterised by active attention, empathy, openness, open-mindedness, respect, and willingness to discover the truth, rather than the searching by every means possible to get a confession, are qualities that play an essential role in the unfolding of an interview (Shepherd 1991; Williamson 1993; St-Yves *et al.* 2004).

Rule 5: knowing how to conclude

Knowing how to conclude means making sure that all points have been covered, that the suspect has nothing to add, and that he has been informed of what will now happen to him. It means staying professional, whether the investigator has obtained a confession or not. It means taking the opportunity to make a good last impression and leave the suspect an open door, a chance or an opportunity to confess – in an hour, the next day or later – to the investigator or someone else. To conclude, it also means remembering that there are rules and that they are the same for everyone (St-Yves *et al.* 2004; St-Yves 2006).

Conclusion

In reality confession is a way to compensate for the lack of material evidence (Baldwin 1993). It is the key to resolving 25–30 per cent of crimes (Baldwin and McConville 1980; Stephenson and Moston 1994; Phillips and Brown 1998; Cassell 1999). It also makes it possible to know and understand what happened, as well as protect against wrongful convictions. It is when confession takes the place of the rest of the investigation that it increases the risks of false confessions (Mucchielli and Clément 2006: 270).

The quest for confession often involves controversial methods, as they sometimes jeopardise the truth and involve risks that can lead to wrongful convictions. In Canada, wrongful convictions due to police interrogations are rare. When they do occur, they are usually the result of statements eventually ruled inadmissible by the court, and when this happens, we cannot always blame the interrogation methods. Most of the time, they are the result of using strategies not allowed by law, liable to tamper with the free and voluntary nature of the statement, or transgress the constitutional rights of the defence or the right to remain silent. Sometimes, it is a matter of using questioning methods that are too suggestive and that can taint the truth and lead to false confessions. Lack of objectivity – commonly called *tunnel vision* – and an unprofessional attitude are other factors that we often find when such mistakes happen.

Commissions of inquiry have given us a chance to learn from our mistakes and to make positive changes. International exchanges made it possible to build bridges between police departments and the academic world, and this has a positive influence on the practice of police interrogation. The recent creation of an international scientific committee[4] that has organised a biannual symposium on investigative police interviews since 2004 makes it possible to promote good practice in police interrogations and to convey ethical principles and rules that aspire to reduce the number of wrongful convictions. All these changes help us to get a little closer to the truth.

Notes

1 'Before 1982, legislation such as the *Canadian Bill of Rights* of 1960 and the *Canadian Human Rights Act* of 1977 was enacted to protect individual rights and freedoms. Several provinces had also enacted human rights legislation to protect civil liberties. These statutes, however, held little precedence over other laws and were always subject to repeal. Entrenching the *Charter of Rights and Freedoms* within the constitution of Canada made it part of the country's supreme law, thus overriding all other statutes inconsistent with the individual rights and liberties it enshrined' (*Statistic Canada*, E-Book, retrieved from www.statcan.ca on 8 January 2007).

2 The Marquis of Queensbury established in the nineteenth century a series of rules (length of rounds, types of punches allowed, use of padded gloves) to make boxing a less dangerous sport.

3 In a recent book, Senese (2005) explains the usefulness of themes and proposes more than 1,600 crime-specific themes.

4 In 2008, the members of the International Scientific Committee were D. Dixon and S. Moston (Australia); A. Leboule and M. Carmans (Belgium); G. Bishop, G. Bruneau, J. Landy, J-R. Laurence, R. Lavigne, M. Pilon, R. Roy and M. St-Yves (Canada); E. Tsui (China); J Py, S. Demarch and B. Soulez (France); S. Soukara (Greece); C. Sellie (Switzerland); R. Bull, A. Griffiths, G.H. Gudjonsson and B. Milne (UK); S. Kassin and R. Fischer (USA).

References

Abric, J.-C. (2003) *Psychologie de la communication: théories et méthodes*. Paris: Armand Colin.

Asch, S.E. (1987) *Social Psychology*. Oxford: Oxford University Press.

Baldwin, J. (1993) 'Police Interviewing Techniques. Establishing the Truth or Proof?', *British Journal of Criminology*, 33: 325–352.

Baldwin, J. and McConville, M. (1980) *Confessions in Crown Court Trials*. Royal Commission on Criminal Procedure Research Study No. 5. London: HMSO.

Borchard, E.M. (1932) *Convicting the Innocent: Sixty-Five Actual Errors of Criminal Justice*. Garden City, NY: Doubleday.

Brandon, R. and Davies, C. (1973) *Wrongful Imprisonment*. London: Allen and Unwin.

Buckley, J.P. (2006) 'The Reid Technique of Interviewing and Interrogation', in T. Williamson (ed.), *Investigative Interviewing: Rights, Research, Regulation*. Cullompton: Willan Publishing, 190–206.

Bull, R. (2006) 'Research on the Police Interviewing of Suspects'. Paper presented at the Best Practices Seminar on Interview Techniques and Training, 23–26 January 2006, Paris.

Cassell, P.G. (1999) 'The Guilty and the "Innocent': An Examination of Alleged Cases of Wrongful Conviction from False Confessions', *Harvard Journal of Law and Public Policy*, 22: 523–603.

Clare, I.C.H. and Gudjonsson, G.H. (1995) 'The Vulnerability of Suspects with Intellectual Disabilities During Police Interviews: A Review and Experimental Study of Decision-making', *Mental Handicap Research*, 8: 110–128.

Deslauriers-Varin, N. (2006) Les Facteurs déterminants dans le processus d'aveu chez les auteurs d'actes criminels. Master's thesis, Université de Montréal.

Deslauriers-Varin, N. and St-Yves, M. (2006) 'An Empirical Investigation of Offenders' Decision to Confess their Crime During Police Interrogation'. Paper presented at the 2nd International Investigative Interviewing Conference, Portsmouth, UK, 5–7 July.

Evans, R. (1993) *The Conduct of Police Interviews with Juveniles*. Royal Commission on Criminal Justice Research Report No. 8. London: HMSO.

Fisher, R.P. and Geiselman, R.E. (1992) *Memory-Enhancing Techniques for Investigative Interviewing*. Springfield, IL: Charles Thomas.

FTP Heads of Prosecutions Committee Working Group (2004) 'Report on the Prevention of Miscarriages of Justice'. Retrieved 8 December 2006 from http://canada.justice.gc.ca/fr/dept/pub/hop/index.html, website.

Geller, W.A. (1992) *Police Videotaping of Suspects' Interrogations and Confessions: A Preliminary Examination of Issues and Practices*. Report to the National Institute of Justice. Washington, DC: Police Executive Research Forum.

Ginet, M. and Py, J. (2001) 'A Technique for Enhancing Memory in Eyewitness Testimonies for Use by Police Officers and Judicial Officers: The Cognitive Interview', *Le Travail Humain*, 64: 173–191.

Grant, A. (1987) *The Audio-Visual Taping Interviews with Suspects and Accused Persons by Halton Regional Police Force, Ontario, Canada: An Evaluation*. Ottawa: Commission de réforme du droit du Canada.

Griffiths, A. and Milne, B. (2006) 'Will It All End in Tiers? Police Interviews with Suspects in Britain', in T. Williamson (ed.), *Investigative Interviewing: Rights, Research, Regulation*. Cullompton: Willan Publishing, 167–189.

Groupe de Travail du Comité FTP des chefs des poursuites pénales (2004) 'Rapport sur la prévention des erreurs judiciaire'. Retrieved from http://canada.justice.gc.ca/fr/dept/pub/hop/index.html, on 8 December 2006).

Gudjonsson, G.H. (1992) *The Psychology of Interrogations, Confessions and Testimony*. Chichester: Wiley.

Gudjonsson, G.H. (2003) *The Psychology of Interrogations and Confessions: A Handbook*. Chichester: Wiley.

Holmberg, U. (2004) Police Interviews with Victims and Suspects of Violent and Sexual Crimes: Interviewees' Experiences and Interview Outcomes. Doctoral dissertation, Stockholm University.

Holmberg, U. and Christianson, S.A. (2002) 'Murderers' and Sexual Offenders' Experiences of Police Interviews and Their Inclination to Admit or Deny Crimes', *Behavioral Sciences and the Law*, 20: 31–45.

Huff, C.R., Rattner, A. and Sagarin, E. (1986) 'Guilty Until Proven Innocent: Wrongful Conviction and Public Policy', *Crime and Delinquency*, 32: 518–544.

Inbau, F.E., Reid, J.E., Buckley, J.P. and Jayne, B.C. (2001) *Criminal Interrogation and Confessions* (4th edn). Gaithersburg, MD: Aspen.

Innocence Project (1986) Retrieved from www.innocenceproject.org on 8 January 2007.

Irving, B. and McKenzie, I.K. (1989) *Police Interrogation: The Effects of the Police and Criminal Evidence Act*. London: HMSO.

Jou, J. and Harris, R.J. (1992) 'The Effect of Divided Attention on Speech Production', *Bulletin of the Psychonomic Society*, 30: 301–304.

Kassin, S.M. and Fong, C.T. (1999) 'I'm Innocent! Effects of Training on Judgments of Truth and Deception in the Interrogation Room', *Law and Human Behavior*, 23: 499–516.

Kassin, S.M. and Gudjonsson, G.H. (2004) 'The Psychology of Confessions: A Review of the Literature and Issues', *Psychological Science in the Public Interest*, 5: 33–67.

Kassin, S.M. and Wrightsman, L.S. (1985) 'Confession evidence', in S.M. Kassin and L.S. Wrightsman (eds), *The Psychology of Evidence and Trial Procedures*. London: Sage, 67–94.

Leo, R.A. (1996) 'Inside the Interrogation Room', *Journal of Criminal Law and Criminology*, 86: 266–303.

Leo, R.A. and Ofshe, R.J. (1998) 'The Consequences of False Confessions: Deprivations of Liberty and Miscarriages of Justice in the Age of Psychological Interrogation', *Journal of Criminal Law and Criminology*, 88: 429–96.

Mann, S., Vrij, A. and Bull, R. (2004) 'Detecting True Lies: Police Officers' Ability to Detect Suspects' Lies', *Journal of Applied Psychology*, 89: 137–149.

Moston, S., Stephenson, G.M. and Williamson, T.M. (1992) 'The Effects of Case Characteristics on Suspect Behaviour During Police Questioning', *British Journal of Criminology*, 32: 23–40.

Mucchielli, L. and Clément, S. (2006) 'Renseignement humain et recherche des aveux: Les compétences relationnelles des enquêtes de police judiciaire', *Cahiers de la sécurité*, 62: 255–285.

Ofshe, R.J. and Leo, R.A. (1997) 'The Decision to Confess Falsely: Rational Choice and Irrational Action', *Denver University Law Review*, 74: 979–1122.

Pearse, J. and Gudjonsson, G.H. (1996) 'Police Interviewing Techniques at Two South London Police Stations', *Psychology, Crime and Law*, 3: 63–74.

Pearse, J., Gudjonsson, G.H., Clare, I.C.H. and Rutter, S. (1998) 'Police Interviewing and Psychological Vulnerabilities: Predicting the Likelihood of a Confession', *Journal of Community and Applied Social Psychology*, 8: 1–21.

Phillips, C. and Brown, D. (1998) Entry into the Criminal Justice System: A Survey of Police Arrests and Their Outcomes. London: Home Office.

Pitt, S.E., Spiers, E.M., Dietz, P.E. and Dvoskin, J.A. (1999) 'Preserving the Integrity of the Interview: The Value of Videotape', *Journal of Forensic Sciences*, 44: 1287–1291.

Py, J., Demarchi, S. and Ginet, M. (2004) 'Comment placer les témoins dans des conditions optimales de restitution de leurs souvenirs d'une scène criminelle?', in M. St-Yves and J. Landry (eds), *Psychologie des entrevues d'enquête: de la recherche à la pratique*. Cowansville, Québec: Éditions Yvon Blais, 169–179.

Rattner, A. (1988) 'Convicted But Innocent. Wrongful Conviction and the Criminal Justice System', *Law Human Behavior*, 12: 283–293.

Redlich, A.D. and Goodman, G.S. (2003) 'Taking Responsibility for an Act Not Committed: The Influence of Age and Suggestibility', *Law and Human Behavior*, 27: 141–156.

Rosenthal, R. and Jacobson, L. (1968) *Pygmalion in the Classroom*. New York: Holt, Rinehart and Winston.

Savage, S. and Milne, R. (2007) 'Miscarriages of Justice – the Role of the Investigative Process', in T. Newburn, T. Williamson and A. Wright (eds), *Handbook of Criminal Investigations*. Cullompton: Willan, 610–627.

Schafer, J.R. and Navarro, J. (2003) *Advanced Interviewing Techniques*. Springfield, IL: Charles C. Thomas.

Senese, L.C. (2005) *Anatomy of Interrogation Themes: The Reid Technique of Interviewing and Interrogation*. Chicago: John E. Reid and Associates, Inc.

Shepherd, E. (1991) 'Ethical Interviewing', *Policing*, 7: 42–60.

Stephenson, G.M. and Moston, S.J. (1994) 'Police Interrogation', *Psychology, Crime & Law*, 1: 151–157.

St-Yves, M. (2004) 'Les Fausses Confessions: comprendre et prévenir', in M. St-Yves and J. Landry (eds), *Psychologie des entrevues d'enquête: de la recherche à la pratique*. Cowansville, Québec: Éditions Yvon Blais, 105–133.

St-Yves, M. (2006) 'The Psychology of Rapport: Five Basic Rules', in T. Williamson (ed.), *Investigative Interviewing: Rights, Research, Regulation*. Cullompton: Willan Publishing, 87–106.

St-Yves, M. and Landry, J. (2004) 'La Pratique de l'interrogatoire de police', in M. St-Yves and J. Landry (eds), *Psychologie des entrevues d'enquête: de la recherche à la pratique*. Cowansville, Québec: Éditions Yvon Blais, 7–30.

St-Yves, M. and Tanguay, M. (2009) 'The Psychology of Interrogation: A Quest for a Confession or a Quest for the Truth?', in M. St-Yves and M. Tanguay (eds), *The Psychology of Criminal Investigations: The Search for the Truth*. Toronto: Carwell, 9–40.

St-Yves, M., Tanguay, M. and Crépault, D. (2004) 'La psychologie de la relation: cinq règles de base', in M. St-Yves and J. Landry (eds), *Psychologie des entrevues d'enquête: de la recherche à la pratique*. Cowansville, Québec: Éditions Yvon Blais, 135–153.

Vrij, A. (2000) *Detecting Lies and Deceit. The Psychology of Lying and the Implications for Professional Practice*. Chichester: Wiley.

Vrij, A. (2004) 'Guidelines to Catch a Liar', in P.A. Granhag and L.A. Strömwall (eds), *The Detection of Deception in Forensic Contexts*. Cambridge: Cambridge University Press, 287–314.

Williamson, T.M. (1990) 'Strategic Changes in Police Interrogation: An Examination of Police and Suspect Behaviour in the Metropolitan Police in Order to Determine the Effects of New Legislation, Technology and Organizational Policies. Ph.D thesis, University of Kent.

Williamson, T.M. (1993) 'From Interrogation to Investigative Interviewing: Strategic Trends in Police Questioning', *Journal of Community and Social Psychology*, 3: 89–99.

Williamson, T.M. (2006a) 'Towards Greater Professionalism: Minimizing Miscarriages of Justice', in T. Williamson (ed.), *Investigative Interviewing: Rights, Research, Regulation*. Cullompton: Willan Publishing, 147–189.

Williamson, T.M. (2006b) 'Principles of Investigative Interviewing: Suspects'. Paper presented at Plenary Session, 2nd International Investigative Interviewing Conference, Portsmouth, UK, 5–7 July 2006.

Chapter 6

Interview and interrogation: a perspective and update from the USA

Randy Borum, Michael G. Gelles and Steven M. Kleinman

Since 11 September 2001, the military and law enforcement agencies of the US (USG) have faced a serious challenge in planning how to reorganise and redeploy their resources against threats from terrorists, extremist factions, and insurgents. Law enforcement has been shifting from its traditional focus on post-incident investigation to focusing on intelligence-driven prevention efforts. Emerging voices within the military establishment have increasingly called for its transformation from a traditional high-tech, equipment-driven battle force into an intelligent system that relies more on understanding the cultural and contextual dynamics of the battle space and that derives more of its actionable intelligence from human sources than from electronic intercepts.

With a renewed interest in, and reliance on, human intelligence (HUMINT), an opportunity exists for the USG to re-examine its policies and practices for interviewing and interrogation to discern whether or not it is relying on best practices that are consistent with American values, international human rights and legal requirements. It is clear that, to protect national security interests, the USG is now – and for the foreseeable future will be – required to gather information from human sources either for purposes of intelligence gathering or for investigations that may lead to criminal prosecution. Broadly speaking, the purpose of these interviews and interrogations is to gather accurate, useful, timely information that furthers security, intelligence, and investigative interests.

After 9/11, the USG's need and demand for effective interview and interrogation methods unfortunately outpaced existing knowledge, capacity and experience. An overwhelming urgency existed, however, to obtain information to protect the homeland, despite a dearth of systemic knowledge about our adversaries' culture and mindset. Troubling reports emerged about certain methods used with detainees in Cuba, Iraq, Afghanistan and elsewhere. As Robert Fein notes, the 'shortfall in advanced, research-based interrogation methods at a time of intense pressure from operational commanders to produce actionable intelligence from high-value targets may have contributed significantly to the unfortunate cases of abuse that have recently come to light' (Fein 2006: xiii).

In this chapter, we will modestly attempt to review a few recent developments in US law and policy for this vital security-related function and to describe a very promising initiative that seeks to chart a course for the future of interrogation, particularly in intelligence-gathering contexts.

Multiple constituencies

At least three types of agencies within the USG have interests in gathering national security information from human sources: law enforcement (including federal as well as state and local), intelligence, and military (Mayer 2005). Each tends to have its own set of information requirements and its own tradition of methods and approaches.

Law enforcement interrogators historically have made a distinction between the concepts of an interview and an interrogation. One commonly understood difference is that the purpose of an interview is to gather information, whereas the primary purpose of an interrogation is to garner a confession from a suspect who is presumed to be guilty. American law enforcement personnel operate explicitly under the legal strictures of the US Constitution, gathering information (which typically must be corroborated) and pursuing confessions for purposes of facilitating a criminal prosecution.

Interrogators from intelligence and military units typically have much different requirements. Although military interrogators may be required to have a 'confession' in order to justify a detainee's continued confinement, in many military interrogations, the confession is regarded as being less central and less useful than 'actionable intelligence' (i.e. definitive information about persons, places, and plans that will inform concrete responses). Intelligence information within this context is used to guide US actions and protect national assets and interests, not principally to provide documentation for criminal prosecution. Because there is usually no subsequent court process for fact-finding, intelligence and military personnel often must act quickly on information they receive, making the accuracy and timeliness of gathered information all the more critical. These differing demands, in part, have led to different trends in interrogation approaches.

The official interrogation approaches currently used by agencies and personnel from the US Intelligence Community have not been proffered in open source documents. Historically, documents such as the KUBARK manual have outlined some of the strategies and techniques – both coercive and non-coercive – that were perhaps used in the 1960s. The nature and extent to which these approaches continue to be used is unclear, although the USG long ago abandoned any official use of KUBARK along with the collateral research programmes on which it was based. Because intelligence officers operate outside the USA and do not interrogate US citizens, many of the constitutional and legal proscriptions that apply unambiguously to law enforcement, may not apply in the same way to intelligence collection. Nevertheless, these agencies do represent the USG and their actions do reflect upon the values and policies of our nation, so their actions in interrogations and human intelligence-gathering operations are a relevant topic of public interest.

More widely recognised and thoroughly documented are the intelligence interrogation policies and tactics of the US military. Most US armed forces have historically relied on *U.S. Army's Field Manual for Intelligence Interrogation*. This manual outlines approximately 17 techniques that have remained relatively intact for more than 50 years across successive editions and despite the fact that no one seems able to produce any research studies or systematic analyses that support their effectiveness. In 2006, this field manual went through its most extensive revision to date. The current version is *U.S. Army Field Manual 2-22.3, Human Intelligence Collector Operations*. In it, 'there are 18 approach techniques that can be employed on any detainee regardless of status or characterization' and one additional 'restricted' technique called 'separation' that is not authorised for use with enemy prisoners of war. The 18 approach techniques, again, are quite similar to those appearing in prior iterations of the manual, though Clarke (2004) observes that 'the chapter on Approach Techniques has been expanded and introduces some additional rapport-building methodologies that support debriefing and elicitation rather than only addressing interrogation in the tactical setting' (p. xx). Prior to the release of the new field manual, the US Army also revised its organisation and operation plan to separate and distinguish the disciplines of HUMINT and counter-intelligence (CI), and changed the official military occupational speciality (MOS) designation from 'Interrogator' to 'HUMINT Collector' (97-E).

Interestingly, perhaps the most hotly debated issues in public discourse over interrogation approaches used by US personnel have centred on what is permissible, rather than what is effective. Intelligence interrogation is sometimes portrayed as an 'across-the-table' battle of wills that is resolved only when the interrogator exerts enough pressure that the suspect or detainee ultimate 'breaks'. The underlying idea behind this blunt and arguably erroneous assumption is that there is a single formula or method for success in getting information and that one just varies the 'level' or degree to comport with the existing rules of engagement. With that assumption, debates over interrogation methods have focused mainly on the amount and kinds of pressures that can permissibly be applied to a subject or detainee.

These policy debates evoked discussion of what rules should bind US operations in human intelligence-gathering activities, how the language of those rules should be interpreted (e.g. how functionally to define what constitutes 'torture'), to whom the rules should apply (e.g. prisoners of war vs. unlawful enemy combatants), and in what settings or venues they might be obtain (e.g. within or outside the USA).

The torture question

At the centre of these debates is what some have called the torture question. The issue is whether and, if so, under what circumstances, it is (or should be) permissible to use highly coercive techniques – including those that produce significant physical pain or enduring and severe psychological distress – to elicit information from uncooperative prisoners. In many ways, this is not a new question for America or any other nation, but the debate has become substantially less theoretical for contemporary Americans in the post 9/11 climate of global insecurity.

At one extreme of the situational continuum is the hypothetical 'ticking bomb' scenario (Brecher 2007; Dershowitz 2008). The hypothetical scenario posits a set of circumstances in which an identified, detained person is 'known' to have specific information about a bomb that has already been activated and set to detonate imminently, and which is certain to cause a large number of (American) deaths and casualties. Given this set of facts, some argue that it should be ethically and legally permissible to do 'anything necessary' to extract information that will save American lives. The commentator Charles Krauthammer has said that under these circumstances 'Not only is it permissible to hang this miscreant by his thumbs. It is a moral duty' (5 December, *The Weekly Standard*). Others argue, however, that the long-term values and interests of the USA would be severely compromised by allowing the end to justify any means even under the most dire circumstances.

The ticking bomb scenario, on its face, is a vexing one. Many scholars, operators and warriors over the years have thoughtfully argued the merits of differing courses of action. The hypothetical itself, of course, is rife with assumptions that run counter to nearly any known 'real-world' intelligence interrogation and that make it a rather poor platform for a broader discussion of US intelligence interrogation policy. In actual practice, interrogators typically cannot be certain, in advance, about whether a given source possesses the information that is needed. Moreover, the assumption that a high degree of pressure or even pain will cause an otherwise uncooperative source to suddenly cooperate in providing accurate, actionable intelligence has not been systematically tested, and certainly runs counter to the experience of many seasoned intelligence interrogators. People may 'talk' under duress, but often the accuracy or reliability of the information they provide would be highly suspect. Just as asset validation has become a vital element in managing HUMINT operations, source veracity remains a critical – and often vexing – element of interrogation operations.

The dilemma extends far beyond the emergent 'ticking bomb' case, however, and involves a range of techniques that may or may not be universally regarded as comprising torture, cruel, inhuman or degrading treatment. The USA agreed in 1994, by signing the UN Convention Against Torture, to extend its domestic prohibition against torture to non-US venues as well. The treaty also bound its participants to 'undertake to prevent ... other acts of cruel, inhuman or degrading treatment or punishment' that might not rise to the level of torture. Yet, when the US Army investigated allegations of detainee abuse at Guantánamo Bay, Cuba (Schmidt Report), it found that detainees were sometimes subjected to loud, noxious music and lights, threats from attack-trained dogs, threats to harm the detainee's family members, questioning for 18–20 hours a day, and various techniques of humiliation, such as sexual tauntings and being led around on a dog leash. Based on these findings from the Army's own report and the array of pictures released showing similar treatment of detainees in Abu Ghraib prison, America's image in the eyes of the world was arguably tainted (Luban 2005). Moreover, there was scant, if any, evidence that the more extreme techniques produced any vital security information, or that other less coercive approaches might not have done as well or better.

Following these events, the US Congress enacted legislation that set discernible parameters around the nature of US interrogation methods and its treatment of detainees in US custody. A main point of contention was whether the provisions should apply only to the US military (or Department of Defense (DOD)) or to all US intelligence and other governmental agencies. Some policymakers argued that intelligence agencies' effectiveness, while operating covertly, would be compromised by a public declaration of what they could or could not do in collecting human intelligence. Nevertheless, Congress eventually passed two laws: the National Defense Authorization Act for FY 2006 (P.L. 109-163) and the Department of Defense Supplemental Appropriations (P.L. 109-48). Both contain identical provisions that require Department of Defense personnel to employ the US Army field manual (FM 2–22.3) guidelines while interrogating detainees, and specifically prohibit cruel and inhuman and degrading treatment or punishment of persons under the detention, custody or control of the USG.

US Senator John McCain, himself a former prisoner of war in Vietnam, proposed an amendment to this legislation that would extend the purview of these boundaries beyond DOD personnel. The McCain Amendment does not require non-DOD agencies, such as non-military intelligence and law enforcement, to employ Army field manual guidelines with respect to the interrogations they conduct. A second provision of the amendment, however, does protect persons in the custody or the control of the US government – regardless of their nationality or physical location – from being subjected to cruel or inhuman or degrading treatment or punishment.

Cruel, inhuman, or degrading treatment or punishment is defined in the amendment to mean the 'cruel, unusual, and inhumane treatment or punishment prohibited by the Fifth, Eighth, and Fourteenth Amendments to the Constitution of the United States, as defined in the United States Reservations, Declarations and Understandings to the United Nations Convention Against Torture and Other Forms of Cruel, Inhuman or Degrading Treatment or Punishment done at New York, December 10, 1984.' This seems fundamentally to allow only techniques that would also be permissible for use by US law enforcement personnel with US citizens. Importantly, that provision applies to not only DOD activities, but also intelligence and law enforcement activities occurring both inside and outside the jurisdiction of the USA, essentially extending the protections of the US Constitution to all persons – regardless of citizenship – under the custody or control of the USG.

Toward a new focus on effectiveness

Resolving a practical or policy-oriented debate over what techniques and approaches can permissibly be used in interrogation is only a first step in determining what approaches *should* be used. The effectiveness of those approaches for acquiring reliable, actionable intelligence is critical. If a source 'talks', but provides unreliable information, the resulting action – at best – may waste valuable resources and – at worst – may erode the strength and resiliency of our security apparatus. The need to understand what approaches, techniques, and strategies are likely to produce accurate, useful information from an uncooperative human source seems self-evident. Surprisingly, however, these questions have received scant scientific attention in the last 50 years. *'Almost no empirical studies in the social and behavioral sciences directly address the effectiveness of interrogation in general practice, or of specific techniques in generating accurate and useful information from otherwise uncooperative persons'* (Borum 2006: 18; emphasis in original).

Historically, within the USA, there has been some divergence of opinion between the law enforcement and the defense/intelligence communities over 'what works' for meeting their respective information requirements, particularly where national security interests are at stake. US law enforcement agents and professionals in the DOD and intelligence community each have had a role in human intelligence collection in the 'global war on terrorism'. Even within the US law enforcement community, however, there are differing views about the relative merits of approaches that emphasise interpersonal influence over psychological pressure. The Reid technique probably continues to be the most influential approach and the predominant model of interrogation used by law enforcement professionals in the USA. Though the Reid technique includes the need to establish 'rapport' during the interview stage, in the interrogation, psychological leverage is garnered less from the relationship itself than from the interrogator's ability to build a suspect's anxiety and to offer psychologically and emotionally appealing alternatives to, and reasons for, confessing.

The range of techniques emphasising influence and persuasion has sometimes been referred to generically as a 'rapport-based' or 'relationship-based' approach. That term, however, may not adequately capture the essence of the approach or what distinguishes it most from other approaches.

According to published anecdotes and declassified material, it appears that a range of interrogation strategies have been successfully employed with al-Qaeda-affiliated persons and other militant Islamist extremists since even before the 1993 attack on the World Trade Centre. Interrogators and agencies have ostensibly attempted to refine these approaches along the way and to integrate 'lessons learned' from their collective experiences in cases such as the 1998 US Embassy bombing in Kenya, the 2000 attack on the USS *Cole*, and the 11 September 2001 attacks. Some in the US law enforcement community believe that experience with detainees in Guantánamo Bay, Afghanistan and Iraq – both positive and negative – generally support the effectiveness of 'rapport-based' methods and reveal the myriad of problems that are associated with more coercive or aggressive tactics. Still, there is no known systematic study of the comparative effectiveness of different approaches that have, thus far, been employed.

It has become quite clear, however, that at least within the foreseeable future, the USA will continue to need critical intelligence from (presumably uncooperative) human sources. In the interest of national security, the future of US interrogation and human intelligence collection methods arguably should be guided, at least in part, by an appraisal of effectiveness that can be integrated within the boundaries set forth by law, ethics, and policy.

A key objective in developing any future approach to interrogation is to provide its practitioners with a useful skill-set for discerning meaningful information within an inherently ambiguous strategic environment. At least for high-value detainees, this future effort is likely to require an adaptable strategic framework, not just the application of certain techniques. An ongoing US-based initiative holds some promise for prompting a next generation of ideas to guide intelligence interrogation.

Educing information: a new era in US intelligence interrogation

While the fundamental interrogation objective of accurate, useful, timely information may be relatively uncontroversial, there is often a divergence of opinion how to accomplish that task most effectively. As a result, the term *interrogation* has come to suggest dramatically different processes involving often radically different means. In an effort to better understand both the art and science of interrogation, an effort is under way to introduce more precision into the language, assumptions, and strategies used in this complex dynamic exchange.

In 2004, Robert Fein, a psychologist serving on the US Intelligence Science Board (ISB), proposed, and subsequently chaired, an ISB study to explore what was currently known about the effectiveness of interrogation, with consideration for what kinds of knowledge might need to be developed and applied in the future to improve the USG's ability to gather accurate, useful information from human sources to protect and advance the security interests of the USA. This initiative was called the Intelligence Science Board Study on Educing Information. In the following section, we will describe a few highlights from the Phase I study and discuss some developments in the use of teams and consultants in intelligence interrogation.

Within the ISB study, interrogation was deliberately framed as a process of *educing information* (EI). The term *educe* was chosen because it denotes a drawing out or elicitation of information, specifically information that may be hidden, unexpressed, or latent. Educing information, therefore, involves deriving meaningful information that might otherwise be unavailable to analysts and decision-makers. The term 'meaningful information' refers to knowledge and understanding that may be 'of interest' to persons, organisations, activities, capabilities, and/or intentions that may affect US national security. This might include, but is not solely limited to 'actionable' information.

Two principal tasks arguably drive the pursuit of meaningful information. The first is managing the information exchange. This involves not only the information the source can provide the interrogator (e.g. information of intelligence value, information that sheds light on the source's interests and motivations, etc.), but also information the interrogator may provide to the source (e.g. current realities outside the detention environment, timeline for release, approval/disapproval of a source's request for additional amenities, etc.).

The second task is managing the relationship. This requires the interrogator to take a wholistic view of the source and of the dynamics between the two of them. Rather than focusing on which techniques to apply, the interrogator continuously assesses, monitors, and integrates a thorough understanding of the source's needs, hopes, fears, and interests as a basis for building a climate of cooperation. Without tending to the relationship, managing the information exchange may become needlessly problematic. But when these two processes work in synergy, it is possible to create a situation in which the source *realistically perceives* that providing accurate and comprehensive information is the best alternative and is in his or her best interests given the present circumstances. Moreover, it may prompt the serendipitous discovery of important operational information that was not even anticipated during the planned interrogation.

Within the EI framework, the operational relationship between the interrogator (often called the 'educing information professional' (EIP) and source is the fulcrum to leverage a climate of cooperation. While the term 'rapport' is commonly used to describe the desired state for a productive interrogation relationship, it has been suggested that the term *operational accord* may be more useful. Operational accord between an interrogator and a source often involves a degree of conformity by the source and/or apparent mutual affinity based on a mutual understanding of – and perhaps even guarded appreciation for – each party's respective concerns, intentions, and desired outcomes.

Findings and a report from Phase I of the *ISB Study on Educing Information* were recently published as a monograph by the National Defense Intelligence College (Fein 2006). The monograph contains a collection of 11 chapters exploring normative and empirical bases for forming an American approach to intelligence interrogation. Chapters include reviews of the relevant social and behavioural science literature, analyses of historical interrogation documents, a review of custodial interrogation studies and practices, explorations of negotiation theory's potential applications to interrogation, and critical essays on barriers and to success and needed research to chart a course for the future of intelligence interrogations.

Toward a team approach to HUMINT collection

Another idea supported by the EI study is the value of using multi-disciplinary teams. The assumption is that a team approach operating within a coordinated systems framework is likely to provide the most effective environment for EI, particularly from high-value sources during long-term custodial detention. Team members' perspectives and input can be integrated to create a working 'case conceptualisation' based on everything that is known about a source, interests, beliefs, and sources of leverage. The team ideally should include an array of relevant subject matter experts to provide advice and counsel on various elements of the EI process. Team members might include intelligence analysts, cultural and linguistic experts, and behavioural science consultants.

Integrating the expertise of psychologists and behavioural scientists into HUMINT collection/interrogation planning has been implemented on a very limited basis. The expertise has been drawn principally from psychologists serving in the military or working for federal law enforcement agencies cooperating with DOD operations. Those consulting in this capacity, which in US military venues are known as 'Behavioral Science Consultation Teams' (BSCT), do not conduct or even manage interrogations, but rather serve as a resource to the interrogator and other members of the team for planning and for monitoring behavioural and relational aspects of the interrogation.

Psychologists' and psychiatrists' involvement in military interrogations has become an issue of substantial professional controversy, however – not from the military or law enforcement agencies – but within the professions themselves. Both the American Psychological Association and the American Psychiatric Association have deliberated over the issue within their respective disciplines, and come to somewhat different conclusions. Both associations agreed without equivocation that members of their profession should not engage in or facilitate torture or any cruel, inhuman or degrading treatment.

The President of the American Psychological Association (then, Ron Levant, PhD) appointed a Task Force on Psychological Ethics and National Security (PENS). The association adopted the PENS Task Force Report as its official position, declaring, in part, that 'Psychologists may serve in various national security-related roles, such as a consultant to an interrogation, in a manner that is consistent with the Ethics Code'. Approximately one year after the PENS Report, the American Psychiatric Association (APA) issued a Position Statement on Psychiatric Participation in Interrogation of Detainees, stating that 'No psychiatrist should participate directly in the interrogation of persons held in custody by military or civilian investigative or law enforcement authorities, whether in the United States or elsewhere. Direct participation includes being present in the interrogation room, asking or suggesting questions, or advising authorities on the use of specific techniques of interrogation with particular detainees.' While the language is clearly prescriptive, the association's president, Steven Sharfstein, MD, clarified that the position statement did not constitute 'an ethical rule' and that individual psychiatrists who did not abide by its provisions 'wouldn't get in trouble with the APA'. Despite some continued dissension within the professions, psychologists and psychiatrists continue to consult in interrogations. In addition to serving as a technical resource, their role in military interrogations now explicitly includes a safety/monitoring function to help ensure that these HUMINT collection activities are conducted in a safe, effective manner.

Conclusions

The eight years since the 11 September attacks on America have been a critical time for intelligence interrogation in the USA and for American personnel throughout the globe. Faced with an emergent threat to the homeland, security forces faced an unprecedented urgency to uncover information that might prevent acts of terrorism or save American lives. It also became increasingly clear that potentially life-saving, actionable intelligence – to the extent that it existed – would be most likely to come from human sources.

The US law enforcement, intelligence and military communities have faced new demands to acquire crucial intelligence from new adversaries in a variety of contexts. Many well-intentioned agencies found themselves lacking detailed, pertinent knowledge of religion or culture, or requisite language skills. Working through acknowledged mistakes and attempting to learn from ongoing experiences, security forces – and the American public – have struggled with the entangled questions of effectiveness and ethics in interrogations.

No large-scale, sweeping changes are yet apparent in the USG's ethos or national strategy for intelligence interrogation. In fact, in late 2007, there was still active debate *within* sectors of the USG about whether specific techniques such as 'waterboarding' would or should constitute 'torture', with little discussion of whether those were even effective, necessary or useful.

Some modest changes, however, have occurred. The US Army's field manual for intelligence interrogation – used throughout the DOD – has undergone a major text revision and has been prescribed through legislation as the doctrinal basis for all authorised military interrogation techniques. The US Congress passed legislation to explicitly prohibit any DOD personnel from participating in torture, cruel, inhuman, or degrading treatment of US detainees. Professional associations have examined the roles that behavioural science and medical professionals may play in consulting in interrogations and have outlined the ethical contours governing their professional conduct when engaged in those activities.

The Intelligence Science Board (ISB) Study on Educing Information has produced the first systematic attempt to look toward the future of interrogations. The early objective of the ISB Study was to examine soberly the science – or lack of science – that might lay beneath nearly a half-century of US doctrine. Although the effectiveness of long-used approaches remains an open question, there was not compelling scientific evidence to support their use or to affirm many of their underlying assumptions. The EI initiative has also probed the research literature in behavioural and social science and begun exploring possible applications from new scientific and relational frameworks, such as social psychology and negotiation theory. Whether any of the study's findings or recommendations will translate into governmental action remains to be seen.

An important question to guide the future of US interrogation policy and practices is arguably: 'What kind of research or knowledge is needed to point us toward the most effective approaches in HUMINT collection?' In attempting to better understand the 'effectiveness' of these efforts, it will likely be necessary not just to explore whether a specific technique does or does not 'work', but to consider how and why different kinds of approaches or strategies might work for certain kinds of detainees, with certain kinds of information, in certain circumstances (or under certain conditions). The future of America's approach to interrogation and HUMINT collection will need to recognise the needs and requirements of expediency while acknowledging the fundamental importance of attaining information that is comprehensive, accurate, reliable and actionable in an operationally relevant context.

References

American Psychiatric Association (2006, May) 'Psychiatric Participation in Interrogation of Detainees: Position Statement'. Retrieved 15 September 2007 from http://www.psych.org/edu/other_res/lib_archives/archives/200601.pdf.

American Psychological Association, Presidential Task Force on Psychological Ethics and National Security (2005) *Report of the American Psychological Association Presidential Task Force on Psychological Ethics and National Security*. Retrieved 10 March 2005, from http://www.apa.org/releases/PENSTaskForceReportFinal.pdf.

Behnke, S. (2006) 'Ethics and Interrogations: Comparing and Contrasting the American Psychological, American Medical and American Psychiatric Association position', *Monitor on Psychology*, 37: 66.

Borum, R. (2004) 'Counterterrorism Training Post-9/11', in R. Gunaratna (ed.), *The Changing Face of Terrorism*. Singapore: Eastern Universities Press, 62–73.

Borum, R. (2006) 'Approaching Truth: Behavioral Science Lessons on Educing Information from Human Sources', in R. Fein (ed.), *Educing Information: Science and Art in Interrogation – Foundations for the Future*. Intelligence Science Board Study on Educing Information Phase 1 Report. Washington, DC: National Defense Intelligence College Press.

Borum, R., Fein, R., Vossekuil, B. and Gelles, M. (2003) 'Profiling Hazards: Profiling in Counterterrorism and Homeland Security', *Counterterrorism and Homeland Security Reports*, 10: 12–13.

Borum, R., Fein, R., Vossekuil, B., Gelles, M. and Shumate, S. (2004) 'The Role of Operational Research in Counterterrorism', *International Journal of Intelligence and Counterintelligence*, 17: 420–434.

Borum, R. and Gelles, M. (2005) 'Al-Qaeda's Operational Evolution: Behavioral and Organizational Perspectives', *Behavioral Sciences and the Law*, 23: 467–483.

Brecher, B. (2007) *Torture and the Ticking Bomb*. New York: Wiley Blackwell.

Clarke, S. (2004) 'USAIC Fields Two New Intelligence Manuals', *Military Intelligence Professional Bulletin*, April–June.

Cunningham, R. and Sarayrah, Y. (1993) *Wasta: The Hidden Force in Middle Eastern Society*. Westport, CT: Praeger.

Dershowitz, A.M. (2002) 'Torture of Terrorists: Is It Necessary to Do and to Lie About It?', in *Shouting Fire: Civil Liberties in a Turbulent Age*. Boston, MA: Little, Brown, 470–479.

Dershowitz, A.M. (2008) *Is There a Right to Remain Silent?: Coercive Interrogation and the fifth Amendment After 9/11*. Oxford: Oxford University Press.

Einesman, F. (1999) 'Confessions and Culture: The Interaction of Miranda and Diversity', *Journal of Criminal Law and Criminology*, 90: 1–48.

Fein, R. (ed.) (2006) *Educing Information: Science and Art in Interrogation – Foundations for the Future*. Intelligence Science Board Study on Educing Informtion Phase 1 Report. Washington, DC: National Defense Intelligence College Press.

Gudjonsson, G. (2003) *The Psychology of Interrogations and Confessions: A Handbook*. New York: Wiley.

Inbau, F., Reid, J., Buckley, J. and Jayne, B. (2001). *Criminal Interrogation and Confessions* (4th edn). Gaithersburg, MD: Aspen.

Knapp, M. and Hall, J. (1997) *Nonverbal Communication in Human Interaction* (4th edn). Orlando, FL: Harcourt Brace.

Leo, R. (1996) 'Inside the Interrogation Room', *Journal of Criminal Law and Criminology*, 86: 266–303.

Lewis, B. (2003) *The Crisis of Islam: Holy War and Unholy Terror*. New York: Modern Library.

Luban, D. (2005) 'Torture, American-Style: This Debate Comes Down to Words vs. Deeds', *Washington Post*, 27 November, B01.

Mayer, J. (2005) 'The Experiment', *New Yorker*, 11 and 18 July.

Navarro, J. (2002) 'Interacting with Arabs and Muslims', *FBI Law Enforcement Bulletin*, 71: 20.

Nydell, M. (2002) *Understanding Arabs: A Guide for Westerners* (3rd edn). Yarmouth, MA: Intercultural Press.

Patterson, E. (2003) CITF: Criminal Investigation Task Force – OSI. *TIG Brief: The Inspector General*, November–December.

Riddell, P. and Cotterell, P. (2003) *Islam in Context: Past, Present, and Future*. Grand Rapids, MI: Baker Academic.

Schafer, J. and Navarro, J. (2004) *Advanced Interviewing Techniques: Proven Strategies for Law Enforcement*. Springfield, IL: Charles C. Thomas.

Walters, S. (2002) *Principles of Kinesic Interview and Interrogation* (2nd edn). Boca Raton, FL: CRC Press.

White, J. (2003) *Defending the Homeland: Domestic Intelligence, Law Enforcement, and Security*. New York: Wadsworth.

Part 2

Current issues in interrogation and investigative interviewing

Chapter 7

A critical analysis of the utilitarian case for torture and the situational factors that lead some people to become torturers

Rod Morgan and Tom Williamson

Introduction

Torture as a means of gaining information or confessional evidence is prohibited by customary international law and is either prohibited by the domestic law of most states or the evidence collected through its use is deemed inadmissible. Yet the practice widely persists, and, in the wake of 9/11, the USA, the world's superpower, has muddied what many had hoped were the clarifying waters by asserting that custodial practices that international and other jurisdictions would almost certainly define as torture, do not reach that threshold. The establishment of, and conditions at, the US detention centre at Guantánamo Bay, Cuba; the revelations regarding the treatment of detainees at Abu Ghraib, Iraq; and the widespread use of 'extraordinary rendition' of suspects to countries where the use of torture is documented and widespread suggest that the balance is tipping back towards allowing greater force to be exerted by military, security and law enforcement agents against persons suspected of having committed or planning serious harm (Danner 2004; Greenberg and Dratel 2004; Rose 2004). It is of course denied by the USA and other states that torture is ever sanctioned: it is asserted that wherever it has occurred it is unauthorised. But the excesses that have been exposed have been encouraged by a political climate more tolerant of coercive methods, and the justification for the practice is utilitarian. It is argued that changed conditions, currently the 'war on terror', make it necessary to allow those whose task it is to collect evidence greater scope to employ coercive methods in order that the public at large be better protected.

Because so much of the contemporary debate about the use of force (both physical and psychological) during the interrogation of suspects is essentially utilitarian, and because, even if the language of human rights is employed – within international human rights law torture is absolutely outlawed – it is clear that among security practitioners utilitarian considerations hold sway, we would argue that merely intoning human rights proscriptions and pointing to legal precedents as to what counts as torture, is inadequate as a basis for preventing the practice. Rather, we must confront the utilitarian case, less often formally defended so much as covertly believed in and practised, that torture or near torture works and is a necessary tool in the armoury of contemporary states.

This chapter is in two parts. In the first part, we consider whether torture or near torture (what some US commentators term 'torture lite' – see Luban 2006) can on utilitarian grounds ever be justified. In the second part, we consider the circumstances in which the use of torture is likely to thrive and who may be drawn into the practice.

Part 1: the utilitarian case for and against torture

The efficacy of torture for establishing the truth (either to prove responsibility for past events or gather intelligence in order to forestall future events) has from the earliest times been doubted. By the same token, whenever the use of torture has been justified, it has generally been on the grounds that either its subjects, because of their individual or class characteristics or their organisational adherence, will not without such methods be persuaded to provide essential information. The totalitarian regimes of the twentieth century covertly resorted to torture to combat counter-revolutionary elements and strike fear into the population generally (Peters 1996: Chapter 4; Evans and Morgan 1998: 13–20). In democratic states, the practice has long been generally abjured, even if the evidence shows it continued in particular situations, notably in post-colonial struggles such as Algeria, Kenya, Northern Ireland and so on. The 'war on terror' is only the latest in a long line of special pleadings for resort to coercive methods. Whether it be proposals for prolonged preventive detention, suspension of the rights normally accorded to suspects, or unusual use of force, the argument is always that a new situation has arisen: the risk and scale of the threat posed is said to be greater, the organisational challenge more complex, the degree to which opponents respect civilised rules of combat diminished. Extreme situations, the argument goes, demand that extreme defensive measures be taken. The state and its innocent citizens have a right to defend themselves. As the *Newsweek* headline had it in the wake of 9/11, it is 'Time to Think About Torture' (Alter 2001).

The test (invariably apocryphal but nonetheless telling) always cited by utilitarian apologists for torture or near torture (the term *moderate physical pressure* is generally preferred) is the ticking bomb scenario or its equivalent. A bomb has been placed in a crowded, but unidentified, public place and could explode at any moment. The perpetrator, or a knowledgeable collaborator, is captured. What methods is the interrogator justified in using in order to obtain information as to the whereabouts of the bomb? Jeremy Bentham (1997), in an essay unpublished in his lifetime, posed this question and answered it unequivocally: in order to rescue innocents from extreme violence, no scruple should be had about applying equal or greater violence to him whose intelligence might save them. The Israeli Landau Commission (1987: para. 3.15), investigating the excesses of the Israeli General Security Services (GSS) during the 1980s, considered the answer self-evident: pressurising suspects would be the lesser evil, what Vice President Dick Cheney has judged to be a 'no-brainer'. Advice prepared by Jay Bybee, now a judge, and endorsed by Alberto Gonzales, then counsel to President George Bush and subsequently Attorney General, referred to the 'choice of evils' arising from such scenarios and found the evil of international terrorism sufficiently compelling to advocate that a variety of safeguards for prisoners be abandoned and more coercive interrogation methods used (Greenberg and Dratel 2004, Memos 6, 7, 14 and 15). The parallel lines of reasoning are clear and make it reasonable that we address these issues without regard to time or place.

In the eighteenth century, at a time when torture remained legally in widespread use, Bentham argued for its retention subject to certain rules:

- It ought not to be used 'without good proof of its being in the power of the prisoner to do what is required of him'.
- It should be used only 'in cases which admit of no delay'.
- The harm to be averted, even in urgent cases, must be great.
- The severity of the torture must be proportionate to the harm to be prevented.
- The use of torture should be regulated and limited by law.

- The type of torture used should be such as to have the fewest long-term effects – that is, it should be of the sort where the 'pain goes off the soonest'. (Bentham 1997: 313–315)

A similar line of reasoning has been followed in contemporary democratic states. In the 1930s, it appears, the US police employed 'third-degree methods', which the Wickersham Commission typified as torture, against organised crime suspects: their use had to be approved by senior officers qualified to judge the seriousness of the threat allegedly posed (Chaffee *et al.* 1931: 174–180). Likewise in the 1980s, the Israeli Landau Commission insisted that 'moderate physical pressure' (which the Commission argued fell short of torture) was justified by the criminal law defence of 'necessity': the methods should be regulated, albeit both the methods that were sanctioned and the agreed regulatory procedure remained secret. The Harvard human rights lawyer, Alan Dershowitz (2001), has recently argued that since, given a 'ticking bomb situation', US security agents would torture 'anyway', it would be better were the practice to be regulated through the issue of 'torture warrants'. Unusual coercive interrogation methods, and the circumstances in which they can officially be used, were in early 2002 approved by the Office of Legal Counsel in the US Justice Department for use in the 'war on terror' (Greenberg and Dratel: Memo 14): whether the methods amount to, or have inevitably spilled over into, torture is disputed (see Danner 2004; Ratner and Ray 2004; Rose 2004), though few who have studied the jurisprudence of the European Court of Human Rights (ECHR) and other bodies would accept the advice accepted by President Bush that torture

> covers only extreme acts. Severe pain is generally of the kind difficult for the victim to endure. Where the pain is physical, it must be of an intensity which accompanies serious physical injury such as death or organ failure. (Danner 2004: 155; Geenberg and Dratel 2004: 213–240)

In fact, it is likely that, were the ECHR asked to consider the question, they would rule that the methods of interrogation and conditions of detention that the Bush administration then approved for terrorist suspects would, in combination and applied for prolonged periods, constitute torture.

Michael Ignatieff (2004a) has controversially argued that facing up to 'lesser evils' is something the age of terrorism makes imperative –

though he also insists that he is contemplating coercive interrogation methods falling short of torture. Like Bentham, Ignatieff wants whatever is to be allowed to be regulated by law. Let us address each of the issues arising from this line of reasoning in turn.

Bentham argued that if, through torture, we could be certain that the subject would do that which it is in the public interest that he be made to do, torture would be more efficacious, and therefore justified on utilitarian grounds, than punishment. The problem with punishment, whose utilitarian justification is deterrence or rehabilitation, is the risk, the future being uncertain, that it will not work, that insufficient or inappropriate punishment has been applied. With torture there is no such risk. The torture stops as soon as the subject complies. But herein also lies the fundamental difficulty. The torturer can *never* be certain that the subject *can* comply. Or that he *has*. We can never be certain that the subject knows that which we have an interest in knowing and, as Aristotle put it, 'those under compulsion are as likely to give false evidence as true' (*Rhetoric* 1376b–1377a).

The obvious response to these objections is that we can never be certain about anything, which is why Bentham argued that the investigator should be as certain as he can be: he should apply an evidential test similar to that sufficient to convict for a serious crime. But how is such a test to be applied in circumstances 'which admit of no delay', while the bomb ticks? In most advanced states, convictions for serious crimes are arrived at with deliberation, following full, thorough and transparent examinations of all the available evidence. These are the very opposite of the frenetic circumstances arising from the ticking bomb, and that is why, as Luban convincingly argues, the ticking bomb scenario is a rhetorical red herring, a 'picture that bewitches us':

> The real debate is not between one guilty man's pain and hundreds of innocent lives. It is the debate between the certainty of anguish and the mere possibility of learning something vital and saving lives. (Luban 2006: 46–7)

Necessity, as the old adage has it, knows no law. It is the most lawless of legal doctrines. An *individual* may do something out of necessity, in the heat of the moment, making an emergency judgement in extreme circumstances. An *individual* may subsequently advance *necessity* in his defence. That is one thing. But to attempt to justify a regular state practice on this basis means standardising allegedly compelling circumstances incapable of standardisation and effective regulation. It means granting security or police personnel a general discretion to use extreme coercive methods in individual cases where there is no necessary urgency, where no specific harm by gathering intelligence from a particular subject can precisely be identified or averted, where the guilt of the subject has not been proved, and where the suspect's capacity to provide information about the alleged threat has to be assumed, possibly reasonably, but not independently tested.

Secondly, even if a genuine ticking bomb situation were to arise, and force were to be used in order to obtain information to dispel the imminent threat, and even were the conduct of the security forces or police subsequently to be excused, that would not mean that the evidence derived from the exercise could subsequently be used in criminal proceedings for past crimes. There is a fundamental difference between averting a future harm and punishing an old one. Allowing evidence collected by force to be used in criminal proceedings creates an *incentive* to apply coercive means to *all* suspects resisting interrogation. It means allowing the security forces and police to treat suspects in a way which, if done by others, constitutes a criminal offence. This was the objection which Lord Donaldson had to the interrogation methods used by the British Army against terrorist suspects in Northern Ireland in the early 1970s (Parker Report 1972). It means licensing the police to use the very practices which the criminal law prohibits and the criminal justice system is ostensibly designed to prevent. This can only mean bringing the system generally into contempt. If the use of force is to be allowed to the police against citizens subject to the presumption of innocence and wishing to preserve their right to silence, it will no longer be clear to citizens that their security is being safeguarded by the system. How will the behaviour of the security forces be distinguishable from that of criminals?

In the case of the detainees at Guantánamo Bay, the US authorities have clearly considered several of the above objections, making the policies they have adopted all the more cynical. They originally determined that the detainees were not covered by the Geneva Conventions, and this, given the open-ended nature of the undeclared non-interstate nature of the 'war on terror', meant, in the absence of the US courts determining the policy unconstitutional (see discussion below), that they could be detained and coercively interrogated without limit of time, with no right of access to the US domestic courts and the forum of public opinion which would accompany such access. They also determined that any criminal proceedings against the detainees should be by way of specially constituted military tribunals without certain protections afforded by the US domestic courts. As Alberto Gonzales advised President Bush when recommending these measures, the president would thus have maximum flexibility in how to deal with these and subsequent detainees and the threat of domestic criminal prosecution would be reduced. The suggestion that these policies would bring criticism from the USA's allies was 'undoubtedly true', but the USA would continue to be able 'to bring war crimes charges against anyone who mistreats U.S. personnel', and most allies would be reassured by claims that the treatment at Guantánamo is humane (Greenberg and Dratel 2004: Memo 7). It is clear that even the USA's staunchest and most supine ally, the UK, was *not* reassured, even if it took four years for a British cabinet minister, Lord Falconer, the Lord Chancellor, to declare that the legal black hole represented by the Guantánamo arrangements is a 'shocking affront to the principles of democracy' (Falconer 2006). Even so, Lord Falconer failed to comment on the conditions and the interrogation methods in use at Guantánamo Bay.

Thirdly, Israel in the 1980s and the USA currently have set limits to the amount of coercion and pain that can be applied, allowing techniques not dissimilar to those used by the British in Northern Ireland (hooding, physical stress positions, sleep deprivation, etc. – see Evans and Morgan 1989; Greenberg and Dratel 2004: Memo 26). By contrast, Bentham set no upper limit to the torture that might be inflicted other than that it should be proportionate and of the sort where the 'pain goes off the soonest'. Why, on utilitarian grounds, should any upper limit be set? There seems no good reason so long as the torture is the lesser of the two evils, the other being the harm prevented. One possible utilitarian reason – that the application of extreme pain might produce unreliable evidence – is implausible. There is now a sufficient corpus of research and case study evidence to demonstrate that even the mildest pressure – pressure so mild that the ordinary citizen might not even interpret it as pressure – can elicit from some vulnerable or suggestible subjects false confessions or misleading information (Royal Commission 1981: 25–6; Gudjonsson 1996).

Rather, contemporary utilitarians fall back on the prevailing human rights culture and the reputation of the state, limits being set so as to contend that the coercion falls short of torture and thus the state is in conformity with its international treaty obligations and international public opinion. This was the position taken by the British in Northern Ireland and by the Landau Commission in Israel, and it is the position taken currently by the US authorities.

But once coercive interrogation methods – sleep deprivation, hooding, dietary manipulation, subjection to temperature extremes, white noise, forcible use of physical stress postures, physical slaps and punches, or threats of all this and worse – have been authorised, all the evidence suggests that setting upper limits becomes a fig leaf for worse. Once the dog is off the leash, the evidence suggests that a legal regulatory framework of the type for which Dershowitz and Ignatieff call does not and will not work, particularly in a 'war on terror' doomsday climate of the sort that Ignatieff suggests we now inhabit. Trained, committed terrorists do not succumb to 'moderate physical pressure'. They are prepared to resist, and often risk much worse treatment from their own organisations if they succumb: this much is clear from the experience of Algeria, Northern Ireland and Palestine. When moderately or even severely coercive methods do not work and the amber light has been given, all the case studies indicate that the security forces go further, much further. The senior US Justice Department officials who prepared the legal advice on interrogation methods for President Bush in 2002 were not inept lawyers. They were highly qualified legal advisers who fully understood the operational interpretation likely to be put on their tough-minded memorandum about the lack of terrorist suspect detainees' rights (Luban 2006).

The evidence that has already emerged from the courts martial already held for both US and British soldiers responsible for prisoners in Iraq is compelling. Near-torture spills over into practices that unequivocally comprise torture, however torture is defined. It is not credible that security forces, operating largely in secret or in theatres where minimal public accountability can routinely be applied, will abide by upper limits. Licensed now to employ coercive methods the rationale for which is the speedy breaking down of detainees' resistance, they will almost certainly step over the line. Lowering the psychological threshold for the use of force almost inevitably leads the dam to be swept away. As one commentator on the Landau Commission's findings has put it: 'If a suspect's body is no longer taboo, what is one blow relative to the sanctity of the cause?' (Kremnitzer 1989: 254). The qualitative Rubicon will have been crossed. The suspect is no longer a subject but an object, not a person but a body, not a citizen but an alien, a reservoir of information to be tapped, a means to an end (Scarry 1984). What begins with tidy intellectual debates about the public interest and lesser evils ends with dirty, hole-in-the-corner contests of will waged in sordid environments by underground officials against demonised *others* whose assumed *evil* and *inhumanity* mean that they do not count in a calculus where, gradually, almost anything goes.

Thus, the ultimate utilitarian objection to torture or near torture is that it corrosively deligitimates the state, and this is Dershowitz' and Ignatieff's rationale for legally regulating more coercive practices. They seek to safeguard the reputation of the state while defending its citizenry from major harm. But Dershowitz sells the pass: he seeks to regulate practices that he argues the state, *in extremis*, will resort to anyway – that is, to regulate that which he concedes is not effectively susceptible to regulation. Ignatieff, by contrast, believes that upper limits can be fixed on the lesser evil of coercive interrogation, thereby protecting the integrity of the state. But Ignatieff deals in generalities. He opposes use of torture – 'if you want to create terrorists, torture is a pretty sure way to do so' (Ignatieff 2004b) – but fails to engage the detail as to what torture comprises. He pirouettes on the slippery semantic slopes of pre-emptive strikes and coercive interrogation.

Because near torture almost inevitably develops into torture and because the truth – despite the torturer's traditional taunts, 'No one will hear you, no one cares about you' – always leaks out, the repercussions ultimately discredit the state. Use of force may initially be supported by popular demand that threats be neutralised and fears assuaged, but the *Other* is ultimately never capable of precise definition and identification in practice. There is always general fallout – the massacre of the innocents, the false confessions, the mistaken identities, the miscarriages of a justice system that no longer seems to deserve the name. This fallout is then capable of being exploited by precisely the groups against whom the state seeks to defend itself. If some suspects are tortured, then those who seek to discredit the state will routinely claim that they have been. And if all opposition group members claim that they have been tortured, why should the police not do that of which they will be accused anyway? One might as well be hung for a sheep as a lamb. Thus is promoted a cycle of disinformation and mistrust. If there are no limits, if the state is engaged in dirty tricks, why should trust be invested in the state and its authority acknowledged?

On all these grounds, we conclude that the *practice* of torture and near torture cannot be justified on utilitarian grounds. There is no consolation here for those who are not persuaded by human rights arguments.

Part 2: torturers in the making

We turn next to the vexed question of who becomes a torturer? To torture another human being is such an abhorrent act that it is easy to assume that the perpetrators are in some way inherently evil. Nothing could be further from the truth: the evidence suggests that torturers are not originally out of the ordinary. We need therefore to consider the power of the situational forces that can turn an ordinary person into someone capable of torturing a fellow human being.

Social psychologists have observed that people have a tendency to underestimate the power of situational forces and that this is typically linked with the tendency to overestimate the role of personality in producing the observed behaviour. This pair of misattributions is referred to as the 'fundamental attribution error' (Ross 1977). In this section, we briefly describe the processes that can, under a set of well-established conditions, transform ordinary people into torturers. Some of the information is based on studies which draw on interviews with men who were torturers and executioners under military regimes in Greece and Brazil (Huggins *et al.* 2002). The studies found no evidence that the future torturers were selected because they were psychopathic or particularly sadistic. Instead they were found to have taken formal and informal training routes. They were typically young recruits to the police or military drawn from rural and politically conservative areas and selected for entry into elite units where torture training took place. They enjoyed privileges not available to their peers and their selection for the unit was an honour. Huggins *et al.* (p. 237) found that in Brazil a component of the training was the harshness of the treatment the recruits received. This desensitised them to pain and suffering, promoted total obedience to authority, created an acceptance of the state's ideology, and energised the men to root out and destroy enemies of the state. Through such means normal men could be shaped to perform the evil that the state required to be carried out.

It is the banality of the process which is most striking, something also observed in studies of Nazi concentration camp guards (Steiner and Fahrenberg 2000) and Hannah Arendt's study of the personality of Adolph Eichmann, whom she observed to be normal. The psychiatrists who examined Eichmann found him to be not merely normal but to have a socially desirable personality (Arendt 1963).

During the Brazilian military regime (1964–85) the need for the state to torture and execute its own citizens found its justification in propaganda centred on a national security ideology that led to the development of supporting organisational structures to carry out the repression. As Huggins *et al.* observe:

> The military regime did what most repressive governments do: it created enemies of the state who must be identified, searched out, collected in secure settings, interrogated if they might have information of value, tortured if they do not comply, and executed when they are of no further value to the state's mission. (Huggins *et al.* 2002: 244)

If the state provides the framework for the transformation from good to evil, what are the social psychological processes leading to that transformation? Social psychological research in the field and laboratory studies show that it is easier for good people to do evil where

- new moralities are created and previous moral considerations over-ridden;
- blind obedience is mandated;
- victims are dehumanised;
- personal and social accountability is neutralised.

The personal standards that guide our behaviour can be changed if the normal constraints are absent, a process termed 'moral disengagement' (Bandura 1990). This can occur when the perpetrators of violence have a distorted perception of the humanity of their victims, seeing them as subhuman enemies against whom violent actions can be taken with impunity because normal systems of accountability and surveillance are absent. The kind of authoritarian regimes in which torture flourishes demand blind obedience. This can absolve participants in state-sponsored violence from a sense of responsibility for what they have done, encouraging further moral disengagement.

Laboratory experiments have shown that, under the right social conditions, untrained, ordinary people will display blind obedience. Milgram notoriously created a laboratory experiment in which subjects were informed that they were taking part in a memory-training exercise. They were shown an electric apparatus that allegedly delivered shocks, ranging on a scale from a mild jolt (15 volts) up to a dangerous level (450 volts), to be applied incrementally each time the learner in the experiment made an error. The learner was out of sight in another room, but could be heard responding to the shocks delivered by the subject. The learners never got the answers right, and the subjects were required to go on delivering the shocks. Prior to the experiment Milgram invited 40 psychiatrists to offer their estimate of the likelihood of participants going to the maximum shock level. The average estimate was 1 per cent. In fact, nearly 64 per cent of the students taking part delivered the maximum shock. Milgram replicated this experiment with over 1,000 people from all walks of life in the USA. In some versions of the experiment, the obedience level reached 90 per cent, thereby demonstrating the power of situational forces in shaping behavioural obedience. The failure of the psychiatrists accurately to predict the outcome can be seen as an example of the fundamental attribution error and demonstrates how easy it is to create blind obedience.

Torture and execution become easier when victims are dehumanised, and are no longer persons but 'animals', 'vermin', 'cockroaches', 'terrorists', 'communists', and other labels that serve to erase their humanity. The absence of accountability results in a process that Zimbardo (1970) terms 'deindividuation'. Anonymity provides a situation where normal restraints are suspended.

Laboratory support for the influence of these four processes was found in the Stanford Prison Experiment (Zimbardo et al. 1973). Here college student volunteers assessed as normal on the basis of psychological tests, clinical interviews and background reports were randomly assigned to play the role of either prisoner or prison guard. By the end of the experiment, the roles assigned for each set of participants led to totally contrasting behaviours. Those subjects assigned to be prisoners were arrested by the city police at their place of residence and booked at the local police station for various felonies before being transferred to a mock prison in the basement of the Stanford University psychology department. Here the subjects were issued with uniforms and given rules created by the guards to follow. The prisoners remained in their cells but the guards worked eight-hour shifts. The experiment was designed to run for two weeks but was terminated after only six days because the simulated prison had become too real. The guards behaved in authoritarian and in some cases even sadistic ways, while the prisoners became passive and totally submissive, experiencing extreme stress reactions. One prisoner had to be released after only 36 hours. The reason was that the guards dehumanised the prisoners through punishment and harassment, and, according to Zimbardo and his colleagues, a process of deindividuation, dehumanisation and moral disengagement unfolded (Huggins et al. 2002: 263). When combined with the results of Milgram's experiment, the Stanford study points to a psychological process whereby the behaviour of ordinary people can be shaped by situational forces such that they are willing to harm and degrade others known to be totally innocent.

So far, the focus of the discussion about the experiment has been on the behaviour of the participants. But Zimbardo and his colleagues point out that the observed behaviour occurred in a context where there were many other actors – city police, a local television station photographer, a Roman Catholic priest who interviewed the prisoners in the presence of the guards and heard their complaints, and parents and friends who visited – whose involvement was intended to lend credibility to the experiment. Despite the ragged appearance of the detainees, these participants did nothing to demand the prisoners' release. The use of torture and summary executions in Brazil likewise did not happen in social isolation. It was situated in a context with many other actors: the trainers who instructed the recruits in the use of torture; the supervisors who selected the officers for this kind of work; the command structure; the technical and maintenance staff who created, serviced and equipped the facilities where torture took place; and the military officers who created the propaganda of a state under threat from enemies that could be dealt with only by recourse to extra-judicial methods. There are social psychological processes that clearly enable ordinary people to turn a blind eye to, or be transformed to commit, acts involving extreme inhumanity: that is, 'anyone could become a torturer or an executioner under a set of quite well-known conditions' (Huggins 2002: 267).

We also need to be alert to the socio-political conditions which facilitate this transformation. To illustrate this, we briefly need to return to the arrangements made by the US government following the events of 9/11 for the detention and questioning of people detained in the 'war on terror', and, in particular, the role of actors such as psychologists and psychiatrists in the interrogation process. The arrangements for dealing with detainees held by the USA has faced its first major legal obstacle. On 29 June 2006, the US Supreme Court delivered its judgment in *Hamden* v. *Rumsfeld*, which halted the plans of the administration to try a selected number of foreign nationals detained at Guantánamo Bay before military commissions. The Supreme Court concluded that the commissions as constituted under a military order signed by President Bush in November 2001 were unlawful on two grounds. First, they had not been authorised by Congress and, secondly, they violated international law and US military law.

On 6 September 2006, President Bush, in response to the *Hamden* ruling, sent to Congress the Military Commissions Act 2006. The proposals in this bill also failed to meet international standards for a fair trial. The administration was unwilling to abandon another aspect of the original military order, namely indefinite detention without charge or trial. On 6 September, President Bush confirmed what had long been speculated in the media, namely that the US Central Intelligence Agency (CIA) had been operating a policy of secret detentions and alternative interrogation techniques, techniques which could be criminal as well as a breach of human rights. The commissions proposed in the bill would have allowed the admission of coerced and hearsay evidence and the exclusion of the defendant from any part of the proceedings in which classified information is admitted. After the invasion of Afghanistan, President Bush decided that common Article 3 of the four Geneva Conventions of 1949 would not apply to al-Qa'ida or Taleban detainees in US custody. The Supreme Court reversed this determination in its *Hamden* ruling. The significance of common Article 3 is that it reflects customary international law applicable to international and non-international conflicts and guarantees minimum standards of humane treatment and fair trial. The Military Commissions Act 2006 contains provisions that would weaken the effect of common Article 3 and allow the pattern of impunity for human rights violations committed by US forces to be reinforced by revising and narrowing the scope of the US War Crimes Act. The administration has also issued a new Army field manual on interrogation which contains strong and welcome prohibitions on abusive interrogation techniques, despite the fact that it appears unwilling to give up the 'alternative interrogation techniques' used by the CIA and other government agencies.

Another example of how far-reaching the socio-political conditions that facilitated torture were can be found in the findings of the Canadian public inquiry into the role of Canadian officials in the deportation and detention of Maher Arar, published on 18 September 2006. Arar, a 34-year-old Canadian telecommunications consultant of Syrian origin, was detained in the USA on 26 September 2002 while changing flights on his journey from Tunisia back home to Canada. He was detained in the USA for 12 days and then on 8 October 2002 was taken from his cell in the middle of the night and flown on a private plane via other US airports and Rome, Italy, to Jordan, where he was beaten and then driven to Syria, where he was detained between 9 October 2002 and 5 October 2003. He was held incommunicado in inhumane detention conditions and tortured. He also heard other prisoners being tortured and screaming. His interrogators appear to have been working on information supplied by Canadian and US intelligence agencies. The findings of the Canadian public inquiry have indicated that much of the information provided by these agencies was inaccurate and had been improperly shared by Canadian police with their US counterparts. The inquiry concluded that 'there is nothing to indicate that Mr Arar committed any offence or that his activities constitute a threat to the security of Canada.' The inquiry also identified three other Canadian nationals of Arab origin who were detained, interrogated and tortured in Syria with the complicity of Canadian and other foreign intelligence agencies.

Another socio-political element that is currently giving rise to concern is the role of qualified professionals in the interrogation process. Where state-sponsored terrorism occurs, the torturer may have the assistance of other professionals who have forsaken their professional ethics in order to take part in dealing with the hated enemy. Medical doctors may be present to revive the victim of torture and nurses may be present to give injections.

A particular issue for the coalition of countries involved in prosecuting the 'war on terror' is the role of psychologists and psychiatrists in interrogating detainees. The controversy is unresolved, with different professional bodies taking different positions on the involvement of their members in interrogation. The clearest statement has been provided by the American Medical Association:

> Physicians must not conduct, directly participate in, or monitor an interrogation with an intent to intervene, because this undermines the physician's role as healer. (Levine 2007: 710)

Another strong statement has been issued by the American Psychiatric Association which holds that:

> No psychiatrist should participate directly in the interrogation of a person held in custody by military or civilian investigative or law enforcement authorities, whether in the United States or elsewhere. Direct participation includes being present in the interrogation room, asking or suggesting questions, or advising authorities on the use of specific techniques of interrogation with particular detainees. (American Psychiatric Association 2006)

More controversial is the position of the American Psychological Association (APA), which appears to be concerned about throwing the baby out with the bath water and does see a role for psychologists, providing it is consistent with the Association's Code of Ethics:

> Psychologists may serve in various national security-related roles, such as a consultant to an interrogation, in a manner that is consistent with the Ethics Code, and when doing so psychologists are mindful of factors unique to these roles and contexts that require special ethical consideration. (APA 2007)

Given that the controversy is linked to the legal ambiguity of places such as Guantánamo Bay, APA members are placed in a difficult position. The debate within the APA has been fuelled by the fact that six out of ten members of a presidential task force endorsed by the APA had ties with the military, four of them having been involved at Guantánamo Bay, at Abu Ghraib Prison, Iraq, or at detention facilities in Afghanistan. The report stated that psychologists could act as consultants to interrogations, but they must report any instances of torture or degrading treatment, and are forbidden to mix the roles of health-care provider and interrogation consultant.

The dilemma is that if psychologists and psychiatrists are excluded from providing advice on interrogations, the practice of interrogators may be crude, ineffective and violate basic human rights. Alternatively, some psychologists and psychiatrists may become so involved with the process that their advice leads to violations of basic human rights. The position of the British Psychological Society (BPS) is that their members are bound by a code of ethics that does not set out specific ethical guidelines on issues such as involvement in interrogation (BPS 2005). At the time of writing, the Royal College of Psychiatrists had yet to announce its policy.

Because of the secretive nature of these security-related interrogations and the closed nature of any military commissions or legal proceedings that follow, it is unlikely that the quality of the interrogation or the advice given by psychologists or psychiatrists will ever be open to critical examination. There therefore seems very little that can be done to monitor the role of these professionals and consider whether their advice is consistent with psychological principles held by the wider psychological or psychiatric communities. The easy option would be to follow the American Psychiatric Association and American Medical Association position and forbid participation in interrogation. A problem resulting from permitting participation is that the regulatory systems are so weak that there would be little control during the interrogation; no opportunity for independent evaluation of what took place; and, in the unlikely event of evidence of malpractice by a professional ever coming to public light, the disciplinary procedures of the various associations and societies would be a weak and ineffective means of sanction. We are therefore likely to see the continuing involvement of both psychologists and (outside the USA) psychiatrists in the interrogation of suspects with the risk that this political endorsement becomes another contextual factor that facilitates the moral disengagement of interrogators. Their practices will have been designed, and sanctioned, by powerful authority figures in the form of psychologists and psychiatrists.

Conclusion

In this chapter, we have critically examined utilitarian justifications for torture (or near torture) in the interrogation of suspects in order to gain evidence. We have concluded that utilitarian arguments do not provide a basis for the violation of customary international law and breaches of human rights. Yet we know that torture is pervasive, is practised in many countries of the world and that the emergence of the 'war on terror' has given a fillip to those who seek to justify its use (Amnesty International 2006: 1–47).

Who becomes a torturer and what processes can transform an ordinary human being so that he or she is able to inflict great cruelty on another human being can be described according to a set of social psychological processes. The fundamental attribution error reminds us that it is easy to judge the disapproved behaviour in terms of the personality of the individual concerned, in this case a torturer who must be evil, rather that the situational forces that shape the behaviour. Laboratory studies indicate that almost anyone could, under a well-known set of circumstances, become a torturer. Finally, we examined the current controversy regarding the role of psychiatrists and psychologists in interrogations in security-related contexts. We noted that the American Medical Association and American Psychiatric Association forbid their members to participate in or monitor an interrogation. The American Psychological Association, responding to a presidential task force report, does allow psychologists to act in various national security-related roles including as consultants in interrogation procedures, providing that their behaviour is consistent with the association's code of ethics. A similar position has been taken by the British Psychological Society. A problem for associations and societies permitting participation in interrogation is the absence of a regulatory regime. This problem is compounded by the closed and secretive nature of the processes for detention, interrogation and prosecution of those who are held in custody as suspects in the 'war on terror'.

References

Alter, J. (2001) 'Time to Think About Torture', *Newsweek*, 5 November.

American Psychiatric Association (2006) 'Psychiatric Participation in Interrogation of Detainees'. 21 May. Retrieved from http://www.psych.org/edu/otherres/libarchives/archives/200601.

American Psychololgical Association (APA) (2007) 'Reaffirmation of the American Psychological Asociation Position Against Torture and Other Cruel, Inhuman, or Degrading Treatment or Punishment and Its Application to Individuals Defined in the United States Code as "Enemy Combatants"'. Retrieved from iwww.apa.org/governance/resolutions/councilres0807.html.

Amnesty International (2006) *Amnesty International Report 2006: The State of the World's Human Rights.* London: Amnesty International, International Secretariat.

Arendt, H. (1963) *Eichmann in Jerusalem: A Report on the Banality of Evil.* London: Viking Press.

Bandura, A. (1990) 'Mechanisms of Moral Disengagement', in W. Reich (ed.), *Origins of Terrorism. Psychologies, Ideologies, Theologies, States of Mind.* New York: Cambridge University Press.

Bentham, J. (1997 [1777–9]) 'Of Torture' (previously unpublished manuscript) ed. by W.T. Twining and P.E. Twining in 'Bentham on Torture', *Northern Ireland Legal Quarterly*, 24: 307–56.

British Psychological Society (BPS) (2005) 'Declaration by the British Psychological Society Concerning Torture and Other Cruel, Inhuman or Degrading Treatment or Punishment', *The Psychologist*, 18: 190.

Chaffee, Z., Pollock, W.H. and Stern, C.S. (1931) 'The Third Degree: Report on Lawlessness in Law Enforcement', *National Commission on Law Observance and Enforcement*, vol IV, no. II. Washington, DC: Government Printing Office.

Danner, M. (2004) *Torture and Truth: America, Abu Ghraib and the War on Terror.* London: Granta.

Dershowitz, A. (2001) 'America Needs Torture Warrants', *Los Angeles Times*, 8 November.

Evans, D. and Morgan, R. (1998) *Preventing Torture: A Study of the European Convention for the Prevention of Torture and Inhuman or Degrading Treatment or Punishment.* Oxford: Clarendon Press.

Falconer, Lord (2006) 'The Role of Judges in a Modern Democracy'. Magna Carta Lecture, Sydney, Australia, 13 September.

Greenberg, K.L. (ed.) (2006) *The Torture Debate in America*. New York: Cambridge University Press.

Greenberg, K.J. and Dratel, J.L. (2004) *The Torture Papers: The Road to Abu Ghraib*. New York: Cambridge University Press.

Gudjonsson, G. (1996) 'Custodial Confinement, Interrogation and Coerced Confessions', in D. Forrest (ed.), *A Glimpse of Hell: Reports on Torture Worldwide*. London: Amnesty International, 36–45.

Huggins, M.K., Garitos-Fatouros, M. and Zimbardo, P.G. (2002) *Violence Workers. Police Torturers and Murderers Reconstruct Brazilian Atrocities*. Berkeley, CA: University of California Press.

Ignatieff, M. (2004a) *The Lesser Evil: Political Ethics in an Age of Terror*. Princeton, NJ: Princeton University Press.

Ignatieff, M. (2004b) 'Lesser Evils', *New York Times Magazine*, 2 May.

Kremnitzer, M. (1989) 'The Landau Commmission Report: Was the Security Service Subordinated to the Law, or the Law to the "Needs" of the Security Service?', *Israeli Law Review*, 24: 216–279.

Landau Commission (1987) *Report of the Commission of Inquiry into the Methods of Investigation of the General Security Service Regarding Hostile Terrorist Activity: Part One*. Jerusalem: Israeli Government.

Levine, M. (2007) 'Role of Physicians in Interrogations', *American Medical Association Journal of Ethics*, 9: 709–711.

Luban, D. (2006) 'Liberalism, Torture and the Ticking Bomb', in K.L. Greenberg (ed.), *The Torture Debate in America*. New York: Cambridge University Press, 35–83.

Morgan, R. (2000) 'The Utilitarian Justification of Torture: Denial, Desert and Disinformation', *Punishment and Society*, 2: 180–196.

Parker Report (1972) *Report of the Committee of Privy Councillors Appointed to Consider Authorised Procedures for the Interrogation of Persons Suspected of Terrorism* (Chairman Lord Parker), Cmnd 4981. London: HMSO.

Peters, E. (1996) *Torture*. Philadelphia: University of Pennsylvania Press.

Ratner, M. and Ray, E. (2004) *Guantánamo: What the World Should Know*. Moreton-in-the-Marsh: Arris.

Rose, D. (2004) *Guantánamo: America's War on Human Rights*. London: Faber.

Ross, L. (1977) 'The Intuitive Psychologist and His Shortcomings. Distortions in the Attribution Process', in L. Berkowitz (ed.), *Advances in Experimental Social Psychology*. New York: Academic Press.

Royal Commission (1981) *Report of the Royal Commission on Criminal Procedure*. London: HMSO.

Scarry, E. (1984) *The Body in Pain*. New York: Oxford University Press.

Steiner, J.M. and Fahrenbert, J. (2000) 'Authorisation and Social Status of Former Members of the Waffen-SS and SS of the Wehrmacht: An Extension and Reanalysis of the Study Published in 1970', *Kölner Zeitschrift für Soziologie und Sozialpsychologie*, 52: 329–348.

Zimbardo, P.G. (1970) 'The Human Choice: Individuation, Reason, and Order Versus Deindividuation, Impulse and Chaos', in W.J. Arnold and D. Levine (eds), *1969 Nebraska Symposium on Motivation.* Lincoln, NE: University of Nebraska Press.

Zimbardo, P.G., Haney, C., Banks, W.C. and Jaffe, D. (1973) 'The Mind is a Formidable Jailer: A Pirandellian Prison', *New York Times Magazine*, 8 April, 38ff.

Chapter 8

Investigative interviewing as a therapeutic jurisprudential approach

Ulf Holmberg

The changing nature of the police interview

Previous research indicates that crime victims' willingness to participate in the legal process largely depends on how they perceive the legal procedure and its actors (Doerner and Lab 1998; Shepherd *et al.* 1999; Yuille *et al.* 1999; Holmberg 2004). Similarly, analyses of recorded police interviews with suspects also indicate that suspects' perceptions of their interviewing officers and the interview itself may affect suspects' willingness to participate in the interview process (Baldwin 1992, 1993; Moston and Engelberg 1993; Moston and Stephenson 1993; Stephenson and Moston 1993; Williamson 1993; Holmberg and Christianson 2002; Kebbell *et al.* 2006). Indeed, fundamental to the success of a crime investigation is the information the police gather from technical and human sources, including witnesses, victims and suspects. The collected information must help to describe what and when a crime occurred, how the crime was accomplished, and why the crime was perpetrated. Without this information, crime victims' and suspects' human rights cannot be safeguarded, the suspected person cannot be fairly prosecuted, the involved people cannot be completely rehabilitated, and the investigation will most likely be dropped. From technical evidence, the investigator may find an important conclusion in the sequence of the crime event, but such technical evidence does not tell the whole story. For example, in the case of the rape and murder of a six-year-old girl named Helene in Sweden, the forensic laboratory concluded that the DNA of the sperm found in the little girl came from the suspect. The suspect denied all allegations, denied any contact with Helene, and did not say anything about how his sperm could be found in the young girl's body. The suspect was convicted of kidnapping the girl, rape and murder only on technical evidence. To describe the criminal act, the consequences of the crime and the intent of the perpetrator, the crime investigation needs accurate descriptions from the people involved, and those who witness the act.

A good police interview is conducted in the framework of the law, is governed by the interview goal, and is influenced by facilitating factors that may affect the elicited report (Yuille *et al.* 1999). In this respect, the characteristics of the interviewer are a dimension that is likely to affect the outcome. Seeing the importance of the police interview, its substance, and significance for the legal process, it is important to examine what interview methods police officers actually use. It is also important to study *how* crime victims, witnesses, and suspects perceive these police interviews as well as under what circumstances these interviewees feel that they have been given a mental space that facilitates an exhaustive narration. From this research, it is most important to take a further step and implement the outcomes into the training of investigative interviewers.

The present chapter discusses the variation of police interviews, from interrogation to investigative interviewing from a therapeutic jurisprudential perspective. By way of introduction, a historical review of interrogation and its manuals is presented. Next, current research on police interview studies is described, and future directions with a therapeutic jurisprudential approach of investigative interviewing are discussed.

From coercion to deception

From antiquity to the first half of the twentieth century, legal actors have used acts of cruelty to discover criminal facts. Suspects have tried to hide their knowledge by silence or lies, and, historically, the method chosen to obtain confessions has been the use of physical and mental force. Münsterberg (1908/1923) argued that threats and torture have been used all over the world and for thousands of years to force suspects to confess. The term 'third degree' was introduced in 1900 to define harsh questioning of a prisoner through mental or physical torture to extract a confession (*Merriam-Webster* 2004). From the first decades of the twentieth century, Münsterberg (1908/1923) described that the 'third degree' – through use of the dazzling light, the cold-water hose and the secret blow – was still being used by the police. Contemporary public opinion was firmly against such methods, and the public were convinced that the 'third degree' was ineffective in bringing out the real truth from suspects. Nevertheless, up to the early 1930s and perhaps longer, the police interview tactic was generally marked by coercion (Leo 1992, 1996).

In Sweden, Hassler (1930) stated that the form of the police interview should be inquisitorial, marked by questions from the police interviewer. The suspect should, in the absence of inflicted pain, threat or deceit, be induced to a voluntary confession. Peixoto (1934) pronounced, from a Brazilian view, that the 'third degree' was inquisitorial and of doubtful value. In the 1930s and 1940s, the use of coercive interviewing methods began to decline (Leo 1992, 1996). Leche and Hagelberg (1945) advised police officers to try to win the interviewee's trust and let the interviewee provide a continuous narration before the police officer began to ask open-ended questions. Leche and Hagelberg also emphasised the necessity for police officers to understand people's emotions and reactions, to have knowledge about the function of human memory, and to understand how a statement could be affected by different circumstances. In order to secure the truth and to judge a witness's veracity, Gerbert (1954) stressed the need to understand a witness's personality. Gerbert stated that some tense witnesses, who appeared to be guilty, were instead reacting to the interview, and these witnesses became relaxed only when they were assured that the interview would be conducted in a fair and impartial way.

In the 1960s, deceptive techniques, tactics and stratagems emerged within the realm of the police interrogation. These methods were based on an uncritical and subjective use of psychological knowledge. One such manual that suggests psychological tactics and methods with respect to the interrogation of suspects is that of the Reid technique by Inbau *et al.* (2001). This manual uses a consciously persuasive tactic to create a conversational rapport in order to win the suspect's trust and obtain the confession. That is, the interrogator leads the suspect into an atmosphere of confidence, and shows sympathy and understanding for the actual criminal behaviour. The interrogator then breaks down the suspect's resistance gradually, sells the advantage of a confession, and cajoles the suspect to a point where close rapport is established. Then, the interrogator puts the suspect in the position of choosing between two possible positions, both of which are incriminating. Whatever alternative the suspect chooses, it will lead to an incriminating confession.

According to the Reid technique, the sole purpose of the interrogation appears to be to obtain a confession, and for some suspects it means to be persuaded to tell the truth (Buckley 2006). Moreover, when the interrogator believes that the suspect has not revealed the truth, the suspect is ready to be interrogated. This phase obliges the interrogator to provide at least 95 per cent of the conversation and not to ask any questions. Weinberg (2002) argues that if the interrogator asks questions, it will reveal uncertainty about the guilt of the suspect, which is not regarded as a good strategy. In several manuals, the interrogation phase is usually seen as a confrontational, confession-seeking process. For example, Benson (2000), Inbau *et al.* (2001) and Starrett (1998) suggest methods which are highly questionable or actually illegal under international law. These are mainly methods involving trickery and/or deceit, but some manuals – for example, Butterfield (2002) advocate methods very close to actual torture, as defined by the UN Universal Declaration of Human Rights Art 5 (UN General Assembly 1948). When coercive interrogation techniques, trickery and deceit are applied by the interrogator, other legal conflicts arise with the principles of voluntariness and the presumption of innocence in the UN covenant on Civil and Political Rights (UN General Assembly 1966 art. 14:2).

If the initial investigation concludes that the suspect is guilty, then the suspect who denies his or her guilt during the interrogation will naturally be considered a liar. The creators of the Reid technique claim that interviewers can be trained to detect lies at an 85 per cent level of accuracy, which exceeds the success rate found in any lie-detection experiment in published research (Kassin 2006). Under circumstances where interrogators work in line with the Reid technique and other similar methods, it is likely that the interrogator will see no need to consider any further the suspect's credibility, and this may signify a miscarriage of justice. The confession-seeking behaviour of legal actors (e.g. a police officer or a prosecutor) may be based on beliefs and presumptions that affect how he or she acts when gathering information from suspects.

Attitudes, beliefs and presumptions

Interviewers' attitudes, beliefs and presumptions may seriously influence the way they actually conduct the interview. Eagly and Chaiken (1998) defined an attitude as a psychological tendency that expresses an evaluation, through some degree of favour or disfavour, of a certain entity. A person is biased towards favourable or unfavourable responses depending on how an attitude object (e.g. an interviewee, an interviewer, or the interview itself) is evaluated, and this may affect the way an interviewer behaves in an interview. Yuille *et al.* (1999) stressed that police interviews should be conducted in a manner that minimises any negative impact on the interviewee, both personally and emotionally. Contrary to Yuille *et al.* but in line with several interrogation manuals, innocent people may be interrogated without evidence of their involvement, but solely on the basis of a police hunch (Kassin 2006). This means that the interrogation is a *guilt-presumptive process* in which biases affect police officers' behaviour, instead of an objective information-gathering process. Such biases may be based on a strong prior presumption of the guilt of the suspect that may influence a police officer's interaction with a suspect, explaining why police officers adopt a confession-seeking interrogating approach (Mortimer and Shepherd 2000). Psychological research has found that when people have formed a belief they become selective when seeking and interpreting new information (e.g. Kassin *et al.* 2003). In this distorted, *selective process*, people strive for information to verify their belief. This process of cognitive *confirmation bias* may make a police officer's beliefs resistant to change, even in the presence of contradictory facts (Nickerson 1998). Innes (2002) argued that during crime investigations police officers may be overwhelmed by the amount of evidence in a case, leading them not to search for new facts that might reveal the whole truth, but instead an officer may search for an amount of evidence that is sufficient to construct a satisfying *internal representation* of the criminal event, and in such a construction, gaps (without evidence) may be filled by imagination and conjecture to fashion a coherent story. Such a construction may feed a presumption of what a victim has been through as well as a suspect's guilt, which in turn may shape the police officer's interviewing behaviour. Kassin *et al.* (2003) conducted an experiment which used students as interrogators to test the hypothesis that guilt presumption affects interviewers' behaviour. This study showed that when interviewers adopted a presumption of guilt rather than innocence, they asked more guilt-oriented questions, and used more techniques and pressure to elicit a confession. Attitudes, beliefs and presumptions may also explain why some police officers act in a statement-taking way (Clarke and Milne 2001) instead of being open-minded when interviewing crime victims. Statement-taking seems to be more automatic than interviewing, which entails a controlled process based on knowledge, knowledge that might be representative of of a strong belief and a presumption. Thus, attitudes, beliefs and presumption may exist in interviews with crime victims as well as in interviews with suspects. The following extract is from an actual victim and represents her perception of the interview process. Further, it shows an example of a police officer's belief or presumption about the development of a rape:

> I don't think he knew how horrible I felt. Sometimes I wondered why I told him about it at all, I guess I'm still wondering. I'm full of big holes and scars. The more we rooted and poked in it, the worse I felt. (Holmberg 1994: 37)

The next quotation comes from a child molester and indicates an interviewer's presumption of guilt:

> He didn't ask a question, in fact, once he asked me, 'Why do you think she [the child] acts like this.' He laid it down, he said to me like this, 'What you have done here', he said, 'that's serious'. (Holmberg 1996: 34)

Obviously, beliefs and preconceived presumptions may affect interviewers' behaviour, in interviews with both crime victims and suspects. One risk of such presumptive behaviour in interviews with crime victims may be that the victim does not have the strength to argue against such opinions, and this in turn may lead to a withdrawal from the case, and result in bad and antitherapeutic feelings. A risk with guilt-presumptive interviews with a suspect, as Zimbardo already in 1967 warned against, is false confessions. This may also lead to bad, antitherapeutic feelings and, not least, miscarriages of justice.

False confession

Several researchers have found a high risk in using persuasive interview techniques, such as Inbau *et al.* (2001) recommended, because they may generate false confessions (e.g. Münsterberg 1908/1923; Zimbardo 1967; Gudjonsson 1992, 1994, 2003; Kassin 2005). Gudjonsson (2003) defined three types of false confession: voluntary, coerced-internalised and coerced-compliant. The voluntary false confession may emanate from an internal pressure, a psychological need to confess falsely to a crime. For example, more than a hundred persons in Sweden were investigated after falsely confessing to the murder of former Prime Minister Olof Palme in 1986 (Detective Superintendent Per-Olof Palmgren, personal communication).

The coerced-internalised false confession refers to a situation in which suspects come to believe, through a police interview, that they have committed a crime. Importantly, in such cases, suspects may have no memories of the alleged event through, for example, drink or drugs, and this lack of memory may sometimes make them more likely to confabulate. In major investigations, suspects may be exposed to several long interviews and they may start to doubt their own memory. Such a situation may occur without any tricks, deceit or pressure from the police officer. The person is cooperative, tries to remember, and without a memory may come to believe that he or she must have committed the crime. By the nature of the questions from the police officers, false memories may be implemented (Nolde *et al*. 1998; Loftus 2003; Steffens and Mecklenbräuker 2007). The creation of false memories occurs because suspects doubt their own autobiographical memory and are in a heightened state of suggestibility. They are cooperative, may be socially isolated and put trust in the police officer who, deliberately or unintentionally, offers hints and cues that lead to false memories. The source of the memory becomes confused, reality is distorted, and there is a fertile base for internalised false confession is created.

A coerced-compliant false confession mirrors a situation in which a person falsely confesses to a crime for some instrumental gain, because of the demands and pressures expressed by the police interviewer. In such a situation, the suspect gives in to explicit coercion in the expectation of receiving some kind of immediate instrumental gain or favour (Gudjonsson 2003; Kassin and Gudjonsson 2004). The motive of a coerced-compliant false confession may be to avoid a threatening situation from which the confessor is desperate to escape. The confessor is completely aware of his or her innocence, and the confession is an act of compliance. An example of this kind of false confession is the case of the Central Park jogger in which five innocent boys confessed to a brutal assault and rape because they believed that they would be released after they had confessed (Kassin 2005). Thus, false confessions may depend on confession-seeking procedures and may appear in different circumstances, a notion that Münsterberg (1908/1925) already articulated in the early days of the past century.

From interrogation to investigative interviewing

The psychologist Dr Eric Shepherd trained police officers of the London Metropolitan Police in communication skills in the early 1980s. Shepherd developed a script for managing any conversation with any person a police officer would be likely to meet. In the context of this training, Shepherd coined the term *conversation management* (CM), which means that a police officer must be aware of and manage the communicative interaction, both verbally and non-verbally (Milne and Bull 1999). CM comprises three phases: (i) the pre-, (ii) the within-, and (iii) the post-interview behaviour phases. The pre-interview phase focuses on how to plan and prepare the forthcoming interview, and the post-interview phase comprises how to evaluate the performed interview. This chapter concerns the within-interview phase, in which the interviewer is encouraged to pay attention to four subphases: greeting, explanation, mutual activity, and closure, abbreviated as GEMAC (Milne and Bull 1999). The *greeting phase* concerns an appropriate introduction of the interviewer, which means establishing rapport. In the *explanation phase*, the interviewer must set out the aims and objectives of the interview, and develop the interview further. *Mutual activity* concerns the elicitation of narration from the interviewee and subsequent questions from the interviewer. *Closure* is the important phase in which the interviewer should create a positive end to the interview, aiming at mutual satisfaction with the content and performance of the session. CM was consistent with the Police and Criminal Evidence Act (PACE) introduced in 1984 in England and Wales, which can be seen as a reaction, by the public, researchers and, to some extent, the police, to criticism of the existing methods used to interrogate suspects (Bull 2000).

In the early 1980s, when Shepherd developed CM in the UK, Fisher and Geiselman (1992) developed the *cognitive interview* (CI) in the USA as a memory-enhancing technique. Studying how police officers conduct their interviews with crime victims and witnesses, Fisher and Geiselman revealed that many officers had no formal training in this area and conducted interviews according to their intuition. The researchers revealed that the most salient features of victim and witness interviews showed a deficiency in the interview structure: almost all questions were direct and no memory-enhancing assistance was given. Universally, the interviewers erroneously interrupted the interviewees, asked too many direct and short-answer questions, and sequenced questions inappropriately.

The first version of CI was based purely on memory theory, but soon Fisher and Geiselman (1992) realised the need to include aspects of social psychology and revised the original CI. The revised version, the enhanced cognitive interview (ECI) comprises several components, and the first, introduction, suggests that the interviewer encourage the interviewee to participate actively in the interview. In this phase, the interviewer develops a rapport with the interviewee by personalising the interview, expressing empathy, and listening actively. This phase also comprises an anxiety-reduction component wherein the interviewer conveys his or her interest in maintaining the interviewee's confidence. The interviewer instructs and encourages the interviewee to describe everything, even details and trivialities, but not to guess. The next phase comprises a *reinstatement of the context of the event.* The reason for reinstating the context is based on the knowledge that human beings remember more when they are in the same state or environment as when the event was encoded (Christianson 1992a, 1992b; Baddeley 1998). By open-ended questions, the interviewer encourages interviewees to search through their memory of the event and to give a *free narration* of what comes to mind. It is important not to interrupt interviewees in their narration. When the memory is drained, the interviewee is instructed to give *the report in a different order*, and thereafter *change perspective* by instructions in an attempt to promote further retrieval. The interviewer also uses witness-compatible questioning to probe certain facts relevant to the investigation. At the end of the interview, *the interviewer reviews what has been reported*, allowing the interviewee to check that what has been reported has also been correctly understood. In the *closure* phase, the interviewer collects background information, extending the functional life of the interview because the interviewee will continue to think about the crime event, and, finally, tries to create a positive last impression.

With the aim of maximising disclosures from crime victims, Shepherd *et al.* (1999) elaborated the CI further, and incorporated aspects from cognitive-behaviour therapy into the CI. The technique, termed *spaced cognitive interview* (SCI), aimed to help crime victims in the event of anxiety-hindered narration. The purpose of SCI is to reduce the crime victim's anxiety by prolonged exposure (PE), which means mental re-experiences of the crime event. Mental re-experience through narratives reduces anxiety originating from traumatic experiences (Pennebaker 1997). Shepherd *et al.* (1999) described a case in which a young woman had been traumatised by an attempted rape. She felt strongly that the man should be stopped, but she did not feel robust enough to tell the police. After two SCI sessions, the young woman was able to give a statement to the police. A police officer is often the first person a traumatised crime victim meets, and Shepherd *et al.* argued that police officers conducting SCI are 'in a unique position to set in train a healing, expressive process' (1999: 139). The authors emphasised that SCI should take place as soon as possible after a crime event has occurred, and in ensuing weeks subsequent SCI sessions should follow. Shepherd *et al.* also argued that prolonged interviews are memory enhancing. Indeed, Brock *et al.* (1999) revealed the information-gathering benefits of conducting multiple interviews (i.e. CI). that comprise more information and more correct information than standard interviews.

Regarding the CI with suspects, Fisher and Perez (2007) have expanded its use to include interviews with cooperative suspects in which the importance of rapport building is emphasised as well as the use of suspect-compatible questioning. Suspect-compatible questioning relates to the suspect's unique mental representation of the crime event, which may vary from focus on the victim to focus on the surroundings. Interviewers are reminded to be sensitive to the suspect's current active mental image. That means that they may have to wait to a later part of the interview to ask investigative relevant details about certain parts of the crime event.

The advent of PACE encouraged further research (e.g. Baldwin 1992) on police interviewing techniques in England and Wales, and this in turn led to investigative interviewing being developed in the early 1990s. The term *interrogation* gave way to 'investigative interviewing' (Milne and Bull 2003), which emphasised and promoted the importance of changing attitudes to the police interview. The PACE was at the heart of the new PEACE model of interviewing, in which the mnemonic 'PEACE' denotes *planning and preparation*; *engage and explain*; *account, clarification and challenge*; *closure*; and *evaluation*, which are all seen as important phases in a good interview (Milne and Bull 1999, 2003; Bull 2000; Bull and Milne 2004). First, interviewers are obliged to plan and prepare themselves carefully before the interview. *Planning and preparation* not only includes reading the case file and being familiar with the facts, but it also encourages police officers to seek knowledge about the individual to be interviewed, in particular, aspects that might complicate or facilitate the interview (e.g. vulnerabilities, religious and cultural aspects, addiction, physical and environmental circumstances). *Engage and explain* is the first phase in the actual interview, in which interviewers inform the suspects about the allegation, their rights, and the procedure to be followed in the interview. Here, it is also most important for interviewers to build rapport, engage suspects, and try to motivate them to provide their perspective on the key events. The aim of this introduction to the interview is to provide suspects with a 'route map' for a fair and just interview of which they are going to be a part. In the phase of *account, clarification and challenge*, suspects are invited to give their account of what happened during the event in question. Interviewers then ask questions about aspects of the suspect's account that need to be clarified and challenge any inconsistencies. The *closure* phase involves interviewers summing up what has been said and checking with suspects that everything has been correctly understood. It is also important to inform suspects, as far as possible, about the next steps in the investigation, and bring the interview to an end on a positive note. A positive closure may prepare the way for a further interview. The final phase of the PEACE model, *evaluation*, requires officers to evaluate the facts revealed in the interview and relate these to pre-existing information and to the aims of the interview. Additionally, is it important for interviewers to evaluate how they have conducted the interview and reflect on how the interview could have been improved. The aim of the PEACE model is to obtain correct and reliable evidence and to discover the truth in a crime investigation. This model emphasises ethical principles, which differentiate this method from other coercive and persuasive approaches to interviewing suspects described earlier. Thus, the key to appropriate behaviour in the within-interview phases of investigative interviewing seems to be acting in a fair way, acting according to ethical principles, and establishing rapport.

Rapport building, a humanitarian approach

Rapport can determine whether an interview will fail or succeed. Rapport certainly makes it easier for a crime victim to provide information in a police interview, as exemplified by this female rape victim's experience of her police interviewer (Holmberg 1994):

> He got me to describe and talk about the details in such an intimate way, like you wouldn't even do with your best friend. It didn't seem like he was being nosy either. He did it for my sake because it was necessary for me, not just for the investigation. (p. 36)

From such a statement, it can be assumed that this police interview signified rapport, which probably contributed to the victim's willingness to narrate the crime event. Thus, establishing rapport is essential to the police interview (Shepherd 1991; Fisher and Geiselman 1992; Kebbell *et al.* 1999; Milne and Bull 1999; Shepherd and Milne 1999; Shepherd *et al.* 1999). Rapport may also 'open doors' and have therapeutic effects. On the other hand, under threatening conditions attitude responses appear automatic (Bargh 1999; Chen and Bargh 1999; Todorov and Bargh 2002), being antitherapeutic and may even 'shut doors', as this convicted rapist's report of his police interview indicates (Holmberg 1996):

> It was easier for me to talk to people who acted properly because people who interview people, they should not punish you, but they can do so just by their way of talking, showing their hate for me as a human being, and at that moment you turn around and return their hate. (p. 35)

This quotation indicates that when the rapist perceived attitudes of being properly treated, the attitude response functioned automatically by making it easy for him to talk; that is, this was a therapeutic way to be interviewed. The quotation also indicates an antitherapeutic experience; when a person perceives an interview marked by hate, the attitude response may function automatically, causing that person to show avoidance and in turn return the hate (Wegner and Bargh 1998; Bargh 1999; Chen and Bargh 1999; Todorov and Bargh 2002).

Fisher and Geiselman (1992) stressed that rapport is established by personalising the interview and showing empathy, while Milne and Bull (1999) emphasised attention and active listening as necessities for rapport building. Collins *et al.* (2002) investigated the results of the three interviewer-attitude conditions, (i) rapport, (ii) abrupt, and (iii) neutral. In the rapport condition, the interviewer showed a gentle, relaxed and friendly approach, and used the interviewee's name. In the abrupt condition, the interviewer spoke in a staccato and harsh tone, did not refer to the interviewee by name, and showed a stiff body posture and indifference. The neutral approach implied that interviewers should be as neutral as they can possibly be in all behavioural aspects. The results showed that participants clearly recognised the rapport approach and felt that better rapport had been established than in the other conditions. In the rapport condition compared to the abrupt and neutral approaches, the interviewees provided more correct items from the dramatic videoclip all participants had previously seen. Additionally, there was no increase in incorrect information in the rapport condition. One may see the neutral approach in the Collins *et al.* study as congruent with the suppression condition in the study by Butler *et al.* (2003), in which the participants saw a film and were subsequently asked to discuss the film in dyads. During the discussions, one subject in each dyad from the so-called suppression group was instructed, via headphones, to suppress feelings and not show any emotion. The control group did not receive such instructions. The results showed that suppressors reacted with an increase in blood pressure, and felt less rapport during the conversation than did the controls. The partners of suppressors liked their partners less in comparison with controls, and they were uninterested in ever speaking with them again. Butler *et al.* (2003) concluded that, at least in some contexts, suppressing emotions disrupts communication and is obstructive to efforts of establishing social bonds.

Ridgeway (2000) argued that rapport exists inherently in a communicative process that comprises ethical parameters. Tickle-Degnen and Rosenthal (1990) offered a conceptualisation of rapport as a construct of non-verbal prototypical components that do not fall into mutually exclusive categories. These components are attentiveness, positivity and coordination, the relative weight of which changes according to the individual's experience of changing levels of rapport in the development of a relationship. From an insider perspective, attention involves feelings of mutual interest and focus, positivity comprises feelings of friendliness and warmth, and coordination involves balance and harmony (Hendrick 1990). Thus, Hendrick stressed that the insider's perspective concerns the phenomenology of feelings that participants perceive in an interaction. Patterson (1990) questioned how rapport can be distinguished from other constructs, such as empathy, and Tickle-Degnen and Rosenthal (1990) declared that rapport is an intrinsic interactional phenomenon of mutual feelings. Without such feelings, genuine rapport cannot exist.

Thus, when rapport is established, interviewees provide more correct information than they do without rapport, and in the latter condition, partners react with dislike and show reluctance to create social bonds. This perspective indicates that attitudes may have an automatic function in rapport building. Researchers have thus pointed out the need for research regarding the relationship between attitudes and the police interview (LeDoux and Hazelwood 1985; Stephenson and Moston 1994; Sear and Stephenson 1997). Many researchers have, however, emphasised the importance of rapport building in police interviews (Shepherd 1991; Fisher and Geiselman 1992; Kebbell *et al.* 1999; Milne and Bull 1999, 2003; Shepherd and Milne 1999; Shepherd *et al.* 1999; Holmberg and Christianson 2002; Holmberg 2004). Contrary to what researchers suggest, Pearse and Gudjonsson (1996) observed 161 recorded police interviews with suspects and found an initial rapport-building process in only 3 per cent of these interviews. Nevertheless, a humanitarian interviewing style promotes rapport building through its underlying notions of empathy and a personalising approach, which Fisher and Geiselman (1992) stressed as rapport facilitating. Ridgeway (2000) argued that rapport is built on ethical parameters, and suggesting that a humanitarian style mirrors such ethical parameters.

A humanitarian interviewing style was identified by Holmberg and Christianson (2002) and Holmberg (2004). Written interviews with 83 convicted murderers and sexual offenders (Holmberg and Christianson 2002) and 178 crime victims of rape or aggravated assault (Holmberg 2004) revealed, through principal components analyses, that these interviewees perceived their police interviews as being either *dominant* or *humanitarian* experiences. In the dominant experience, these interviewees perceived their interviewers as impatient, rushing, aggressive, brusque, nonchalant, unfriendly, deprecating and condemning. In the humanitarian experience, the interviewees characterised their interviewers as cooperative, accommodating, positive, empathic, helpful and engaging. Additionally, Holmberg and Christianson (2002) found, by logistic regression analysis, a significant positive relation between the humanitarian interviewing style and the offenders' admissions of crime, while there was a weak, non-significant relation between a dominant approach and the offenders' denials of crime. According to the sample, the odds of admissions were between 1.62 and 6.29 times greater when participants perceived humanitarian attitudes than for those who were met with dominance. Furthermore, in the study about crime victims' experiences of police interviews, Holmberg (2004) found that 51 per cent of the victims provided all information remembered, and consequently, 49 per cent consciously omitted information about the crime event. A logistic regression analysis showed that it was 60 per cent more likely that crime victims who perceived a humanitarian interview would provide all information remembered compared with those who experienced a dominant interviewing style. In fact, it was 30 per cent less likely that crime victims who perceived a dominant interviewing approach would provide all information remembered.

Moreover, Tickle-Degnen and Rosenthal (1990) described rapport as prototypical components comprising attentiveness, positivity and coordination. Hendrick (1990) viewed these components as feelings of mutual interest and focus (attention), feelings of friendliness and warmth (positivity), and balance and harmony (coordination). The humanitarian interviewing style suggests the advantages of operationalising rapport from an insider perspective. Showing personal interest, creating personal conversation, and being helpful in the humanitarian interviewing style mirrors the feelings of interest and focus in the attention component of rapport (cf. the quotation above). Friendliness and warmth in the rapport component positivity are in line with positive attitude and empathy in the humanitarian interviewing style. The coordination component of rapport, with feelings of balance and harmony, is in line with cooperative and accommodating behaviour in the humanitarian interviewing approach. Cooperation needs balance; otherwise, communication in the interview will be more one-way, and harmony presupposes a certain amount of accommodating behaviour. Thus, the humanitarian interviewing style offers, from an insider perspective, an operationalisation of rapport as an intrinsic interactional phenomenon with mutual feelings that, according to Tickle-Degnen and Rosenthal (1999), distinguish rapport from other constructs (e.g. empathy).

The humanitarian interview attitude promotes rapport, and may automatically serve as an instrumental or adjustment function in the sense that the interviewee provides all available information in the interview, and this is supported by the research of Collins *et al.* (2002) and Butler *et al.* (2003). Additionally, Benneworth (2003) demonstrated, in line with the humanitarian approach, that a police officer who surrenders the floor by using open-ended questions about relationships and assists the suspect in re-creating an emotional history facilitates admission. Such an approach enhances the individual's prospects for rehabilitation and psychological well-being, in line with therapeutic jurisprudential practice (Wexler 1996a, 1996b, 2000; Winick 2000; Petrucci *et al.* 2003).

Therapeutic jurisprudence

Therapeutic jurisprudence (TJ) is a growing movement within the philosophy of law and within the legal and judicial practice areas. Its roots can be seen as anchored to the American legal realism developed in the first half of the twentieth century. Already in 1908,

Roscoe Pound, a Harvard jurist, criticised the existing jurisprudence, which he called a mechanical jurisprudence (MJ) that conceptualised the law as an autonomous discipline (Finkelman and Grisso 1996). Pound proclaimed that MJ 'lived' its own sovereign life and that the consequences of a crime were only seen in legal terms. Sociological jurisprudence (Finkelman and Grisso 1996; Dow 2000) then developed as a reaction against MJ. Sharing much with sociological jurisprudence, TJ focuses on human problems and conflicts and urges police officers, prosecutors and other legal actors to understand that conflicts produce social and psychological effects on the individuals involved. TJ sees the law and its procedures as therapeutic agents because the law and its execution (e.g. an investigative interview) often generate therapeutic or antitherapeutic consequences (Petrucci *et al.* 2003). In the late 1980s, Professor David Wexler and Professor Bruce Winick founded TJ based on mental health law. By this perspective, the law and the execution of legal procedures came to be seen in the context of the behavioural sciences (Petrucci *et al.* 2003).

The purpose of TJ is to execute legal procedures such that they promote the social and psychological well-being of the individual involved in a juridical action (Wexler 1996b). The idea is that legal actors can use theories and empirical knowledge from the behavioural sciences to influence the practice of the law. In this way, jurisprudence may be seen as a therapeutic tool to promote psychological well-being in the legal practice.

Police officers may also mistakenly interview interviewees in a dominant, antitherapeutic, counter-productive way, and may awaken their avoidance and withdrawals. Such avoidance and withdrawal needs to be treated through *meta-communication*, that is, to communicate about the communication, so that hindrances may be identified and resolved. In this way, the police interviewer, and the interviewee may be aware of their own and each other's cognitions and meta-cognitive experiences that are based on misperceptions, misinterpretations and neglected needs (Salonen *et al.* 2005). The meta-communicative analysis may reveal the interviewee's need to talk about the crime event. By talking about hindrances and needs, the investigator may effect a second-order change of the problem (Watzlawick *et al.* 1974), after which interviewees may express their view of what happened. An investigator's failure to make such an effort may contribute to more persistent resistance and problem avoidance by the interviewee.

Thus, criminal behaviour and subsequent police interviews relate not only to legal issues, but also to social and psychological aspects, as described by TJ (Finkelman and Grisso 1996; Wexler 1996a). TJ and the humanitarian approach, as revealed by Holmberg and Christiansoon (2002) and Holmberg (2004), both promote the physiological and psychological well-being of the individual involved in the juridical action. This may be explained by the fact that both have an interest in treating all parties in the legal process as human beings by recognising their behaviour and needs (Wexler 1996b). In this perspective, all interviewees are included: victims, witnesses, suspects, police officers, prosecutors, and anyone in the process. Additionally, TJ and the humanitarian approach provide a problem-oriented approach comparable to ethical interviewing (EI) (Shepherd 1991) and cognitive interviewing (Fisher and Geiselman 1992; Fisher and Perez 2007). Shepherd argued that the EI approach lends itself to professional investigation. This approach rests on ethical principles, signifying that individuals show respect for and treat each other as equals with the same right to dignity, self-determination, and free choice. It also emphasises empathy, which means people treating each other from the perspective of mutual understanding, signifying a therapeutic demeanour.

Contrary to the perspective of mutual understanding is the dominant, which is considered antitherapeutic because it may hinder an interviewee's ability to re-create the context of an event (Christianson 1992a; Fisher and Geiselman 1992; Fisher 1995; Baddeley 1998). Interviewing a suspect in the humanitarian style promotes rapport and therefore allows the interviewee to provide information (Collins et al. 2002; Butler et al. 2003). The humanitarian approach enhances the individual's prospects for rehabilitation and psychological well-being, and this is in line with TJ (Wexler 1996a, 1996b, 2000; Winick 2000; Petrucci et al. 2003).

Psychological well-being and a sense of coherence

The 'meaning of life' is a multi-dimensional construct of people's perception of their life, and it is positively correlated with well-being and can be empirically measured (Auhagen 2000). Zika and Chamberlain (1992) and Debats et al. (1995) have studied the meaning of life with several measures and with combinations of qualitative and quantitative methods. The research results show that the meaning of life is mainly positively associated with psychological well-being, and Debats et al. (1995) suggest a salutogenic approach in studies of mental health. Antonovsky's construct, 'sense of coherence' (SOC), based on a salutogenic perspective, offers an appropriate way to define and an instrument to measure the meaning of life and psychological well-being (Auhagen 2000). Congruent with Auhagen, Gana (2001) argues that SOC measures an individual's well-being and coping capacity. Gana studied 193 adults and showed that an individual's adverse and stressful experiences had no direct effect on psychological well-being but did so indirectly by a mediator, the SOC. Gana concluded that the effects of stressful events on psychological well-being are buffered in the SOC, which Antonovsky (1984, 1987) postulated as a global orientation.

Comprehensibility, manageability, and *meaningfulness* are the components that construct the SOC (Antonovsky 1984). The first, the cognitive component comprehensibility, refers to the degree to which individuals perceive information, about themselves and the social environment, as structured, predicable and comprehensible. The second instrumental component, manageability, refers to whether individuals perceive their personal and social resources as sufficient to cope with demands posed by internal and external stimuli. The third motivational component, meaningfulness, is the emotional counterpart of comprehensibility; it refers to how individuals feel that their lives make sense emotionally and to the extent that they perceive stressful experiences as requiring them to invest time, energy and effort. According to a person's world-view, the SOC is relatively stable over time. However, traumatic events often change how individuals perceive their life and, consequently, also change their SOC (Schneider *et al.* 2000; Snekkevik *et al.* 2003). Such changes become more prominent after severe multiple traumas. Moreover, Snekkevik *et al.* also found that low SOC was associated with psychological distress, anxiety and depression. On the other hand, Pallant and Lae (2002) showed that the other end of the scale, a high SOC, relates to lower scores on perceived stress and negative affectivity and to higher scores on positive affectivity and life satisfaction. Furthermore, Pallant and Lae have found that the short, 13-item form of the SOC (see Antonovsky 1987) has high reliability, construct validity and incremental validity and is useful for well-being measures. Thus, the measure of sense of coherence seems to be an appropriate instrument to measure the psychological well-being in TJ.

Crime, investigative interviewing and psychological well-being

If we rely upon TJ and psychological well-being, will suspects as well as crime victims differ in their sense of coherence depending on experiences of a crime and how they perceived their police interviews? First, murderers and sexual offenders with experiences of maltreatment and abuse in childhood have shown lower psychological well-being in terms of sense of coherence than murderers and sexual offenders without such experiences (Holmberg *et al.* 2007). The authors also show that, with control for childhood maltreatment, offenders who experience a humanitarian police interview and may have feelings of being highly respected were associated with a significantly higher SOC. Those who felt themselves less respected showed a lower SOC. Moreover, Holmberg *et al.* also report that murderers and sexual offenders who admit their crime showed a significantly higher SOC than deniers. That means that being highly respected in police interviews and admitting crimes relates to higher psychological well-being, but the authors point out that there is no direction of causality revealed, but just an association. Of course, it may be possible that a police interviewer's humanitarian approach to an interviewee causes the interviewee's feelings of being respected, and to admit committing a crime, and that in turn, generates a high SOC. It may also be possible that the original source of the humanitarian experiences may be the interviewees themselves, because if they behave in a humanitarian and respectful way, the police interviewer might respond in the same way, resulting in an admission and a high SOC. Someone may argue that an interviewee's experiences of humanity and respect may be an expression of a police officer's interviewing strategy to obtain a confession. Holmberg *et al.* explain that this might be true in some cases. However, it is likely that an offender in the study of Holmberg and Christianson (2002), who might have been treated by a simulated humanitarian approach, later realised these circumstances after the conviction. After a year or more in prison, the convict would consequently report a perception of low SOC based on bitterness.

Another study that supports the finding that being respected relates to a high SOC is a study of crime victims' experiences of police interviews. Holmberg and Olsson (2007) investigated 83 crime victims' (domestic violence or burglary) experiences of their police interviews. To measure their experiences of the police interview, the questionnaire previously used by Holmberg and Christianson (2002) and Holmberg (2004) was used. Psychological well-being was measured by Antonovsky's (1984) short form of SOC. A principal component analysis revealed that these crime victims perceived their interviews as *humanitarian* or *dominant,* almost identical with Holmberg and Christianson's (2002) and Holmberg's (2004) previous findings. Moreover, crime victims who perceived a high humanitarian approach from their police interviewer reported a significantly higher SOC than those who perceived a low humanitarian approach. Preliminary results from extended and ongoing analyses of a previous study by Holmberg (2004) show that crime victims who provided all information remembered during their police interview report a higher SOC than victims who consciously omitted information. Even here, as in the research on murderers' and sexual offenders' psychological well-being, it is only possible to talk about relations, and not causality. However, humanity in police interviews is associated with crime victims' narration. It may be seen from the investigative perspective also that a TJ humanitarian approach promotes psychological well-being.

Summary and visions of the future

Humanity and respect in police interviews that encourage crime victims to provide all information remembered from a crime event, and promote admissions from suspects, should not be seen only from a investigative and legal perspective. Additionally and most important, it is likely that police interviews conducted in line with a humanitarian, ethical and rapport-based TJ promote experiences whereby a crime victim, as well as a suspect, may work through the crime committed. Thus, such experiences may enhance the memory as well as facilitate the rehabilitation and the psychological well-being of the interviewee.

When interviews with suspects are discussed, the suspect's confession is often in focus. In some jurisdictions, a confession has a decisive value and is seen as a conclusive proof and may simplify a legal proceeding, whereas in other jurisdictions a confession has no value at all. A confession should not be seen superficially as a key to solve and close a case, because often confession-seeking behaviour has been related to coercion, deception, tricks and stratagems that sometimes are contrary to human rights and TJ and are obviously antitherapeutic. Such procedures may hinder suspects from telling their story, may hinder or complicate rehabilitation, and make it difficult for suspects to take responsibility for a crime. Such a situation and similar demeanour may complicate crime victims' right to a legal as well as a human compensation.

There is a need for further research on psychological well-being in TJ because the studies presented in this chapter showed only a relationship between perceptions of the police interview and psychological well-being. It is important to define this concept and find methods to measure psychological well-being in the legal context because it will offer a greater opportunity to develop legal methods and procedures. This chapter and its referred studies indicate that psychological well-being in a legal context can be measured, and further research suggests the use of different standardised instruments to identify more deeply psychological well-being in TJ. The humanitarian/dominant investigative distinction can be nicely situated within the conceptual framework of TJ and this calls for empirical work to aid the understanding of the law in action. Furthermore, the use of the SOC concept is very much in keeping with TJ's call for researchers to explicate and justify their measures of psychological well-being for the benefit of the people involved in legal actions. Thus, the hope of this chapter is that it will shed light on how the TJ perspective can contribute to the further development of investigative interviewing and the work of law enforcement in general.

References

Antonovsky, A. (1984) 'The Sense of Coherence as a Determinant of Health', in J.D. Matarazzo, S.M. Weiss, J.A. Herd, N.E. Miller and S.M. Weiss (eds), *Behavioral Health: A Handbook of Health Enhancement and Disease Prevention.* Chichester: Wiley.

Antonovsky, A. (1987) *Unrevealing the Mystery of Health.* San Francisco: Jossey-Bass.

Auhagen, A.E. (2000) 'On the Psychology of Meaning of Life', *Swiss Journal of Psychology*, 59: 34–48.

Baddeley, A. (1998) *Human Memory: Theory and Practice.* Boston, MA: Allyn and Bacon.

Baldwin, J. (1992) *Video Taping Police Interviews with Suspects – An Evaluation* (Police Research Series Paper 1). London: Home Office Police Department.

Baldwin, J. (1993) 'Police Interview Techniques: Establishing Truth or Proof?', *British Journal of Criminology*, 33: 325–352.

Bargh, J.A. (1999) 'The Cognitive Monster: A Case Against the Controllability of Automatic Stereotype Effects', in S. Chaiken and Y. Trope (eds.), *Dual Process Theories in Social Psychology.* New York: Guilford Press, 361–382.

Benneworth, K. (2003 July) Who 'Tells the Story' in the Police-Paedophile Investigative Interview and the Encouragement of Suspect Denial. Paper presented at the Psychology and Law International, Interdisciplinary Conference, Edinburgh, UK.

Benson, R. (2000) *Ragnar's Guide to Interviews, Investigations, and Interrogations.* Boulder, CO: Paladin Press.

Brock, P., Fisher, R.P. and Cutler, B.L. (1999) 'Examining the Cognitive Interview in a Double-Test Paradigm', *Psychology, Crime and Law*, 5: 29–45.

Buckley, J.P. (2006) 'The Reid-Technique of Interviewing and Interrogation', in T. Williamson (ed.), *Investigative Interviewing: Rights, Research, Regulation.* Cullompton: Willan Publishing.

Bull, R. (2000) 'Police Investigative Interviewing', in A. Memon and R. Bull (eds), *Handbook of the Psychology of Interviewing.* Chichester: Wiley, 279–292.

Bull, R. and Milne, R. (2004) 'Attempts to Improve Police Interviewing of Suspects', in G.D. Lassiter (ed.), *Interrogations, Confessions and Entrapment.* New York: Kluwer, 181–196.

Butler, E.A., Egloff, B., Wilhelm, F.H., Smith, N.C., Ericson, E.A. and Gross, J.J. (2003) 'The Social Consequences of Expressive Suppression', *Emotion*, 3: 48–67.

Butterfield, R. (2002). *The Official Guide to Interrogation.* Philadelphia: Xlibris Corporation.

Chen, M. and Bargh, J.A. (1999) 'Consequences of Automatic Evaluation: Immediate Behavioral Predispositions to Approach or Avoid the Stimulus', *Personality and Social Psychology Bulletin*, 25: 215–224.

Christianson, S-Å. (1992a) *The Handbook of Emotion and Memory: Research and Theory.* Hillsdale, NJ: Lawrence Erlbaum.

Christianson, S-Å. (1992b) 'Remembering Emotional Events: Potential Mechanisms', in S-Å Christianson (ed.), *The Handbook of Emotion and Memory: Research and Theory.* Hillsdale, NJ: Lawrence Erlbaum Associates Publishers, 307–342.

Clarke, C. and Milne, R. (2001) *National Evaluation of the PEACE Investigative Interviewing Course.* Home Office, UK, Police Research Award Scheme, Report No: PRSA/149. Retrieved from http://www.homeoffice.gov.uk/peace_interviewcourse.pdf.

Collins, R., Lincoln, R. and Frank, M.G. (2002) 'The Effect of Rapport in Forensic Interviewing', *Psychiatry, Psychology and Law*, 9: 69–78.

Debats, D.L., Drost, J. and Hansen, P. (1995) 'Experiences of Meaning of Life: A Combined Qualitative and Quantitative Approach', *British Journal of Psychology*, 86: 359–375.

Doerner, W.G. and Lab, S.P. (1998). *Victimology.* Cincinnati, OH: Anderson.

Dow, D.R. (2000) 'The Relevance of Legal Scholarship: Reflections on Judge Kozinski's Musings', *Houston Law Review*, 37: 329–340.

Eagly, A.H and Chaiken, S. (1998) 'Attitude Structure and Function', in D.T. Gilbert, S.T. Fiske and G. Lindzey (eds), *The Handbook of Social Psychology, vol. 2.* Boston, MA: McGraw-Hill, 307–342.

Finkelman, D. and Grisso, T. (1996) 'Therapeutic Jurisprudence: From Idea to Application', in D.B. Wexler and B.J. Winick (eds), *Law in a Therapeutic Key.* Durham, NC: Carolina Academic Press, 587–598.

Fisher, R.P. (1995) 'Interviewing Victims and Witnesses of Crime', *Psychology, Public Policy and Law*, 1: 732–764.

Fisher, R.P. and Geiselman, R.E. (1992) *Memory-enhancing Techniques for Investigative Interview: The Cognitive Interview*. Springfield, IL: Charles C Thomas.

Fisher, R.P. and Perez, V. (2007) 'Memory-Enhancing Techniques for Interviewing Crime Suspects', in S.Å. Christianson (ed.), *Offenders' Memories of Violent Crimes*. Chichester: Wiley, 329–354.

Gana, K. (2001) 'Is Sense of Coherence a Mediator Between Adversity and Psychological Well-being in Adults?', *Stress and Health*, 17: 77–83.

Gerbert, K. (1954) 'The Psychology of Expression and the Technique of Criminal Interrogation', *Jahrbuch fuer Psychologie und Psychotherapie*, 2: 85–98.

Gudjonsson, G.H. (1992) *The Psychology of Interrogations, Confessions and Testimony*. Chichester: Wiley.

Gudjonsson, G.H. (1994) 'Investigative Interviewing: Recent Developments and Some Fundamental Issues', *International Review of Psychiatry*, 6: 237–246.

Gudjonsson, G.H. (2003) *The Psychology of Interrogations and Confessions*. New York: Wiley.

Hassler, Å. (1930) *Föreläsningar över den Svenska kriminalprocessen, I*. Stockholm: A.B. Nordiska Bokhandeln i Distribution.

Hendrick, C. (1990) 'The Nature of Rapport', *Psychological Inquiry*, 4: 312–315.

Holmberg, U. (1994) *Samtal med sexualbrottsoffer: Hur har kvinnorna upplevt kommunikationen med olika resurspersoner*. Report series 1994: 1. Kristianstad: Kristianstad University.

Holmberg, U. (1996) *Sexualbrottsförövares upplevelser av polisförhör*. Report series 1996: 7. Kristianstad: Kristianstad University.

Holmberg, U. (2004) 'Crime Victims' Experiences of Police Interviews and their Inclination to Provide or Omit Information', *International Journal of Police Science and Management*, 6: 155–170.

Holmberg, U. and Christianson, S.Å. (2002) 'Murderers' and Sexual Offenders' Experiences of Police Interviews and their Inclination to Admit or Deny Crimes', *Behavioural Sciences and the Law*, 20: 31–45.

Holmberg, U., Christianson, S.Å. and Wexler, D. (2007) 'Interviewing Offenders: A Therapeutic Jurisprudential Approach', in S.Å. Christianson (ed.), *Offenders' Memories of Violent Crimes*. Chichester: Wiley, 355–371.

Holmberg, U. and Olsson, B. (2007, July) 'Crime Victims' Psychological Well-being Related to Police Interviews and Questions from the Prosecutor'. Paper presented at the 30th International Congress on Law and Mental Health, Padua, Italy.

Inbau, F.E., Reid, J.E., Buckley, J.P. and Jayne, B.C. (2001) *Criminal Interrogation and Confessions* (4th edn). Sudbury: Jones and Bartlett.

Innes, M. (2002) 'The "Process Structure'" of Police Homicide Investigations', *British Journal of Crimonology*, 42: 669–688.

Kassin, S.M. (2005) 'On the Psychology of Confession: Does Innocence Put Innocents at Risk?', *American Psychologist*, 60: 215–228.

Kassin, S.M. (2006) 'A Critical Appraisal of Modern Police Interrogations', in T. Williamson (ed.), *Investigative Interviewing: Rights, Research, Regulation*. Cullompton: Willan Publishing.

Kassin, S.M., Goldstein, C.C. and Savitsky, K. (2003) 'Behavioral Confirmation in the Interrogation Room: On the Dangers of Presuming Guilt', *Law and Human Behavior*, 27: 187–203.

Kassin, S.M. and Gudjonsson, G.H. (2004) 'The Psychology of Confessions: A Review of the Literature and Issues', *Psychological Science in the Public Interest*, 5: 33–67.

Kebbel, M.R., Hurren, E.J. and Mazzerolle, P. (2006) *An Investigation into the Effective and Ethical Interviewing of Suspected Sex Offenders*. Trends and Issues in Crime and Criminal Justice, no. 32. Canberra: Australian Institute of Criminology, 1–5.

Kebbell, M.R., Milne, R. and Wagstaff, G.F. (1999) 'The Cognitive Interview: A Survey of its Forensic Effectiveness', *Psychology, Crime and Law*, 5: 101–115.

Leche, E. and Hagelberg, V. (1945) *Förhör i brottmål*. Stockholm: P.A. Nordstedt and Söners.

LeDoux, J.C. and Hazelwood, R.R. (1985) 'Police Attitudes and Beliefs Toward Rape', *Journal of Police Science and Administration*, 13: 211–220.

Leo, R.A. (1992) 'From Coercion to Deception: The Changing Nature of Police Interrogation in America', *Crime, Law and Social Change*, 18: 35–59.

Leo, R.A. (1996) 'Criminal Law: Inside the Interrogation Room', *Journal of Criminal Law and Criminology*, 86: 266–303.

Loftus, E.F. (2003) 'Make-Believe Memories', *American Psychologist*, 11: 867–873.

Merriam-Webster Dictionary (2004) Merriam-Webster OnLine. Retrieved from http://www.m-w.com.

Milne, R. and Bull, R. (1999) *Investigative Interviewing: Psychology and Practice*. Chichester: Wiley.

Milne, R. and Bull, R. (2003) 'Interviewing by the Police', in D. Carson and R. Bull (eds), *Handbook of Psychology in Legal Contexts*. Chichester: Wiley, 111–125.

Mortimer, A. and Shepherd, E. (2000) 'Frames of Mind: Schemata Guiding Cognition and Conduct in the Interviewing of Suspected Offenders', in A. Memon and R. Bull (eds), *Handbook of the Psychology of Interviewing*. Chichester: Wiley, 293–316.

Moston, S. and Engelberg, T. (1993) 'Police Questioning Techniques in Tape Recorded Interviews with Criminal Suspects', *Policing and Society*, 3: 223–237.

Moston, S. and Stephenson, G.M. (1993) 'The Changing Face of Police Interrogation', *Journal of Community and Applied Social Psychology*, 3: 101–115.

Münsterberg, H. (1908/1923) 'On the Witness Stand: Essays on Psychology and Crime', *Classics in the History of Psychology*. An Internet resource developed by Christopher D. Green (ed.), York University, Toronto, Ontario. Retrieved from http://psychclassics.yorku.ca/Munster/Witness/detection.htm.

Münsterberg, H. (1908/1925) 'On the Witness Stand: Essays on Psychology and Crime', *Classics in the History of Psychology'*. An internet resource developed by Christopher D. Green (ed.), York University, Toronto, Ontario. Retrieved from http://psychclassics.yorku.ca/Munster/Witness/confessions.htm.

Nickerson, R.S. (1998) 'Confirmation Bias: A Ubiquitous Phenomenon in Many Guises', *Review of General Psychology*, 2: 175–220.

Nolde, S.F., Johnson, M.K. and Raye, C.L. (1998) 'The Role of Prefrontal Cortex During Tests of Episodic Memory', *Trends in Cognitive Sciences*, 2, 399–406.

Pallant, J.F. and Lae, L. (2002) 'Sense of Coherence, Well-Being, Coping and Personality Factors: Further Evaluation of the Sense of Coherence Scale', *Personality and Individual Differences*, 33: 39–48.

Patterson, M.L. (1990) 'On the Construct Validity and Developmental Course of Rapport', *Psychological Inquiry*, 4: 320–321.

Pearse, J. and Gudjonsson, G.H. (1996) 'Police Interviewing Techniques at Two South London Police Stations', *Psychology, Crime and Law*, 3: 63–74.

Peixoto, A. (1934) 'The Interrogation and Confessions in the Judiciary Process', *Revista de Criminologia Buenos Aires*, 21: 383–395.

Pennebaker, J.W. (1997) *Opening Up: The Healing Power of Expressing Emotions*. New York: Guilford Press.

Petrucci, C.J., Winick, B.J. and Wexler, D.B. (2003) 'Therapeutic Jurisprudence: An Invitation to Social Scientists', in D. Carson and R. Bull (eds), *Handbook of Psychology in Legal Contexts*. Chichester: Wiley, 579–601.

Ridgeway, B.J. (2000) 'The Hermeneutical Aspects of Rapport', *Dissertation Abstracts International Section A: Humanities and Social Sciences, 2000 Feb.,* 60 (7-A), 2527 (University microfilms No. AEH9937686).

Salonen, P., Vauras, M. and Efklides, A. (2005) 'Social Interaction – What Can It Tell Us about Metacognition and Coregulation in Learning?', *European Psychologist*, 10: 199–208.

Schneider, U., Büchi, S., Sensky, T. and Klaghofer, R. (2000) 'Anotonovsky's Sense of Coherence: Trait or State?', *Psychotherapy and Psychosomatis*, 69: 296–302.

Sear, L. and Stephenson, G.M. (1997) 'Interviewing Skills and Individual Characteristics of Police Interrogators', *Issues in Criminology and Legal Psychology*, 29: 27–34.

Shepherd, E. (1991) 'Ethical Interviewing', *Policing*, 7: 42–60.

Shepherd, E. and Milne, R. (1999) 'Full and Faithful: Ensuring Quality Practice and Integrity of Outcomes in Witness Interviews', in A. Heaton-Armstrong, E. Shepherd and D. Wolchover (eds), *Analysing Witness*

Testimony: A Guide for Legal Practitioners and Other Professionals. London: Blackstone Press, 124–145.

Shepherd, E., Mortimer, A., Turner, V. and Watson, J. (1999) 'Spaced Cognitive Interviewing: Facilitating Therapeutic and Forensic Narration of Trauma Memories', *Psychology, Crime and Law*, 5: 117–143.

Snekkevik, H., Anke, A., Stanghelle, J.K. and Fugl-Meyer, A.R. (2003) 'Is Sense of Coherence Stable After Multiple Trauma?', *Clinical Rehabilitation*, 17: 443–454.

Starrett, P. (1998) *Interview and Interrogation – for Investigations in the Public or Private Sector*. San Clemente CA: LawTec Publishing.

Steffens, M.C. and Mecklenbräuker, S. (2007) 'False Memories: Phenomena, Theories, and Implications', *Journal of Psychology*, 215: 12–24.

Stephenson, G.M. and Moston, S.J. (1993) 'Attitudes and Assumptions of Police Officers When Questioning Criminal Suspects', *Issues in Criminological and Legal Psychology*, 18: 30–36.

Stephenson, G.M. and Moston, S.J. (1994) 'Police Interrogation', *Psychology, Crime and Law*, 1: 151–157.

Tickle-Degnen, L. and Rosenthal, R. (1990) 'The Nature of Rapport and Its Nonverbal Correlates', *Psychological Inquiry*, 4: 285–293.

Todorov, A. and Bargh, J.A. (2002) 'Automatic Sources of Aggression', *Aggression and Violent Behavior*, 7: 53–68.

UN Universal Declaration of Human Rights, UN General Assembly, 1948, Art 5, 9.

UN Covenant on Civil and Political Rights, UN General Assembly, 1966 art. 14:2 (presumption of innocence).

Watzlawick, P., Weakland, J. and Fisch, R. (1974) *Change: Principles of Problem Formation and Problem Resolution*. New York: Norton.

Wegner, D.M. and Bargh, J.A. (1998) 'Control and Automaticity in Social Life', in D.T. Gilbert, S.T. Fiske and G. Lindzey (eds), *The Handbook of Social Psychology* (4th edn). Boston: Oxford University Press, 446–496.

Weinberg, C.D. (2002) *Effective Interviewing and Interrogation Techniques*. San Diego: Academic Press.

Wexler, D.B. (1996a) 'Therapeutic Jurisprudence and Changing Conceptions of Legal Scholarship', in D.B. Wexler and B.J. Winick (eds), *Law in a Therapeutic Key*. Durham, NC: Carolina Academic Press, 597–610.

Wexler, D.B (1996b) 'Reflections on the Scope of Therapeutic Jurisprudence', in D.B. Wexler and B.J. Winick (eds), *Law in a Therapeutic Key*. Durham, NC: Carolina Academic Press, 811–829.

Wexler, D.B. (2000) 'Practicing Therapeutic Jurisprudence: Psychological Soft Spots and Strategies', in D.P. Stolle, D.B. Wexler and B.J. Winnick (eds), *Practicing Therapeutic Jurisprudence: Law as a Helping Profession*. Durham, NC: Carolina Academic Press, 45–67.

Williamson, T.M. (1993) 'From Interrogation to Investigative Interviewing: Strategic Trends in Police Questioning', *Journal of Community and Applied Psychology*, 3: 89–99.

Winick, B.J. (2000) 'Therapeutic Jurisprudence and the Role of Counsel in Litigation', in D.P. Stolle, D.B. Wexler and B.J. Winnick (eds), *Practicing Therapeutic Jurisprudence: Law as a Helping Profession*. Durham, NC: Carolina Academic Press, 309–324.

Yuille, J.C., Marxsen, D. and Cooper, B. (1999) 'Training Investigative Interviewing: Adherence to the Spirit, as well as the Letter', *International Journal of Law and Psychiatry*, 22: 323–336.

Zika, S. and Chamberlain, K. (1992) 'On the Relation Between Meaning in Life and Psychological Well-Being', *British Journal of Psychology*, 83: 133–145.

Zimbardo, P.G. (1967) 'The Psychology of Police Confessions', *Psychology Today*, 1: 17–20, 25–27.

Chapter 9

Increasing cognitive load in interviews to detect deceit

Aldert Vrij,[1] Ronald Fisher, Samantha Mann and Sharon Leal

Existing protocols to detect deceit

In the ideal world, lie detection would be possible by merely observing someone. For example, professionals could walk around at airports and could spot those who have something to hide by looking for signs of erratic behaviour. Alternatively, heat-detection cameras could be installed at airports that could identify potential wrongdoers by measuring people's tonic arousal. Indeed, 'SPOT' teams (Screening Passengers by Observation Technique) that look for signs of erratic behaviour are now employed at airports in the USA and will be employed at airports in the UK (*Sunday Times* 20 August 2006: 7), and researchers have further recommended to install heat-detection cameras at airports for lie detection purposes (Pavlidis *et al.* 2002). Although we can understand why airports, and probably many other institutions, find those lie detection methods appealing, we believe that their success will be limited. Our main concern is that those techniques imply that the mere fact of hiding something, or other forms of lying, result in unique patterns of non-verbal behaviours or physiological responses. Deception research has convincingly demonstrated that this is not the case (DePaulo *et al.* 2003; Vrij 2008). Therefore, to detect lies, a person must be interviewed. Interview protocols thus need to be designed with the goal of devising questions or tasks that elicit differential responses in liars and truth tellers. Those different responses could subsequently be detected by observers.

Three such interview protocols are used to date, but they all have limitations. The two most widely used interview protocols are the

Control Question Polygraph Test, which measures physiological responses (Raskin and Honts 2002), and the Behaviour Analysis Interview, which measures verbal and nonverbal responses (Inbau *et al.* 2001; Vrij *et al.* 2006a). These protocols are based on the assumption that liars are afraid of being caught, and hence will be particularly aroused when answering key questions (e.g. 'Did you take the money?'). According to the National Research Council (2003), however, this underlying assumption is theoretically weak. Liars do not necessarily show more arousal during the key questions: they may be unconcerned about the key questions or they may have trained themselves to avoid revealing any arousal to the questions. Conversely, truth tellers may show signs of arousal when answering the key questions. The mere fact of being accused of wrongdoing or concern about being unable to convince the examiner of their innocence could make truth tellers aroused.

Another approach to detecting deception, as exemplified by the Guilty Knowledge Polygraph Test (GKT) (Lykken 1998), is based upon the premise that people orient toward personally significant stimuli. For instance, people may attend to a conversation only when their names are mentioned. This principle can be applied to lie detection. Suppose a body was found in the living room, but the suspect denies any knowledge of the crime. The suspect could be asked where the body was found: was it in the kitchen, in the bedroom, in the living room, or in the dining room? If the suspect has actually committed the crime, he or she may show an orienting response when the correct alternative is mentioned. Orienting responses are associated with increased arousal (Lykken 1998), the occurrence of P300 waves (Rosenfeld 2002), and greater activation of specific parts of the brain (Spence *et al.* 2001). According to the National Research Council (2003), the orienting response premise is theoretically more plausible than the earlier described premise of arousal due to the fear of being caught. However, the National Research Council concluded that lie detection based upon the orienting response is also not without theoretical problems. Their main concern is that reactions to familiar and unfamiliar stimuli should be thought of as a continuum rather than a dichotomy (as suggested by GKT polygraphers). That is, an examinee may show enhanced responses even to unfamiliar stimuli. Suppose that the murderer used a revolver and suppose that the innocent examinee owns an unregistered pistol. That examinee might show enhanced responses to questions that mention handguns among the alternatives, even if he or she has no concealed knowledge about the murder weapon. Moreover, interview protocols designed to demonstrate orienting responses may be difficult to apply. They can be used only when the examiner possesses specific knowledge about the crime (such as where the body was found). Furthermore, measuring orienting responses requires analysing physiological responses (skin conductance, EEG, brain scans) that often can be assessed only with impractically sophisticated and expensive equipment.

Using cognitive load as a tool to detect deceit

Given the theoretical weakness of the fear-based approach and the practical difficulties of the orienting approach, we developed another approach to discriminate between liars and truth tellers (Vrij *et al.* 2006c; Vrij 2008). This novel approach is based on the premise that, in most interviews, lying is cognitively demanding.[2] Several aspects of lying contribute to this increased mental load. First, formulating the lie itself may be cognitively demanding. Liars must need to make up their stories and must monitor their fabrications so that they are plausible and adhere to everything the observer knows or might find out. In addition, liars must remember their earlier statements, so that they appear consistent when retelling their story, and know what they told to whom. Liars should also avoid making slips of the tongue, and should refrain from providing new leads.

A second aspect of lying that adds to mental load is that liars are typically less likely than truth tellers to take their credibility for granted (DePaulo *et al.* 2003; Kassin and Gudjonsson 2004; Kassin and Norwick 2004; Kassin 2005). There are at least two reasons for this. The stakes (i.e., negative consequences of getting caught and positive consequences of getting away with the lie) are sometimes higher for liars than for truth tellers. Smugglers are probably keener to make an honest impression on customs officers than non-smugglers, because the negative consequences for having to open their suitcases are much higher for smugglers than for non-smugglers. In addition, truth tellers typically assume that their innocence shines through (illusion of transparency) (Gilovich *et al.* 1998; Kassin and Gudjonsson 2004; Kassin and Norwick 2004; Kassin 2005). As such, liars will be more inclined than truth tellers to monitor and control their demeanour so that they will appear honest to the lie detector (DePaulo and Kirkendol 1989). Monitoring and controlling their own demeanour should be cognitively demanding for liars.

Third, because liars do not take credibility for granted, they may monitor the *interviewer's* reactions more carefully in order to assess whether they are getting away with their lie (Buller and Burgoon 1996; Schweitzer *et al.* 2002). Carefully monitoring the interviewer also requires cognitive resources. Fourth, liars may be preoccupied by the task of reminding themselves to act and role-play (DePaulo *et al.* 2003), which requires extra cognitive effort. Fifth, liars have to suppress the truth while they are lying and this is also cognitively demanding (Spence *et al.* 2001). Finally, while activation of the truth often happens automatically, activation of the lie is more intentional and deliberate, and thus requires mental effort (Gilbert 1991; Walczyk *et al.* 2003; Walczyk *et al.* 2005).

The assumption that lying is cognitively demanding is supported by deception research. In a typical deception study, participants are allocated randomly to a truth-telling or lying conditions. Truth tellers are asked to describe honestly (i) their feelings toward someone else, (ii) their attitudes about controversial issues, (iii) a film they have just seen, or (iv) a staged event, including transgressions, in which they have participated. Liars are requested to describe feelings or attitudes they do not endorse, or to distort what happened in the film or during the staged event. To raise the stakes, participants are sometimes offered incentives if they appear convincing. A meta-analysis of more than 100 experimental laboratory studies revealed that liars show more signs of cognitive load: they decrease their movements and stutter more (DePaulo *et al.* 2003). A similar pattern was found in police interviews with real-life suspects, whose lies were accompanied by signs of cognitive load: increased pauses, decreased blinking, and, for males, decreased hand and finger movements (Mann *et al.* 2002; Vrij and Mann 2003). Moreover, police officers who were shown a selection of these police interviews, while being unaware that some of these clips contained lies and others contained truths, reported that they thought that the suspects were having to think harder than when they lied than when they were telling the truth (Mann and Vrij 2006;[3] see also Landström *et al.* 2005, 2007).

Converging with the pattern of increased cognitive load during deception, experimental studies in which participants were asked directly to assess their own cognitive load during interviews consistently showed that mock suspects found lying to be more cognitively demanding than truth telling (Vrij *et al.* 1996; Vrij *et al.* 2006b; White and Burgoon 2001; Granhag and Strömwall 2002; Gozna and Babooram 2004; Caso *et al.* 2005; Hartwig *et al.* 2006; Strömwall *et al.* 2006; Vrij *et al.* 2001b; Vrij and Mann 2006). Moreover, research examining brain activities during truth telling and lying (by using MRI scanners) has shown that lying is associated with activating executive 'higher' brain centres such as the prefrontal cortex (Spence *et al.* 2004). Finally, Vrij *et al.* (2001) asked police officers to detect deceit either directly ('Is the person lying?') or indirectly ('Is the person having to think hard?'). (In the indirect condition, the police officers were not informed that some suspects were lying and others were telling the truth.) The police officers were able to discriminate between liars and truth tellers, albeit only in the indirect condition. Moreover, only in the indirect condition did they pay attention to the cues that actually discriminated between the truth tellers and liars (e.g. a decrease in hand movements). In all, several findings converge on the claim that lying is more cognitively demanding than truth telling.

The greater cognitive demand experienced by liars than truth tellers could be exploited by a lie detector to discriminate more effectively between them. Liars, whose cognitive resources will be depleted by the more demanding act of lying, will have fewer cognitive resources left over to answer the lie detector's questions than will truth tellers. As a result, liars will be particularly debilitated when they are required to engage in cognitively demanding tasks. Liars should then reveal even more signs of cognitive load, such as increased stuttering, longer pauses, inconsistent answers, reduced blinking, and decreased movements. These signs of cognitive load are noteworthy, because observers can recognise them without using complex or expensive equipment (Vrij *et al.* 2001a; Vrij 2004; Vrij *et al.* 2004).

Lie detectors can manipulate cognitive demand strategically by varying the format of the interview. The police, and perhaps other professionals, commonly use two types of interview formats: information-gathering and accusatory (Moston *et al.* 1992). In the information-gathering style, interviewers ask suspects to give detailed statements about their activities through open questions (e.g. 'What did you do between 3 pm and 4 pm?'). Generating detailed responses to such open questions can be cognitively challenging. By comparison, in the accusatory style, interviewers confront suspects with an accusation (e.g. 'I think you have committed the crime'). This typically results in a short denial (e.g. 'No, I didn't do it'), which is not cognitively challenging. We should therefore expect that, compared to the accusatory style of interview, the information-gathering style (a) will be more cognitively demanding, and (b) will discriminate better between liars and truth tellers.

Both of these predictions were supported in experimental laboratory studies. The cognitive demand prediction was tested by Vrij *et al.* (2006b), whereby participants took part in a staged event and then were interviewed about their experiences in either an information-gathering or accusatory style. When asked to describe their cognitive processes, the participants reported that information-gathering interviews were cognitively more demanding than accusatory interviews. The discrimination prediction was examined in two parallel experiments that used a similar experimental procedure to Vrij *et al.* (2006b). Participants took part in a staged event and lied or told the truth about the event in a subsequent information-gathering or accusatory interview. Both experiments showed that information-gathering interviews yielded more discriminating cues to deception than did accusatory interviews. In information-gathering interviews, the liars' statements included fewer details (measured with criteria-based content analysis (CBCA) and reality monitoring (RM) than the truth tellers' statements, whereas no differences were found in the amount of detail given by liars and truth tellers in the accusatory interviews (Vrij *et al.* in press). Moreover, liars made fewer hand movements than truth tellers in information-gathering interviews, whereas no difference in hand movements was found in accusatory interviews (Vrij 2006).

As we noted earlier, information-gathering interviews are perceived as cognitively demanding. Interviewing procedures that introduce additional cognitive load should therefore be particularly debilitating in information-gathering interviews. We will describe several examples of how interviewers can take advantage of this principle to distinguish between liars and truth tellers. Because the strategies may vary as a function of the evidence available, we will distinguish between cases in which the lie detector has no evidence against the suspect and cases in which the lie detector does have some evidence.

Lie detection when no evidence is available

One way to increase cognitive load in an information-gathering interview is by asking interviewees to recall their activities in reverse order (Fisher *et al.* 2002). Alternatively, interviewees could be instructed to make direct eye contact with the interviewer when recounting their story (Beattie 1981). Both of these instructions are cognitively demanding, and hence, we expect to improve discrimination between both liars and truth tellers within an information-gathering style of interview. We found evidence for this hypothesis in our 'reverse order' lie detection study (Vrij *et al.* 2006c). Truth tellers took part in a staged event and recalled this event in a subsequent interview. Liars, on the other hand, did not take part in the event but pretended that they had in the subsequent interview. Truth teller and liars either recalled the event in chronological 'normal' order, or in reverse order. In the latter condition, they first described what happened at the end of the event, then what happened just before that, and so on. Police officers either saw video clips of the interviews with the participants who recalled their story in chronological order, or saw video clips of the interviews with participants who recalled their story in reverse order. In general, the ability to detect the truths and lies by the police officers who saw the chronological interviews was poor: They classified only 50 per cent of the truths and 42 per cent of the lies correctly (total accuracy rate was 46 per cent). The police officers who saw the reverse order interviews performed remarkably better: they classified 56 per cent of the truths and 59 per cent of the lies correctly (58 per cent total accuracy). In itself, a 59 per cent lie detection accuracy in the reverse order interviews may not appear high, but an increase from 42 per cent (chronological order interviews) to 59 per cent (reverse order interviews) is substantial. There is also anecdotal evidence to support the reverse order technique. Investigators who use this technique told us that suspects sometimes give themselves away by their obviously non-credible stories that are often replete with inconsistencies.

Because liars are typically motivated to get away with their lies, they may take measures to prevent them from being caught. For example, liars could anticipate being interviewed about their activities, and therefore could prepare a fabricated alibi beforehand. If so, the liar may not experience profound cognitive load while answering open-ended questions in the information-gathering interview. Lie detectors could easily make the interview setting more cognitively demanding for such liars by asking detailed follow-up questions (e.g. 'You mentioned that you went to the gym last night. Who else was there?'). Answering such detailed questions should be more difficult for (even) well-prepared liars than for truth tellers if the questions force the suspect to address details that they have not previously prepared. Suspects would then have to elaborate spontaneously, which is cognitively demanding. Obviously, suspects could always decide just to stick to their prepared alibis and not provide any further information (e.g. 'Sorry, I didn't notice who else was at the gym'). This is unlikely, however, because not being able to elaborate on a previous statement looks suspicious, which is something that liars attempt to avoid.

A particularly sophisticated alibi for suspects would be to describe an event that they have actually experienced before, albeit not at the time they claim. Thus, creating a false alibi by mentioning the gym (example above) would be particularly useful if the suspect has indeed been to that gym before. The interviewer should be aware of this. Questions such as 'What exercises did you do at the gym?' are then easy to answer for the suspect. Instead, the interviewer should ask time-specific questions (e.g. 'Describe who else was there?'), as this is the only aspect of the event the suspect lies about.

Lie detection when some evidence is available

In many settings, such as airport settings, lie detectors may not have any evidence they could use to check the veracity of a statement. However, in other cases, such as police interviews, some evidence may be available. For example, sometimes a police detective has evidence, such as fingerprints or CCTV footage, that could link a suspect to a crime. Two recent studies examined how police officers can present incriminating evidence against a suspect in a strategic fashion, to increase cognitive load. Traditionally (Inbau *et al.* 2001), police present such evidence at the beginning of the interview (e.g. 'A videotape shows that you were in Commercial Road on Saturday evening at 8 pm'). The lying suspect must then fabricate an alibi that is consistent with the factual evidence. We acknowledge that this may be a difficult task, particularly if the suspect is taken by surprise that the police have such evidence. The suspect's task can be made even more cognitively demanding, however, if the interviewer withholds the evidence and, instead, encourages the suspect to talk first about his whereabouts on Saturday night. Lying suspects may implicate themselves if their alibi precludes their being in Commercial Road on Saturday night, and then they are confronted with the videotaped evidence that places them in the unmentioned location. Hartwig *et al.* (2005) conducted an experiment and manipulated the timing of evidence presentation (either before or after suspects were given the opportunity to give their false alibi). Lies were more readily detected by observers when the interviewer presented the evidence at a later stage (62 per cent accuracy) than at an earlier stage of the interview (43 per cent accuracy). In the late-evidence condition, guilty suspects' statements were significantly more inconsistent with the evidence than were innocent suspects' statements, whereas in the early evidence condition, liars and truth tellers were not significantly different.

Furthermore, the observers indeed picked up these inconsistencies: As the number of inconsistencies in a statement increased, the more likely the observer was to assess the suspect as guilty, and the more correct the observer was.

Lie detectors' judicious use of questions to increase cognitive demands can take on other strategies, for example, by limiting the number of acceptable explanations suspects can offer to account for the current situation. In problem-solving terms, the difficulty of the task is inversely related to the number of acceptable solutions (the size of the solution set). Suppose, for example, that the suspect's car was noticed near the crime scene just after the crime took place, but the suspect did not refer to the car in his alibi. After being confronted with this piece of evidence, the suspect may reply that he used the car on that particular day, thereby adapting his story to match the evidence. However, suppose that the interrogator does not reveal the evidence at this stage but asks some questions about the evidence instead (e.g. 'Did you use your car that day?'). When confronted with the evidence after these questions, the suspect has fewer opportunities to escape (reduced size of solution set), if he has already told the interviewer that he did not use his car on that particular day. The solution set would be reduced even further if the suspect indicated that he did not lend the car to anyone else, and that nobody else has keys to his car (van den Adel 1997). Hartwig *et al.* (2006) tested this 'strategic-use-of-evidence' technique in their experiment. Police officers interviewed mock suspects about a mock crime (half of the suspects were guilty of committing the mock crime). Prior to these interviews, half of the police officers were trained in how to use the strategic-use-of-evidence (SUE) technique. Trained officers obtained a considerably higher deception detection accuracy rate (85.4 per cent) than did untrained interviewers (56.1 per cent). This study also demonstrated that the SUE technique is cognitively demanding for liars. Lying suspects reported experiencing significantly more cognitive demand during their interviews than truth tellers, particularly when interviewed by trained officers who employed the SUE technique.

Final thoughts

We conclude this chapter by discussing three points that are relevant to our new lie detection protocol.

Disguising behaviours

Liars may well attempt to avoid displaying signs that might increase suspicion (Hocking and Leathers 1980), which most people, probably including liars, believe are signs of increased arousal (Strömwall *et al*. 2004). Therefore, as research has shown, liars are particularly inclined to disguise signs of arousal (Strömwall *et al*. 2006). If they do this successfully, lie detection based on focusing on arousal cues will be difficult. However, focusing on liars' cognitive behaviours, which should not be influenced by liars' behavioural presentation strategies, may prove to be more effective.

Cognitive demand assumption

Is lying always more difficult than truth telling in information-gathering interviews? Take for example an interviewee who is asked in July about his whereabouts during a particular day in February. Truth tellers may have more difficulty in remembering and recalling their whereabouts during that day than liars, who merely have to recall a fabricated alibi. However, this does not necessarily mean that lying is easier than truth telling in such a situation. We explained in this chapter that 'storytelling' is only one of the six aspects that comprise cognitive load for liars in information-gathering interview settings. The other five aspects of cognitive load (monitoring and controlling one's own behaviour, monitoring the lie detector, preoccupation with reminding themselves to act, inhibition of the truth, and activation of the lie) probably still affect liars more than truth tellers, and, as a result, an information-gathering interview about an event that happened a while ago may still be more challenging for liars than for truth tellers.

Finally, unlike the arousal and orienting-response interview protocols, which are specifically designed for lie detection purposes, the cognitive approach could serve a wider purpose. It uses an information-gathering interview style, which is regarded as an effective interview strategy in general (Fisher *et al*. 2002), because it encourages interviewees to give their side of the story and provides the interviewer with a wealth of information. An information-gathering interview also forms the core of the ethical framework of police interviewing, which is the suspect interview style that is promoted in the UK (Williamson, 1993, 1994).

Acknowledgement

This project was sponsored by grants from the Economic and Social Research Council (RES-000-23-0292 and RES-000-22-1632).

Notes

1 Correspondence concerning this chapter should be addressed to Aldert Vrij, University of Portsmouth, Psychology Department, King Henry Building, King Henry 1 Street, Portsmouth PO1 2DY, United Kingdom or via email: aldert.vrij@port.ac.uk

2 Outside an interview context, lying is not always difficult, and sometimes it is even easier to lie than to tell the truth (McCornack 1997). Suppose a friend gives you a present for your birthday that you don't like. In this case it is probably easier to pretend that you like the present than to say that you don't like it.

3 Interestingly, the suspects looked *less* nervous when they lied than when they told the truth according to the police officers. Note that this finding demonstrates a potential problem associated with arousal-based lie detection tools.

References

Beattie, G.W. (1981) 'A Further Investigation of the Cognitive Interference Hypothesis of Gaze Patterns During Conversation', *British Journal of Social Psychology*, 20: 243–248.

Buller, D.B. and Burgoon, J.K. (1996) 'Interpersonal Deception Theory', *Communication Theory*, 6: 203–242.

Caso, L., Gnisci, A., Vrij, A. and Mann, S. (2005) 'Processes Underlying Deception: An Empirical Analysis of Truths and Lies When Manipulating the Stakes', *Journal of Interviewing and Offender Profiling*, 2: 195–202.

DePaulo, B.M. and Kirkendol, S.E. (1989) 'The Motivational Impairment Effect in the Communication of Deception', in J.C. Yuille (ed.), *Credibility Assessment*. Dordrecht: Kluwer, 51–70.

DePaulo, B.M., Lindsay, J.L., Malone, B.E., Muhlenbruck, L., Charlton, K. and Cooper, H. (2003) 'Cues to Deception', *Psychological Bulletin*, 129: 74–118.

Fisher, R.P., Brennan, K.H. and McCauley, M.R. (2002) 'The Cognitive Interview Method to Enhance Eyewitness Recall', in M.L. Eisen, J.A. Quas and G.S. Goodman (eds), *Memory and Suggestibility in the Forensic Interview*. Mahwah, NJ: Lawrence Erlbaum Associates, 265–286.

Gilbert, D.T. (1991) 'How Mental Systems Believe', *American Psychologist*, 46: 107–119.

Gilovich, T., Savitsky, K. and Medvec, V.H. (1998) 'The Illusion of Transparency: Biased Assessments of Others' Ability to Read One's Emotional States', *Journal of Personality and Social Psychology*, 75: 332–346.

Gozna, L. and Babooram, N. (2004) 'Non-traditional Interviews: Deception in a Simulated Customs Baggage Search', in A. Czerederecka, T. Jaskiewicz-Obydzinska, R. Roesch and J. Wojcikiewicz (eds), *Forensic Psychology and Law*. Krakow, Poland: Institute of Forensic Research, 153–161.

Granhag, P.A. and Strömwall, L.A. (2002) 'Repeated Interrogations: Verbal and Nonverbal Cues to Deception', *Applied Cognitive Psychology*, 16: 243–257.

Hartwig, M., Granhag, P.A., Strömwall, L. and Kronkvist, O. (2006) 'Strategic Use of Evidence During Police Interrogations: When Training to Detect Deception Works', *Law and Human Behavior*, 30: 603–619.

Hartwig, M., Granhag, P.A., Strömwall, L.A. and Vrij, A. (2005) 'The Strategic Use of Disclosing Evidence', *Law and Human Behavior*, 29: 469–484.

Hocking, J.E. and Leathers, D.G. (1980) 'Nonverbal Indicators of Deception: A New Theoretical Perspective', *Communication Monographs*, 47: 119–131.

Inbau, F.E., Reid, J.E., Buckley, J.P. and Jayne, B.C. (2001) *Criminal Interrogation and Confessions* (4th edn). Gaithersburg, MD: Aspen.

Kassin, S.M. (2005) 'On the Psychology of Confessions: Does Innocence Put Innocents at Risk?', *American Psychologist*, 60: 215–228.

Kassin, S.M. and Gudjonsson, G.H. (2004) 'The Psychology of Confessions: A Review of the Literature and Issues', *Psychological Science in the Public Interest*, 5: 33–67.

Kassin, S.M. and Norwick, R.J. (2004) 'Why People Waive their Miranda Rights: The Power of Innocence', *Law and Human Behavior*, 28: 211–221.

Landström, S., Granhag, P.A. and Hartwig, M. (2005) 'Witnesses Appearing Live Versus on Video: Effects on Observers' Perception, Veracity Assessments and Memory', *Applied Cognitive Psychology*, 19: 913–933.

Landström, S., Granhag, P.A. and Hartwig, M. (in press) 'Children's Live and Videotaped Testimonies: How Presentation Mode Affects Observers' Perception, Assessment and Memory', *Legal and Criminological Psychology*, 12: 333–348.

Lykken, D.T. (1998) *A Tremor in the Blood: Uses and Abuses of the Lie Detector*. New York: Plenum Trade.

Mann, S. and Vrij, A. (2006) 'Police Officers' Judgements of Veracity, Tenseness, Cognitive Load and Attempted Behavioural Control in Real Life Police Interviews', *Psychology, Crime and Law*, 12: 307–319.

Mann, S., Vrij, A. and Bull, R. (2002) 'Suspects, Lies and Videotape: An Analysis of Authentic High-Stakes Liars', *Law and Human Behavior*, 26: 365–376.

McCornack, S.A. (1997) 'The Generation of Deceptive Messages: Laying the Groundwork for a Viable Theory of Interpersonal Deception', in J.O. Greene (ed.), *Message Production: Advances in Communication Theory*. Mahwah, NJ: Lawrence Erlbaum, 91–126.

Moston, S.J., Stephenson, G.M. and Williamson, T.M. (1992) 'The Effects of Case Characteristics on Suspect Behaviour During Police Questioning', *British Journal of Criminology*, 32: 23–39.

National Research Council (2003) *The Polygraph and Lie Detection*. Committee to Review the Scientific Evidence on the Polygraph. Washington, DC: National Academic Press.

Pavlidis, J., Eberhardt, N.L. and Levine, J.A. (2002) 'Seeing Through the Face of Deception', *Nature*, 415: 35.

Raskin, D.C. and Honts, C.R. (2002) 'The Comparison Question Test', in M. Kleiner (ed.), *Handbook of Polygraph Testing*. London: Academic Press, 1–48.

Rosenfeld, J.P. (2002) 'Event-Related Potentials in the Detection of Deception, Malingering, and False Memories', in M. Kleiner (ed.), *Handbook of Polygraph Testing*. London: Academic Press, 1–48.

Schweitzer, M.E., Brodt, S.E. and Croson, R.T.A. (2002) 'Seeing and Believing: Visual Access and the Strategic Use of Deception', *International Journal of Conflict Management*, 13: 258–275.

Spence, S.A., Farrow, T.F.D., Herford, A.E., Wilkinson, I.D., Zheng, Y. and Woodruff, P.W.R. (2001) 'Behavioural and Functional Anatomical Correlates of Deception in Humans', *NeuroReport*, 12: 2849–2853.

Spence, S.A., Hunter, M.D., Farrow, T.F.D., Green, R.D., Leung, D.H., Hughes, C.J. and Ganesan, V. (2004) 'A Cognitive Neurobiological Account of Deception: Evidence from Functional Neuroimaging', *Philosophical Transactions of the Royal Society of London*, 359: 1755–1762.

Strömwall. L.A., Granhag, P.A. and Hartwig, M. (2004) 'Practitioners' Beliefs About Deception', in P.A. Granhag and L.A. Strömwall (eds), *Deception Detection in Forensic Contexts*. Cambridge: Cambridge University Press, 229–250.

Strömwall, L.A., Hartwig, M. and Granhag, P.A. (2006) 'To Act Truthfully: Nonverbal Behaviour and Strategies During a Police Interrogation', *Psychology, Crime and Law*, 12: 207–219.

Van den Adel, H.M. (1997) *Handleiding verdachtenverhoor* ('Interviewing suspects manual'). Den Haag: VUGA-Uitgeverij.

Vrij, A. (2003) 'We Will Protect Your Wife and Child, but Only If You Confess: Police Interrogations in England and The Netherlands', in P.J. van Koppen and S.D Penrod (eds), *Adversarial Versus Inquisitorial Justice: Psychological Perspectives on Criminal Justice Systems*. New York: Plenum, 55–79.

Vrij, A. (2004) 'Why Professionals Fail to Catch Liars and How They Can Improve', *Legal and Criminological Psychology*, 9: 159–181.

Vrij, A. (2006) 'Challenging Interviewees During Interviews: The Potential Effects on Lie Detection', *Psychology, Crime and Law*, 12: 193–206.

Vrij, A. (2008) *Detecting Liers and Deceit: Pitfalls and Opportunities*. Chichester: Wiley.

Vrij, A. and Mann, S. (2003) 'Deception Detection', in P.W. Halligan, C. Bass and D.A. Oakley (eds), *Malingering and Illness Deception*. Oxford: Oxford University Press, 348–362.

Vrij, A. and Mann, S. (2006) 'Criteria-Based Content Analysis: An Empirical Test of its Underlying Processes', *Psychology, Crime and Law*, 12: 337–349.

Vrij, A., Edward, K. and Bull, R. (2001a) 'Police Officers' Ability to Detect Deceit: The Benefit of Indirect Deception Detection Measures', *Legal and Criminological Psychology*, 6: 185–197.

Vrij, A., Edward, K. and Bull, R. (2001b) 'Stereotypical Verbal and Nonverbal Responses While Deceiving Others', *Personality and Social Psychology Bulletin*, 27: 899–909.

Vrij, A., Evans, H., Akehurst, L. and Mann, S. (2004) 'Rapid Judgements in Assessing Verbal and Nonverbal Cues: Their Potential for Deception Researchers and Lie Detection', *Applied Cognitive Psychology*, 18, 283–296.

Vrij, A., Fisher, R., Mann, S. and Leal, S. (2006c) 'Detecting Deception by Manipulating Cognitive Load', *Trends in Cognitive Sciences*, 10: 141–142.

Vrij, A., Mann, S. and Fisher, R.P. (2006a) 'An Empirical Test of the Behaviour Analysis Interview', *Law and Human Behavior*, 30: 329–345.

Vrij, A., Mann, S. and Fisher, R. (2006b) 'Information-Gathering vs Accusatory Interview Style: Individual Differences in Respondents' Experiences', *Personality and Individual Differences*, 41: 589–599.

Vrij, A., Mann, S., Fisher, R., Leal, S., Milne, B. and Bull, R. (2008) 'Increasing Cognitive Load to Facilitate Lie Detection: The Benefit of Recalling an Event in Reverse Order', *Law and Human Behavior*, 32: 253–265.

Vrij, A., Mann, S., Kristen, S. and Fisher, R. (2007) 'Cues to Deception and Ability to Detect Lies as a Function of Police Interview Styles', *Law and Human Behavior*, 31: 499–518.

Vrij, A., Semin, G.R. and Bull, R. (1996) 'Insight into Behaviour During Deception', *Human Communication Research*, 22: 544–562.

Walczyk, J.J., Roper, K.S., Seemann, E. and Humphrey, A.M. (2003) 'Cognitive Mechanisms Underlying Lying to Questions: Response Time as a Cue to Deception', *Applied Cognitive Psychology*, 17: 755–744.

Walczyk, J.J., Schwartz, J.P., Clifton, R., Adams, B., Wei, M. and Zha, P. (2005) 'Lying Person-to-Person About Live Events: A Cognitive Framework for Lie Detection', *Personnel Psychology*, 58: 141–170.

White, C.H. and Burgoon, J.K. (2001) 'Adaptation and Communicative Design: Patterns of Interaction in Truthful and Deceptive Conversations', *Human Communication Research*, 27: 9–37.

Williamson, T. (1993) 'From Interrogation to Investigative Interviewing: Strategic Trends in Police Questioning', *Journal of Community and Applied Social Psychology*, 3: 89–99.

Williamson, T. (1994) 'Reflections in Current Police Practice', in D. Morgan and G.M. Stephenson (eds), *Suspicion and Silence: The Right to Silence in Criminal Investigations*. London: Blackstone, 107–116.

Chapter 10

Detecting deceit: current issues

Peter Bull

Introduction

Whether deception can be detected from non-verbal cues is the focus of this chapter. Traditional research on cue identification, it will be argued, is based on an old-fashioned and outmoded view of non-verbal communication, implemented through inappropriate laboratory techniques derived from experimental psychology. In contrast, contemporary research on interpersonal communication is an interdisciplinary endeavour; it draws on a wide range of academic disciplines, which this laboratory tradition simply ignores. Of particular importance is the focus on studying the fine details of social interaction through the analysis of film, audiotape and videotape recordings. Because such research is based on the detailed ('micro') analysis of both speech and non-verbal behaviour, it has become known as microanalysis (Bull 2002).

The aim of this chapter is to discuss the application of microanalysis to cue identification in deception detection. The chapter is divided into four main sections:

1 principles of microanalysis
2 critical review of research on non-verbal behaviour and deception detection
3 illustrative example of an interview with Tony Blair
4 how microanalysis can be applied to deception research.

I. Microanalysis

Microanalysis represents not only a distinctive methodology but also a distinctive way of thinking about communication (Bull 2002). Undoubtedly, this form of analysis has facilitated discoveries which otherwise simply would not be possible. Indeed, the effect of the video recorder has been likened to that of the microscope in the biological sciences. Without recorded data that can repeatedly be examined, it is simply not possible to perform the kind of highly detailed analysis of both speech and non-verbal communication characteristic of the microanalytic approach.

But microanalysis did not develop simply as a consequence of innovations in technology. Film technology had been available since the beginning of the twentieth century; two of the earliest pioneers of cinematography, Muybridge and Marey, had a particular interest in analysing and recording movement patterns in animals and humans (Marey 1895; Muybridge 1899, 1901). The extensive use of this technology in the study of human social interaction has only developed in the past few decades, but its use reflects fundamental changes in the way in which we think about human communication (Kendon 1982). Thus, microanalysis can be seen as not only a distinctive methodology but also a distinctive way of thinking about communication.

Research on interpersonal communication has been conducted in a wide variety of academic disciplines, most notably social psychology, psychiatry, anthropology, linguistics, sociology, ethology and, of course, communication. Within these disciplines, a number of distinctive approaches may be distinguished: in particular, conversation analysis (e.g. Sacks 1992), discourse analysis (e.g. Potter and Wetherell 1987), speech act theory (Austin 1962), ethology (e.g. Fridlund 1997), and the social skills approach (e.g. Hargie 1997).

Within these approaches, there are both important differences of emphasis as well as outright disagreements, but also some fundamental similarities. Some of the most important disagreements have been concerned with methodology, on how to conduct the research. Traditionally, one of the main planks of academic psychology has been a belief in the value of the experimental method, and for many years this approach typified social psychological research on interpersonal communication. Intrinsic to the experimental method is a belief in the importance of quantification and the use of inferential statistics. An important consequence of a quantitative approach is the need for categorisation. The advantage of this procedure is that it allows the researcher to reduce observed behaviour to frequencies or rates of occurrence, rather than attempting a detailed description of each event. These data can then be subjected to some sort of analysis by inferential statistics. Hence, a salient feature of this approach has been a preoccupation with the development of coding systems.

The use of the experimental method in communication research has been subjected to intensive criticism by those who favour naturalistic observation and a qualitative approach. One target of criticism has been the artificiality of the data obtained in laboratories, where the participants either knew or suspected that they were being recorded for the purpose of an experiment. Although these problems are not insurmountable, the use of naturalistic observation has increasingly become the preferred method of making observations in communication research. The use of coding systems has also been criticised, on the grounds that such procedures are typically arbitrary and reductionist, and distort the data to fit into preconceived categories (Psathas 1995). Furthermore, it is claimed that context and meaning are only dealt with in so far as they are specified in the category system (Psathas 1995). Researchers in both conversation analysis and discourse analysis have also become increasingly concerned not to 'impose' preconceived categories on the data, but to make use of the ways in which people categorise themselves, as manifested in their own discourse (van Dijk 1997).

These methodological disputes are one instance of an ongoing disagreement within communication research. They have substantial implications for research on deception detection, which are discussed further below. It is important to be aware that communication scholars do have these significant disagreements. But it is also important to be aware that they do share a number of common assumptions. Thus, it is possible and useful to discern certain basic themes which represent a novel and distinctive way of thinking about communication, which has been termed the microanalytic approach (Bull 2002). These themes are listed below:

1 *Communication is studied as it actually occurs.* This marked a radical shift from the traditional concern with the study of communication in terms of what it should be – in terms of, for example, its efficiency, clarity or persuasiveness.

2 *Communication can be studied as an activity in its own right.* This feature contrasts with more traditional approaches, which were

concerned with the study of communication not for its own sake but as a means of investigating other social processes, such as leadership, interpersonal relationships or power structures.

3 *All features of interaction are potentially significant.* A further distinguishing feature has been the expansion of what behaviour can be regarded as communicative. The remarkable development of interest in non-verbal communication can be regarded as one such manifestation. So, too, is the extraordinary detail in which conversation analysts seek in their transcripts to represent as exactly as possible the way in which conversation sounds. The underlying assumption is that all features of interaction are potentially significant, and therefore should not be dismissed out of hand as unworthy of investigation.

4 *Communication has a structure.* Although interaction may seem at first sight to be disorderly or even random, it cannot be assumed to be so, and one of the tasks of the investigator is to analyse whether an underlying structure can be discerned.

5 *Conversation can be regarded as a form of action.* According to speech act theory, language does not simply describe some state of affairs or state some facts: it is in itself a form of action. This proposal has been profoundly influential. It underlies a great deal of research on the functions of conversation, on the ways in which conversational actions are accomplished.

6 *Communication can be understood in an evolutionary context.* This proposal is central to ethological and sociobiological approaches to communication analysis. Outside those traditions, it has had comparatively little influence; this is not a concern of approaches such as conversation analysis or discourse analysis. However, it has been of importance for social psychologists who study emotional expression.

7 *Communication is best studied in naturally occurring contexts.* This proposal is common to almost all approaches. The prime exception is experimental social psychology, whose proponents have traditionally made extensive use of laboratory-based experimentation as a means of studying communication. However, the trend in social psychology in recent years has also been towards naturalistic analysis.

193

8 *Communication can be regarded as a form of skill.* This proposal represents one of the main contributions of the social psychological approach to communication. Indeed, it has been so influential that the term 'communication skills' has passed into the wider culture.

9 *Communication can be taught like any other skill.* A related proposal is that communication can be taught like any other skill. This again has been highly influential in the wider culture; social or communication skills training has been widely used in a variety of personal and occupational contexts.

10 *Macro-issues can be studied through microanalysis.* Also of particular importance for the wider culture is the assumption that major (or macro) social issues such as racism, politics or feminism can be analysed through microanalysis.

This microanalytic approach has significant implications for research on deception detection, which is reviewed in the next section.

2. Research on non-verbal behaviour and deception detection

(a) Deception detection

There is a long tradition of research intended to assess how well observers can detect deception. For example, Kraut (1980) reviewed 21 studies of deception detection. In most of these studies, the accuracy rate ranged from 45 per cent to 60 per cent. The mean (average) rate was 57 per cent, where 50 per cent would be expected by chance alone. Kraut's review was published in 1980, and many further studies have appeared since then. Thus, Vrij (2000) reviewed an additional 39 studies of deception detection by what he calls laypeople (i.e. people who were not professionally involved in lie detection, such as police officers). Again, the majority of accuracy rates fell in the range 45–60 per cent, with a mean accuracy rate of 57 per cent.[1] A recent study (Porter *et al.* 2007) compared the performance of motivated observers (offered a monetary/gift incentive for accurate lie detection) with that of unmotivated observers (no performance incentive). Motivated observers actually performed significantly less accurately (46 per cent) but more confidently than the unmotivated observers (60 per cent).

Overall, this research suggests that people are not very good at spotting lies; their performance is not much above what might be expected by chance. However, there are a number of reasons for treating this conclusion with caution. One problem with averaging accuracy rates over a large number of studies is that it can lead us to underestimate the skills of more perceptive observers. Although average performance in lie detection is unimpressive, research has shown that there do seem to be people who are good at this task. For example, Ekman and O'Sullivan (1991) investigated the deception detection accuracy of a number of different groups, some of whom might be expected by virtue of their occupation to be good at lie detection. They found that neither police officers, polygraphers, judges nor psychiatrists performed significantly better than college students or indeed better than chance. But there was one exception. Secret service agents achieved 64 per cent accuracy, and were significantly better than all the other groups. Some of them achieved remarkably good results: over half achieved 70 per cent or higher, some even 80 per cent. A further study (Ekman *et al.* 1999) focused on other groups with a special interest in deception detection. These included federal officers, sheriffs and clinical psychologists; their accuracy rates were comparable to the secret service agents (68–73 per cent).

The performance of these 'high-flyers' at deception detection is of both theoretical and practical interest. Through analysing the skills and techniques of these more perceptive observers, it may be possible not only to acquire a deeper theoretical understanding of deception detection but also to impart that knowledge to less perceptive observers in the form of appropriate training procedures.

Specifically with regard to the secret service agents, it has been hypothesised that the nature of their job enhances their attention to non-verbal cues, resulting in higher levels of accuracy (Ekman and O'Sullivan 1991). Other research supports the putative significance of non-verbal cues. One study of skilled lie detectors (O'Sullivan and Ekman 2004) found that most of them had had unusual childhoods, where the ability to read non-verbal cues of emotion might have been decidedly advantageous. Thus, some (brought up in the USA) did not speak English until grade school; some were children of alcoholics; some (unlike most of their peers) had mothers who went out to work. Another study (Etcoff *et al.* 2000) was conducted of patients with speech aphasias, who suffered severe deficits in comprehending spoken sentences following damage to the left cerebral hemisphere. These patients achieved high levels of deception detection accuracy from facial expressions, possibly due to the attention they learned to pay to non-verbal indicators. In a further study, Ekman and Friesen (1974) asked nurses to watch two films, one a pleasant landscape and the other showing amputations and treatment of severe burns. The nurses were asked honestly to describe their reactions to the landscape, but to conceal any negative feelings in response to the stress film. Results showed that whereas four highly trained facial analysts correctly identified almost all deceptive and honest communications, untrained observers did no better than chance in detecting deception from the face.

Ekman and his colleagues have also identified what they call *micro-expressions*. *Micros* are brief facial expressions of emotion that may only last a fraction of a second before being suppressed. So, for example, someone might be extremely surprised by a novel piece of information, but not wish others to be aware of this. Although on hearing this news the person might start to raise his/her eyebrows and start to let his/her mouth fall open, both movements might be quickly inhibited. However, a skilled observer might notice the micro-expressions, and would also be highly sceptical if the other person subsequently denied feeling surprised. Skill in recognising these micros has been formally tested by showing pictures of facial expressions at very short exposures (1/25th of a second). One study showed a significant positive correlation between the ability to identify micro-expressions and deception detection accuracy for college students (Frank and Ekman 1997), and another for professional lie catchers (Ekman and O'Sullivan 1991).

Thus, despite the overall conclusion that people are not very good at spotting lies, research evidence also shows that skill in perceiving non-verbal cues is significantly correlated with accuracy in deception detection. But what are the non-verbal cues that indicate someone is lying? There is an extensive research literature on cue identification, which is discussed below.

(b) Identifying non-verbal cues of deception

In his book *Detecting Lies and Deceit,* Vrij (2000) summarises the literature on non-verbal behaviour during deception. Vrij organises this review in terms of the conventional distinction between vocal and non-vocal non-verbal behaviour. Vocal behaviour refers to all of the actions involved in producing speech, whereas non-vocal behaviour refers to communicative activities other than speech (e.g. facial expressions and body movements). The verbal elements in conversation are taken to mean the actual words used (as distinct from all vocal considerations as to how they might be pronounced). Thus, non-verbal behaviour refers to all vocal and non-vocal behaviour that is not verbal in the sense defined above (Laver and Hutcheson 1972).

Vrij (2000: 36–37) tabulates 44 studies concerned with non-vocal non-verbal behaviour during deception. These comprise facial characteristics (gaze, smiling, blinking) and various forms of body movement (e.g. movements of the head, trunk, arms, hands and fingers, and also what are called self-manipulations and illustrators). Self-manipulations involve body contact movements, such as scratching the head or the wrists. Illustrators are movements directly tied to speech, believed to amplify and elaborate the verbal content of the message.

Vrij (2000) tabulates the results according to whether these behaviours increase or decrease during deception, or show no relationship with it. These results, he concludes, show a very confusing pattern. From detailed inspection of the table, the only indicator of deception appears to be movement inhibition: liars tend to move their arms, hands, fingers, feet and legs less than do truth tellers. Even this is not to suggest that everybody inhibits movement when lying, but only that the majority of liars do this. For example, from an overview of his own experiments Vrij reports that whereas 64 per cent of 181 participants showed a decrease in hand, finger and arm movements during deception, 35 per cent showed an actual increase in these movements (Vrij and Akehurst 1996; Vrij et al. 1997). Vrij goes on to suggest two possible explanations for movement inhibition. One is that the decrease in movement might be the result of lie complexity. Because liars have to think hard to lie, cognitive overload inhibits their non-verbal behaviour. Another possibility is that in seeking to make an honest impression, liars move very deliberately and try to avoid non-essential movements. Again, this might result in movement inhibition.

Vrij (2000) reports that all other non-verbal behaviours (e.g. gaze aversion, smiling, self-manipulations, shifting positions and eye blinks) do not seem to be reliable indicators of deception. For example, according to popular belief, liars typically look away (Vrij 2000). This belief is not unreasonable, given that liars may be nervous or have to think hard, and gaze aversion is associated with both nervousness and cognitive overload (Vrij 2000). But the data Vrij reports reveal no consistent pattern: some studies show an increase in gaze, others a decrease, and most no effect at all. Vrij proposes that gaze aversion may not be a reliable indicator of deception, because it is so easy to control. Thus, it is not very difficult for liars to look their conversational partners straight in the eye should they so wish. This might not, however, be the case under the influence of strong emotion, a point Vrij does not consider.

Overall, the results of Vrij's (2000) review suggest that non-verbal behaviour tells us relatively little about how to identify deception. In stark contrast, the studies reviewed above in Section 2(a) show that skill in perceiving non-verbal cues is significantly correlated with accuracy in deception detection. One possible explanation for the contradictory nature of these findings lies in the methodological problems that beset cue identification research. In this chapter, it will be argued that such research is so methodologically flawed that there is little that can be safely concluded about what specific non-verbal cues are indicative of deception. These methodological problems are discussed below.

(c) Methodological problems in cue identification research

Vrij (2000) discusses a number of methodological problems with laboratory-based experimental studies of non-verbal behaviour and deception. One is what Frank and Ekman (1997) have called the issue of stake or interest. People asked to tell lies in laboratory experiments do not face any serious consequences if found out. Conversely, real-life lies if detected can have very serious consequences. Fear of those consequences may be manifest in non-verbal behaviours that give clues that deception is taking place. Vrij (2000) fully acknowledges this problem. He recognises that laboratory experiments may simply not make people nervous enough to display non-verbal behaviours indicative of deception.

A second problem is that the coding systems used to analyse non-verbal behaviour may not be sufficiently fine-grained to pick up deception cues. For example, in Vrij's (2000) table of non-verbal behaviour research, no relationship is shown between smiling and deception. But, as Vrij points out, Ekman and his colleagues have identified a significant distinction between what they call felt and false smiles (e.g. Ekman and Friesen 1982). Felt smiles include all smiles in which a person actually experiences a positive emotion. They involve the action of two muscles: the *zygomatic major*, which pulls the lip corners towards the cheekbone, and the *orbicularis oculi*, which raises the cheek and produces bagged skin below the eyes and crow's-feet at the eye. In a false smile, the action of the *orbicularis oculi* is absent. That is to say, false and felt smiles are perceptibly different. Furthermore, studies by Ekman and his colleagues have shown that false smiles are used more in deception than felt smiles (e.g. Ekman and O'Sullivan 1991).

A third problem stems from the way in which the data are analysed. Vrij (2000) points out that some researchers do not measure the frequency of occurrence of behaviours during lying and truth-telling; instead they measure their temporal duration. In Vrij's view (p. 39), duration is not a sufficiently detailed measure; this might explain why some researchers have found non-verbal differences between truth tellers and liars, while others have not.

In fact, both frequency and duration as the mode of analysis are seriously open to criticism. From the contemporary microanalytic perspective, such research is seriously flawed by its characteristic use of crude 'code and count' forms of quantification. No attention is paid to the structuring of non-verbal behaviour and speech, even though their close interdependence has been demonstrated time and time again by microanalytic research (e.g. Bavelas and Chovil 2000; Kendon 2004). Thus, there is a substantial literature demonstrating that non-verbal behaviour is highly synchronised with speech – in terms of vocal stress (e.g. Pittenger *et al.* 1960; Bull and Connelly 1985), syntax (Lindenfeld 1971) and meaning (e.g. Scheflen 1964; Kendon 2004). Furthermore, the meaning of non-verbal behaviour can often be understood only through its relationship to speech. Thus, gesture may be used to parse the structure of discourse, indicating, for example, what is prominent or focal in speech. Again, it may be used to indicate how an utterance is to be taken: for example, whether it is to be taken as a request, a plea, an offer, an invitation, or a refusal (Kendon 2004).

None of these structural features show up in studies where the analyst simply codes and counts up the number of times a non-verbal behaviour occurs, irrespective of what the person is saying. This important methodological issue of communicational structure is addressed by none of the studies of non-verbal behaviour reviewed by Vrij (2000). From this perspective, it is unsurprising that the results of his review are so confused and contradictory. In his conclusions about non-verbal cue identification, Vrij is both circumspect and cautious. Indeed, his readers might understandably conclude that non-verbal cues tell us little as to whether a person is engaged in deception. But from a microanalytic perspective on communication research, this conclusion is seriously open to dispute. Given that the methodology of these studies is so open to criticism, it is debatable whether anything can be concluded from them at all. Furthermore, this conclusion directly contradicts the research reviewed in Section 2(a) above, which indicates that skill in perceiving non-verbal cues correlates significantly with accuracy in deception detection. In short, to identify specific non-verbal cues to deception requires much more sophisticated and sensitive research. Vrij's conclusions are open to dispute not because they are too cautious but because they are insufficiently critical of traditional methodologies.

3. An illustrative example: an interview with Tony Blair

To further illustrate this argument, it is useful to discuss one case study in some detail. The example elaborated below is drawn from a televised interview with Tony Blair (UK prime minister 1997–2007) conducted on BBC's *Question Time* (28 April) during the 2005 British general election. The day after the interview, the *Daily Mail* ran a story claiming that it provided spectacular evidence of Tony Blair's deceitfulness. This was because he was so visibly and obviously sweating.

In humans, sweating is primarily a means of temperature regulation; it has a cooling effect due to the latent heat of evaporation of water. It may also be increased by nervousness and nausea, and decreased by cold. Sweating is obviously an ambiguous signal, but in this respect, it is typical of non-verbal behaviour in general. For example, gaze aversion can occur for a variety of reasons. It may be due to shyness, or to cognitive planning (e.g. Beattie 1979) (i.e. looking at another person when thinking may be too distracting); it may also indicate that the speaker wishes to keep the speaking turn (Kendon 1967). To analyse the particular functions of gaze aversion, it needs to be studied in situated context, with reference to what is actually being said. Thus, the frequency or duration with which people avert their gaze may not tell us very much about whether they are being deceitful. But if a person averts gaze in response to one highly sensitive question, that particular instance of gaze aversion might be highly significant in that particular context.

These same considerations apply to the significance of Tony Blair's sweating in this interview. There can be no doubt that he was sweating, it was palpably visible on his forehead. Of course, he could just have been too hot! Closer analysis shows that he starts to sweat in relation to a series of questions about making an appointment with a general practitioner. One lady in the audience (Diana Church) relates how her GP had asked her to bring her son back for an appointment in a week. She was told by the receptionist that no bookings could be made more than 48 hours ahead. This procedure had been adopted by many GP practices in order to meet the government's target for a maximum 48-hour wait. By not allowing people to make appointments more than 48 hours in advance, GP practices could claim that they were meeting government targets. Tony Blair was unaware of this. The interviewer David Dimbleby specifically asked him, 'Is this news to you?' Blair replied, 'I have to say that is news to me that doctors are insisting you have to come within the 48 hours.' He later went on to say 'The system obviously shouldn't work in that way', and that he would look into it.

None of this contextual information appeared in the *Daily Mail*'s report of the interview. It simply focused on Tony Blair's 'oodles of sweat' as clear evidence that he was lying. But from an alternative perspective, Blair could be seen as caught in a situation probably familiar to anyone who speaks in public. That is to say, he was caught on the hop by a question for which he was ill-prepared and unable to give a proper answer. Thus, his sweating might be seen as evidence not of deceit but of panic. None of this information on the social context or the content of speech appeared in the *Daily Mail*'s 'analysis' of Tony Blair's sweating. Their observations were decontextualised, and made no allowance for the potential multiple meanings of non-verbal behaviour.

Although it is easy to castigate the *Daily Mail* for its superficiality, its underlying logic is arguably no different from the experiments on non-verbal behaviour and deception described in Section 2(b) above. If the *Daily Mail*'s attack on Blair seem crass, so, too, are those studies of non-verbal behaviour and deception in which the investigator simply tots up the number of gestures, irrespective of their social context or the content of what is being said.

4. Microanalysis and deception detection

The main proposal of this chapter is that in analysing the role of non-verbal behaviour in deception detection, a radically new approach is required, more in line with contemporary thinking on communication analysis. Time and time again, microanalytic studies have demonstrated the close interdependence between speech and non-verbal behaviour (e.g. McNeill 1992; Beattie 2003; Kendon 2004). Given this close interconnectedness, their separation would appear to be highly artificial. In particular, hand and facial gestures may be seen as visible acts of meaning, and arguably should be treated as part of natural language (Bavelas and Chovil 2000). Kendon makes this point when he subtitles his book on gesture 'visible action as utterance' (Kendon 2004). Bavelas and Chovil (2000) referred to 'face-to-face dialogue', and argue for what they term an integrated message model in which audible and visible communicative acts are treated as a unified whole.

This more recent perspective of language and gesture as a single integrated system differs radically from the notion of 'body language' – a communication process utilising signals made up of body movements, regarded by its adherents as separate from and beyond speech (McNeill 1992). Traditional research on non-verbal behaviour and deception (e.g. those studies reviewed by Vrij (2000)) implicitly assumes this old-fashioned notion of 'body language'. No reference is made to the content of what is said, or the social context in which communication occurs. Admittedly, Vrij and Mann (2004) have recently argued that lie detection can be improved by combining verbal and non-verbal/auditory cues. Furthermore, Vrij *et al.* (2004) demonstrated that this resulted in more correct classification of liars and truth tellers than the use of either speech or non-verbal behaviour alone. Even so, Vrij *et al.*'s analysis did not treat speech and non-verbal behaviour as a single integrated system; they were still utilised as independent sources of information.

In developing an integrated perspective on the analysis of deceptive communication, particular use could be made of micro-expressions (e.g. Frank and Ekman 1997). The evidence described in Section 2a above suggests that micro-expressions may provide important clues to deception. There are at least two ways in which their analysis could be incorporated into an integrated message perspective: in terms of inappropriateness and inconsistency.

Consider the following example. A suspect in a police murder enquiry is a close relative of the victim. In an interview, the suspect comments on the lack of progress by the police in the case. If the suspect was a relative of the victim, one might expect to see expressions of anger or sadness as he talks. In fact, a brief smile is discernible; the suspect actually looks pleased that no progress has been made. This would be neither appropriate for a close relative nor consistent with what is being said. This is not to suggest that such cues should be regarded as evidence, but they might provide useful pointers in an investigation that some sort of deception is taking place.

Another way of developing this approach is through recent work on gesture (Beattie 2003). Like a number of the authors cited above (McNeill 1992; Bavelas and Chovil 2000; Kendon 2004), Beattie has argued that hand and and arm movements are intimately connected with speaking and thinking. As a consequence, they reflect our thoughts; indeed, they may provide us with a glimpse of hidden, unarticulated thoughts; that is to say, they make thought visible. Beattie and Shovelton (1999a, 1999b, 2001) ran a series of experiments based on video recordings of participants narrating cartoon stories. These descriptions were then replayed either with speech or with speech and gestures to another set of participants, who were subsequently asked a series of detailed questions about the stories. For example, in one experiment (Beattie and Shovelton 1999a), observers were asked questions about the actions and objects described in the cartoons. These questions covered such things as the identity of people or objects reported, as well as their size, shape and relative position, and the nature of any actions described and the speed of such actions. Results consistently showed that participants who saw the gestures got significantly more information about the original story than those who heard only the speech.

Beattie (2003) went on to argue that the precise form of a gesture may provide important clues to deception. Through gesture, a speaker may unwittingly provide information that either is not contained in speech or even directly contradicts it. Beattie reports one anecdotal example of an executive at a meeting who, as she described how sales started to soar after an advertising campaign, made a *downward* gesture with her hand that seemed to contradict what she was saying. When Beattie asked specifically whether sales had soared or actually declined, she admitted with embarrassment that sales had actually declined immediately after the campaign.

Another example of this kind of gestural 'leakage' can be seen in an interview between President Bush and Sir David Frost (broadcast 16 November, 2003). In the context of the Iraq War, Frost asked Bush about his relationships with President Chirac and Chancellor Schroeder. In his reply, Bush said, 'We're not going to agree on every issue.' As he did so, he moved his hands apart, as if to indicate the distance between himself and the two European leaders. Then Bush said, 'But a Europe which works closely with America and an America which works closely with Europe means the world will be better off.' As he said 'A Europe which works closely with America', he joined his hands, but only by touching the tips of his two index fingers. To illustrate this point, Bush could have joined his hands in a number of ways – by, for example, interlacing his fingers, or by one hand clasping the other. This would have suggested a much greater degree of closeness. In contrast, wagging the index finger is characteristically used in argument. Touch the hands by the index fingers suggested a rather greater degree of distance and rivalry between Bush and the European leaders than Bush's choice of words would have acknowledged.

In short, the analysis of both micro-expressions and of hand gesture suggests ways in which non-verbal behaviour can be integrated with speech in an integrated message model.

Conclusions

Research on deception detection suggests that people are not very good at spotting lies, although skill in perceiving non-verbal cues does significantly enhance performance. Research intended to identify non-verbal cues indicative of deception has been notably disappointing; the findings are often confused and contradictory. In this chapter, it has been argued that the methodology of this research is old-fashioned and out of date. It fails to reflect contemporary thinking about interpersonal communication. The alternative proposed here is an integrated message perspective, in which speech and non-verbal behaviour are treated as a unified whole. Through the microanalysis of non-verbal cues in relation to both social context and the content of speech, we should be able to evaluate much more effectively the utility of non-verbal cues in detecting deception.

Note

1 It should be noted that a new edition of Vrij's book was to be published in 2008, although this was not available at time of going to press.

References

Austin, J. (1962) *How to Do Things with Words*. Cambridge, MA: Harvard University Press.

Bavelas, J.B. and Chovil, N. (2000) 'Visible Acts of Meaning: An Integrated Message Model of Language in Face-to-Face Dialogue', *Journal of Language and Social Psychology*, 19: 163–194.

Beattie, G.W. (1979) 'Contextual Constraints on the Floor-Apportionment Function of Speaker-Gaze in Dyadic Conversations', *British Journal of Social and Clinical Psychology*, 18: 391–392.

Beattie, G.W. (2003) *Visible Thought: The New Psychology of Body Language*. Hove, East Sussex: Routledge.

Beattie, G.W. and Shovelton, H. (1999a) 'Do Iconic Hand Gestures Really Contribute Anything to the Semantic Information Conveyed by Speech? An Experimental Investigation', *Semiotica*, 123: 1–30.

Beattie, G.W. and Shovelton, H. (1999b) 'Mapping the Range of Information Contained in the Iconic Hand Gestures that Accompany Spontaneous Speech', *Journal of Language and Social Psychology*, 18: 438–462.

Beattie, G.W. and Shovelton, H. (2001) 'An Experimental Investigation of the Role of Different Types of Iconic Gesture in Communication: A Semantic Feature Approach', *Gesture*, 1: 129–149.

Bull, P. (2002) *Communication Under the Microscope: The Theory and Practice of Microanalysis*. London: Psychology Press.

Bull, P.E. and Connelly, G. (1985) 'Body Movement and Emphasis in Speech', *Journal of Nonverbal Behaviour*, 9: 169–187.

Ekman, P. and O'Sullivan, M. (1991) 'Who Can Catch a Liar?', *American Psychologist*, 46: 913–920.

Ekman, P., O'Sullivan, M. and Frank, M. (1999) 'A Few Can Catch a Liar', *Psychological Science*, 10: 263–266.

Ekman, P. and Friesen, W.V. (1974) 'Detecting Deception from the Body or Face', *Journal of Personality and Social Psychology*, 29: 288–298.

Ekman, P. and Friesen, W.V. (1982) 'Felt, False and Miserable Smiles', *Journal of Nonverbal Behaviour*, 6: 238–252.

Etcoff, N.L., Ekman, P., Magee, J.J. and Frank, M.G. (2000) 'Lie Detection and Language Loss', *Nature*, 405: 139.

Frank, M.G. and Ekman, P. (1997) 'The Ability to Detect Deceit Generalises Across Different Types of High-Stake Lies', *Journal of Personality and Social Psychology*, 72: 1429–1439.

Fridlund, A.J. (1997) 'The New Ethology of Human Facial Expressions', in J.A. Russell and J.M. Fernández-Dols (eds), *The Psychology of Facial Expression*. New York: Cambridge University Press, 103–129.

Hargie, O.D.W. (1997) 'Interpersonal Communication: A Theoretical Framework', in O.D.W. Hargie (ed.) *The Handbook of Communication Skills* (2nd edn). London: Routledge, 29–63.

Kendon, A. (1967) 'Some Functions of Gaze Direction in Social Interaction', *Acta Psychologica*, 26: 22–63.

Kendon, A. (1982) 'Organization of Behaviour in Face-to-Face Interaction', in K.R. Scherer and P. Ekman (eds), *Handbook of Methods in Nonverbal Behaviour Research*. Cambridge: Cambridge University Press, 440–505.

Kendon, A. (2004) *Gesture: Visible Action as Utterance*. Cambridge: Cambridge University Press.

Kraut, R.E. (1980) 'Humans as Lie Detectors: Some Second Thoughts', *Journal of Communication*, 30: 209–216.

Laver, J. and Hutcheson, S. (eds) (1972) *Communication in Face-to-face Interaction*. Harmondsworth: Penguin.

Lindenfeld, J. (1971) 'Verbal and Nonverbal Elements in Discourse', *Semiotica*, 3: 223–233.

Marey, É.J. (1895) *Movement*. New York: D. Appleton.

McNeill, D. (1992) *Hand and Mind. What Gestures Reveal About Thought*. Chicago: University of Chicago Press.

Muybridge, E. (1957 [1899]). *Animals in Motion*. New York: Dover Publications.

Muybridge, E. (1957 [1901]) *The Human Figure in Motion*. New York: Dover Publications.

O'Sullivan, M. and Ekman, P. (2004) 'The Wizards of Deception Detection', in P.A. Granhag and L. Stromwell (eds), *The Detection of Deception in Forensic Contexts*. Cambridge: Cambridge University Press, 269–286.

Pittenger, R.E., Hockett, C.F. and Danehy, J.J. (1960) *The First Five Minutes: A Sample of Microscopic Interview Analysis*. Ithaca, NY: Martineau.

Porter, S., McCabe, S., Woodworth, M. and Peace, K.A. (2007) '"Genius Is 1% Inspiration and 99% Perspiration" … Or Is It? An Investigation of the Impact of Motivation and Feedback on Deception Detection', *Legal and Criminological Psychology*, 12: 297–309.

Potter, J. and Wetherell M. (1987) *Discourse and Social Psychology: Beyond Attitudes and Behaviour*. London: Sage.

Psathas, G. (1995) *Conversation Analysis: The Study of Talk-in-Interaction*. Thousand Oaks, CA: Sage.

Sacks, H. (1992) (ed. G. Jefferson) *Lectures on Conversation*. Cambridge, MA: Blackwell.

Scheflen, A.E. (1964) 'The Significance of Posture in Communication Systems', *Psychiatry*, 27: 316–331.

Van Dijk, T.A. (1997) *Discourse as Structure and Process*. Discourse Studies: A Multidisciplinary Introduction, Volume 1. London: Sage.

Vrij, A. (2000) *Detecting Lies and Deceit*. Chichester: Wiley.

Vrij, A. (in press) *Detecting Lies and Deceit: Pitfalls and Opportunities*. Chichester: Wiley.

Vrij, A. and Akehurst, L. (1996, August) 'Hand Movements During Deception: Some Recent Insights'. Paper presented at the Sixth European Conference on Psychology and Law, Sienna, Italy.

Vrij, A., Akehurst, L., Soukara, S. and Bull, R. (2004) 'Detecting Deceit via Analyses of Verbal and Nonverbal Behaviour in Children and Adults', *Human Communication Research*, 30: 8–41.

Vrij, A. and Mann, S. (2004) 'Detecting Deception: The Benefit of Looking at a Combination of Behavioural, Auditory and Speech Content Related Cues in a Systematic Manner', *Group Decision and Negotiation*, 13: 61–79.

Vrij, A., Winkel, F.W. and Akehurst, L. (1997) 'Police Officers' Incorrect Beliefs About Nonverbal Indicators of Deception and its Consequences', in J.F. Nijboer and J.M. Reijntjers (eds), *Proceedings of the First World Conference on New Trends in Criminal Investigation and Evidence*. Lelystad: Koninklijke Vermande, 221–238.

Index